The How-To Book of the

BIBLE

*Everything You Need to Know
But No One Ever Taught You*

Karl A. Schultz

Our Sunday Visitor Publishing Division
Our Sunday Visitor, Inc.
Huntington, Indiana 46750

Nihil Obstat: Rev. Michael Heintz
Censor Librorum

Imprimatur: ✠ John M. D'Arcy
Bishop of Fort Wayne-South Bend
June 3, 2004

The *nihil obstat* and *imprimatur* are declarations that a work is free from doctrinal or moral error. It is not implied that those who have granted the *nihil obstat* and *imprimatur* agree with the contents, opinions, or statements expressed.

The Scripture citations used in this work are taken from the *Catholic Edition of the Revised Standard Version of the Bible* (RSV), copyright © 1965 and 1966 by the Division of Christian Education of the National Council of the Churches of Christ in the United States of America. Used by permission. All rights reserved.

English translations of the documents of the Second Vatican Council, papal documents, and other Vatican documents are from the Vatican website, www.vatican.va.

Every reasonable effort has been made to determine copyright holders of excerpted materials and to secure permissions as needed. If any copyrighted materials have been inadvertently used in this work without proper credit being given in one form or another, please notify Our Sunday Visitor in writing so that future printings of this work may be corrected accordingly.

Our Sunday Visitor Publishing Division
Our Sunday Visitor, Inc.
200 Noll Plaza
Huntington, IN 46750

ISBN: 1-59276-095-3 (Inventory No. T147)
LCCN: 2004107356

Cover design by Tyler Ottinger
Interior design by Sherri L. Hoffman

PRINTED IN THE UNITED STATES OF AMERICA

Table of Contents

Introduction

WHY READ THE BIBLE?

The Bible is a timeless human and divine treasure. It is western civilization's most influential and revered book, with a personal message for everyone. Along with sacred Tradition, it is the fundamental source of revelation for the Catholic Church.

If you're not sure what you want out of the Bible, or how to get it, this book can help you. You will discover ways of experiencing the Bible according to your needs.

The contemporary relevance of the Bible and its diverse applications are often overlooked. It is the book of healing and human potential par excellence. It is a handbook on human relationships and sexuality. Who is more credible on these subjects than the Source of life and love?

The Bible's correspondence to life underlies the fascination and respect it evokes. Simultaneously idealistic and realistic, it addresses life's ups and downs like no other book. This life-centeredness, along with its inspired nature, make it indispensable for Christians who seek to fulfill their vocations and potential.

BEFRIENDING THE BIBLE

Friendship with the Bible develops slowly. There is a learning and feeling-out process, just as in any significant relationship or endeavor. Sometimes a biblical passage will seem as if it is addressed directly to you. Other times, it will seem to have nothing to do with your life. Passages that initially confound you may end up among your favorites. In each chapter, I'll highlight appealing and important passages that will help you develop an expanding favorites list.

As with human friends, the Bible can not only delight, but leave a sour or uncertain taste. Some persons have undergone such confusing and bitter experiences that even picking up the Bible is a challenge. This book will help you address these issues and become comfortable with the Bible.

WHO THIS BOOK IS FOR

This book is for all persons who wish to have a better understanding of the Bible and the distinctly Catholic approach. Because of progress in ecumenism and biblical studies, Catholics, Orthodox, and Protestants can read, pray, and share the Bible in ways unheard of a half century ago. Some passages are interpreted differently, but those differences are beyond the scope of this book.

I believe that the Catholic approach to the Bible will enrich both Catholics and non-Catholics seeking to expand their horizons and deepen their understanding of Scripture.

In accordance with its "how-to" designation, this book provides practical guidance on reading, praying, interpreting, appreciating (e.g., its contribution to literature, art, and society), and applying (to life) the Bible. It is designed to help you holistically encounter the Bible privately and in a group and liturgical setting. Accordingly, it is not only for beginners, but for all persons seeking to enrich their interactions with Scripture. Actually, we're all beginners with respect to the Bible. Each time we encounter it, we can discover something new.

BOOK OBJECTIVES

This book is designed to:
1) Familiarize you with the Bible as a whole, while highlighting its key parts and themes. The latter is a good starting point for exploring the rest of the Bible.

The book is filled with biblical quotations, references, and highlighted passages. These illustrate my points and facilitate looking up the passages and experiencing them yourself. The ideal is to read the Bible alongside this book. There is no substitute for direct contact with the Bible.

2) Relate the Bible to life and vice-versa.

The Bible comes to life when you discover it in life and apply it to life. God hasn't gone on sabbatical after inspiring the Bible! God's initiative in salvation (biblical) and personal (our lives) history is the Bible's fundamental theme.

3) Reveal the accessible riches and most important passages of the Old Testament. Many people feel that the Old Testament is harsh, antiquated, and cryptic. Consequently, they feel intimidated or disinterested. My goal is to help you overcome any apprehensions and develop an affection for the Old Testament. You'll discover that much of it is timeless and stimulating.

We'll build up to the Old Testament by first encountering background information, interpretive methods, and the New Testament. This will increase your confidence and create anticipation.

4) Discover the energy and support available in learning the Bible with others.

Just as the Bible evolved within a community, so you refine your understanding of the Bible through exposure to the thoughts and experiences of others. This primarily occurs through classes, dialogue, and group interaction, but it also encompasses literary and software resources. I'll address each of these in the book.

HOW THIS BOOK IS ORGANIZED

Section I: How to Read the Bible

You'll encounter the Bible in your and its own context. You'll learn why and how the Bible arose, and how its development parallels yours. You'll discover which translation(s) and background resources meet your needs. You'll encounter various approaches to reading the Bible and how to choose among them. You'll learn Judaism's and Christianity's oldest models for experiencing the Bible in a holistic manner.

Section II: How to Read the New Testament

You'll encounter the context and central themes, events, and passages of the New Testament, and discover their relevance to your life. You'll learn accessible principles and methods for interpreting the New Testament in a competent and fulfilling manner.

Section III: How to Read the Old Testament

You'll survey the geographic, political, and cultural context of the Old Testament, and encounter its key events, concepts, characters, and passages. You'll see yourself in its timeless stories and characters. You'll discover how the Old Testament sheds light on the New Testament.

Appendix

A detailed bibliography lists some of the finest accessible resources on the Bible.

ICONS

Given the Bible's natural adaptation to art, and the Church's promotion of such, it seems fitting for this book to have icons. Similar types of information that occur periodically throughout the book are identified by the following icons:

What Does It Mean?

Explains essential terms and concepts, and provides a basic biblical vocabulary.

The Bible Says What?

Explains confusing passages or concepts that have traditionally given readers difficulty.

Peak Passages

Presents biblical passages that have been influential in both individual spirituality and Church teachings.

Wrestling with the Word

The Bible provides questions more than answers. This icon signifies reflection questions and thought-provoking comments that will help you internalize and assimilate the Bible, and make personal applications. You will soon learn how to develop your own questions and recognize those the Bible is posing, and thereby enter into fruitful dialogue with the Bible.

Sacred Humor

The Bible uses word plays, irony, and sarcasm to inject levity and enhance interest and memorization. I'll point out instances of biblical humor and inject my own playful observations.

Humor lightens an intense topic and provides refreshing breaks in the text. When we fail to live up to biblical and human ideals, it is therapeutic to laugh at ourselves and life. Humor is a profoundly human and divine characteristic whose role in the Bible and Christian spirituality is often overlooked, particularly within contemporary Catholicism.

Saints and Sages on the Bible

Insights from credible commentators on the Bible.

Signs of the Times: The Bible Today

Cites examples of the Bible's timeless and contemporary relevance, and helps you recognize the Bible's correspondence to life, and your situation in particular.

INTERFAITH LANGUAGE CONSIDERATIONS

Because of their familiarity, I will use the traditional B.C. and A.D. designations instead of the abbreviations "B.C.E." (before the common era) and "C.E." (the common era), and which are commonly used in interfaith circles.

For reasons explained in Chapter Two, I will use the traditional name "Old Testament" rather than the more ecumenical term, "Hebrew Bible," with the understanding that "old" is a chronological term without any connotations of inferiority.

REFERENCING THE BIBLE CHAPTER AND VERSE

The Bible was not divided into chapters until the publishing of the Paris Bible in 1226 under the direction of Stephen Langton, Archbishop of Canterbury. Verse numbering is generally attributed to Robert Estienne, who purportedly enumerated the Greek New Testament in 1550 and his French translation three years later.

TRANSLATION USED AND BIBLICAL ABBREVIATIONS

This book uses the Revised Standard Version, Catholic Edition. In cases where the translation is wooden or uses archaic language (thee's and thou's), I will use another translation and denote this next to the biblical citation.

You do not need to use the same translation to follow along. Abbreviations of biblical books vary slightly by translation, but are easy to decipher. The table of contents of most Bibles displays their abbreviation system.

DECIPHERING A BIBLICAL REFERENCE

A biblical reference begins with the abbreviation of the biblical book. For example, Gen refers to Genesis; the abbreviation is not followed by a period.

A number before the abbreviation indicates the first, second, or third book of that title. For example, 3 Jn refers to the third letter of John, 2 Kings refers to the second book of Kings.

After the biblical abbreviation comes the chapter. For example, Mt 3 refers to the third chapter of Matthew.

If the reference points to a specific verse, it will continue with a colon, then the verse number. For example, Job 3:2 means the second verse of chapter three of Job.

A series of verses within the same chapter are designated by a hyphen. For example, Lev 3:1-6 means verses one through six of the third chapter of Leviticus.

A sequence of chapters within the same book are also designated by a hyphen. 1 Kings 3-6 means the third through sixth chapters of the first book of Kings. Remember, a colon is necessary to designate a verse.

Discontinuous verses within the same chapter are separated by commas. For example, Lk 3:1, 6, 7 means the first, sixth, and seventh verses of chapter three of Luke's Gospel.

Different chapters are distinguished by semicolons. For example, Gen 3:7; 7:8, means the seventh verse of chapter three of Genesis and the eighth verse of chapter seven. Deut 3;7;9 means the third, seventh, and ninth chapters of Deuteronomy. Remember, a colon is necessary to indicate a verse.

If more than one biblical book is referenced, it will be contained in a separate designation and separated by a semicolon, for example, Jn 3:3; Ex 1:2.

Decipher this one: Gen 4:5-8; 7:4,7; 10:1.

It refers to the book of Genesis, verses five through eight of chapter four, verses four and seven of chapter seven, and verse one of chapter ten.

The letters "f." or "ff." following a biblical reference means the verse designated and the verse/verses that follow. Scholars use this with the assumption that the reader will know from the context how far to read.

The term "cf." means cross reference, and precedes a passage that is referenced but not quoted. If a passage is quoted verbatim, it will not be preceded by a "cf." For example, cf. Ezek 34:15 ff. refers the reader to God's statement uttered through Ezekial that he will be Israel's shepherd. God's proclamation is followed by a lengthy explanation that does not lend itself to a precise stopping point, hence the "ff." designation. The reader can then determine how much of the passage he wishes to read.

When a reference ends in a, b, or c, it refers to the first, second, or third part of a verse that is lengthy or reflects a break in thought.

The most prominent example of this is Gen 2:4, in which the first half of the verse, identified as Gen 2:4a, concludes the first creation story (Gen 1:1-2:4a), and the second half of the verse, Gen 2:4b, begins the second (Gen 2:4b-3:24).

It is the biblical text that is inspired, not the verse numbering system. Occasionally, we encounter passages in which verse or chapter breaks are questionable.

SYMBOLS SUMMARY

Remember what the symbols mean:

:   A colon indicates a verse designation will follow.

- A hyphen indicates a continuous sequence of verses or chapters.
, A comma preceded by a colon and a number indicates a discontinuous sequence of verses within the same chapter.
; A semicolon designates a different chapter within the same book, or indicates that a different book is being referenced.
cf. precedes a non-quoted biblical reference.
f. or ff. means the cited verses and following.
a, b, or **c** following a verse number indicates only part of that verse.

FEEDBACK

Your feedback is part of my continuing education. I utilize it and greatly appreciate your time and thoughtfulness. You can contact me at my Web site (www.karlaschultz.com) or e-mail address (karlaschultz@juno.com), or by writing Genesis Personal Development Center, 3431 Gass Avenue, Pittsburgh, PA 15212-2239. The telephone number is (412) 766-7545.

DEDICATION

This book is dedicated to Mom, Dad, and Big T. I love and miss you always.

KARL A. SCHULTZ

Section One

How to Read the Bible

Chapter One

——— The Contents of the Bible ———

┌─ Contents of this Chapter ────────

- Learn the components of the Old and New Testament.
- Discover why Jewish, Protestant, Catholic, and Orthodox canons of the Old Testament differ.
- Encounter ancient Jewish writings that were excluded from the Bible by both Jews and Christians.
- Learn about the first major translation of the Bible.

WHAT IS THE BIBLE?

The word "Bible" comes from the Greek phrase *ta biblia*, which means books or scrolls (cf. 2 Mac 8:23; Dan 9:2). The Bible is actually not one book, but many. The earliest passages in the Bible (from the book of Exodus) date to the late thirteenth century B.C. (the time of Moses), while the last book in the New Testament was probably composed between A.D. 100 and 125. I use the qualifier "probably" because dating the Bible is an inexact science, given its antiquity and the lack of surviving date-specific records.

For Christians, the Bible is divided into two parts, the Old Testament and the New Testament. The word testament is a synonym for covenant. For ecumenical reasons, the Old Testament is often referred to as the Hebrew Bible or the Jewish

Scriptures. However, that terminology is imprecise in a Catholic context — as discussed below, the list of books in the Hebrew (and Protestant) Bible differs from that in the Catholic and Orthodox Bible.

The terms First and Second Testament are also used in place of Old and New. However, this dispenses with the integral term "new" that is used in both the Hebrew (cf. Jer 31:31-34) and Christian sections (cf. Lk 22:20; 1 Cor 11:25; Heb 8:8-13) of the Bible to describe God's covenant with his people.

WHAT DOES IT MEAN?

 You will encounter references in Bible footnotes to the biblical "canon." Canon originally meant reed, and also referred to a standard or measuring stick. It became the term used to describe the list of books in the Bible.

COMPONENTS OF THE OLD TESTAMENT

Catholics divide the Old Testament into three sections: the historical books, the wisdom books, and the prophetic books.

The historical books include, in the following order:

Genesis	Judges	Nehemiah
Exodus	Ruth	Tobit
Leviticus	1 & 2 Samuel	Judith
Numbers	1 & 2 Kings	Esther
Deuteronomy	1 & 2 Chronicles	1 & 2 Maccabees.
Joshua	Ezra	

The wisdom books include:

Job	Song of Songs
Psalms	Wisdom (of Solomon)
Proverbs	Sirach.
Ecclesiastes	

The prophetic books include:

Isaiah	Hosea	Nahum
Jeremiah	Joel	Habakkuk
Lamentations	Amos	Zephaniah
Baruch	Obadiah	Haggai
Ezekiel	Jonah	Zechariah
Daniel	Micah	Malachi.

DISPUTED WRITINGS

The composition of the Old Testament is not uniform among Christians and Jews. Protestants and Jews exclude the following books from their Old Testament canon (list of inspired books): Tobit, Judith, 1 and 2 Maccabees, Sirach (Ecclesiasticus), Wisdom (of Solomon), Baruch, and parts of Esther and Daniel.

The Greek/Eastern Orthodox Church includes the above books while adding 1 Esdras, Psalm 151, 3 Maccabees (with 4 Maccabees in an appendix), and the Prayer of Manasseh. The Russian Orthodox Church adds 1 and 2 Esdras, Psalm 151, and 3 Maccabees.

WHAT DOES IT MEAN?

The term *apocrypha* (Greek for "hidden") is used by Protestants to describe the disputed writings. Catholics refer to these as the deuterocanonical (second canon) books because they were composed later than the rest of the Old Testament. Unlike the Protestant tradition, Catholics consider these to be as authoritative and inspired as the rest of the Old Testament.

Catholics use the term *apocryphal* and Protestants use *pseudepigrapha* (Greek for "false writings") to describe books universally excluded from the canon.

REJECTED WRITINGS

Widely circulated Jewish apocryphal writings include the Assumption of Moses, Jubilees, 4 Esdras, The Testament of Twelve Patriarchs, and 1 Enoch. Prominent exclusions from the New Testament canon include the Gospel of Peter, the Gospel of the Hebrews, the Protoevangelium of James, and the book of most interest to scholars, the Gospel of Thomas.

THE BIBLE SAYS WHAT?

 Some passages in the Bible make reference or contain parallels to the apocryphal writings. For example, Jude (probably the least read New Testament book) contains an allusion to 1 Enoch, and refers to a legendary dispute between the archangel Michael and Satan over Moses' body that is described in the Assumption of Moses.

The New Testament-related apocryphal writings are the sole source of non-biblical details that have become part of Catholic tradition. These include Peter's request to be crucified upside down, the names of the thieves on the cross (Dismas and Gestas), the names of Mary's parents (Joachim and Anna), and Veronica's wiping of the face of Jesus.

HOW DID THE DISPUTED BOOKS ARISE?

Subsequent to the fall of the northern (721 B.C.) and southern (587 B.C.) kingdoms of Judaism, and for socio-economic reasons as well, Jewish people began living in communities outside of the promised land (parts of modern-day Israel, Jordan, Syria, and Lebanon — also referred to as Palestine and Canaan). The lands the Jews dispersed/migrated to, and the process itself, are referred to as the Diaspora, or "the Dispersion," the Greek word's translation.

When Alexander the Great conquered most of the Near East in the mid-fourth century B.C., he and his successors brought Greek language, religion, and culture. The Jewish people living in the Diaspora eventually could no longer understand Hebrew. Having had their temple destroyed by the Babylonians in 587 B.C., they were now in danger of losing their Scriptures.

To address this need, a third century B.C. translation of the Old Testament into Greek was undertaken by Jewish scholars in Alexandria, Egypt, the seat of Greek culture in the Near East. This is referred to as the Septuagint, from the Greek word for seventy, and is often denominated as LXX (the Roman numerals for seventy).

According to a legend recorded in the *Letter of Aristeas*, seventy-two scholars translated the Old Testament into Greek in seventy-two days, and came up with identical translations.

This tale and numeric symbolism convey the high esteem in which the translation was held. As evidenced by the Dead Sea Scrolls (second century B.C. fragments of Old Testament books discovered between 1947 and 1956), different versions of the Septuagint existed, and underwent periodic revision.

The Septuagint contained additional books written in Greek (the books of Sirach and Tobit were available, at least in part, in Hebrew and Aramaic respectively) that circulated widely but were eventually excluded from the Jewish canon, probably because they were composed after the latest books in the Jewish canon, at which point the Jews believed God had ceased revealing himself in inspired books. The list of books in the Jewish canon was determined definitively between the late second and early third centuries A.D.

The New Testament authors frequently quote or draw from the Septuagint. For example, the apex of the passion narrative in Matthew draws directly from a passage in the Wisdom of Solomon (cf. Mt 27:41-43; Wis 2:17-20).

DOUBTS ABOUT THE DEUTEROCANONICAL BOOKS

Although doubts over the canonicity of the deuterocanonical books were raised sporadically in the early centuries of Christianity, including by Origen (the Church's first biblical scholar), St. Athanasius (whose doubt may have reflected his Jewish teachers' influence), and St. Jerome (translator of the Bible into Latin in the late fourth and early fifth century), they were used extensively in the preaching, teaching, and worship of the early Church. The book of Sirach became known as Ecclesiasticus ("Church book" in Latin) because it was used so extensively in the liturgy and in Christian moral teachings.

The only significant theological principle in the disputed books that is absent from the other canonical books is that of intercession for the dead (cf. 2 Macc 12:39-45), upon which the Catholic teaching of purgatory is partially based.

In response to rejection of the disputed books by the Protestant reformers, on April 8, 1546, the Council of Trent definitively defined the Old Testament canon as we have it today.

Protestant recognition of the value of the Apocrypha as edifying spiritual reading is indicated by inclusion of the books in an appendix in several modern Protestant translations.

SIGNS OF THE TIMES: THE BIBLE TODAY

 Familiarity with the purpose and context of the Septuagint, the first important translation of the Bible, alerts us to a parallel with modern life. Like the Jews of Jesus' time and the centuries immediately before, most Christians know the Bible only in translation. Like the Diaspora Jews, we live far from the Holy Land in a highly secular culture that is smitten with tantalizing philosophies (in our day, secular humanism and New Age spirituality), and are subject to discrimination or even persecution from persons both within and outside of our faith community.

COMPOSITION OF THE NEW TESTAMENT

Protestants, Catholics, and Orthodox share the same New Testament canon. The New Testament begins with the four

Gospels: Matthew, Mark, Luke, and John. Immediately following is Acts of the Apostles, an account of the activities of the early Church, particularly the apostles Peter and Paul. It was written by the evangelist Luke as a companion to his Gospel.

Following these are the letters of Paul in order of decreasing length, beginning with books written to a community: Romans, 1 and 2 Corinthians, Galatians, Ephesians, Philippians, Colossians, 1 and 2 Thessalonians, 1 and 2 Timothy, Titus, and Philemon.

After Paul's letters comes Hebrews, traditionally (but with doubts beginning in the early Church) ascribed to Paul due to references to Timothy in Heb 13:23, but whose authorship is a mystery, and the so-called catholic (universal) or general letters: James, 1 and 2 Peter, 1, 2, and 3 John, and Jude. Unlike most of Paul's letters, these are not identified with any particular Christian community. The New Testament closes with Revelation (traditionally known as Apocalypse), the most cryptic book in the Bible.

BEGINNING AND ENDING WITH JESUS CHRIST

One of the most famous quotations on the Bible in Catholic tradition comes from St. Jerome, the Church's first great translator of the Bible: "Ignorance of the Scriptures is ignorance of Christ."

When I was in college, I took a course on Catholicism in which the priest ended the first session with the statement, "Roman Catholicism begins with Jesus Christ," followed by a lengthy pause. I expected him to continue by mentioning the sacraments, saints, Mary, the popes, bingo (just kidding), etc., but instead, he continued in a solemn and steady manner, "and it ends there, too."

In that spirit, Catholics view the Bible as an opportunity to encounter Jesus both individually and as a community through the inspiration of the Holy Spirit. In so doing, we discover the love and will of our heavenly father.

St. Teresa of Ávila emphasized that we come to God through the human Jesus. The New Testament is that story, and the Old

Testament prepares us for such. In the next chapter, we will refine our understanding of a fundamental biblical term for itself and Jesus, the word of God.

Chapter Two

The Word of God

Now that we know the contents of the Bible, we should consider what it means to refer to the Bible as the word of God, its fundamental designation by believers. The concept of "word" is essential to an understanding of both the human and divine dimensions of the Bible. A comprehension of the power of words, the most basic level of communication, is integral to an understanding of human development and relationships.

The ancient Hebrew conception of the divine and human word underscores the Bible's relevance to spiritual and human development. In the next chapter, we will further explore how the divine and human came together in the formation of the Bible, and how its development mirrors ours.

THE POWER OF THE HUMAN WORD

The ancient Hebrew concept of word (in Hebrew, *dabar*) was much more dynamic than ours. A word was not only an utterance, but an entity of meaning and action.

We live in an era of high technology communications, yet have lost touch with the most basic level of language, words. Society has become largely indifferent to the integrity of words. When was the last time you heard the expression "A man's word is his bond"? Personal, business, community, and global relationships break down when human words are devalued.

The Hebrews respected the power of words so much that they used a special word, "Amen," to communicate agreement. When Jesus, an individual (cf. Num 5:22; Tob 8:6), or the community (cf. Neh 8:6; Jdt 13:20) wish to give extra affirmation to something, they say "amen, amen." Several of the Psalms (cf. Ps 72:19; 89:52) end with two "Amens."

Since the Bible stresses truthfulness and fidelity to human words, imagine the respect and power it attributes to God's word.

WRESTLING WITH THE WORD

To what persons, beliefs, and commitments in my life would I append a double amen?

Is my word my bond? Can others put their trust in it?

Do I believe that God's word can be trusted, that his promises in the Bible can be counted upon (cf. Jas 1:5-7)? Am I willing to take risks for God, as he has for me?

THE HEBREW NOTION OF THE DIVINE WORD

With God's word, the dynamic character of *dabar* takes on even greater significance. The Hebrews understood God's word as something alive and effective. It got things done, and evoked a response. God's word contained meaning, willpower, and energy.

It was not simply an utterance or a collection of letters. God's word was his way of communicating with human beings, acting in the world, and inviting a response.

PEAK PASSAGES

"Is not my word like fire, says the LORD, and like a hammer which breaks the rock in pieces?" (Jer 23:29; cf. Heb 4:12-13).

"For as the rain and the snow come down from heaven, and return not thither but water the earth, making it bring forth and sprout, giving seed to the sower and bread to the eater, so shall my word be that goes forth from my mouth; it shall not return to me empty, but it shall accomplish that which I purpose, and prosper in the thing for which I sent it" (Is 55:10-11).

"All flesh is like grass and all its glory like the flower of grass. The grass withers, and the flower falls, but the word of the LORD abides for ever" (1 Pet 1:24-25; cf. Is 40:8).

JESUS, GOD'S WORD PAR EXCELLENCE

Building upon the Hebrew concept of word, the Gospel and first letter of John used the Greek word *logos* ("word") to describe Jesus' pre-existence and foundational role in creation (cf. Jn 1:1-18; 1 Jn 1:1-4). John presents Jesus as the meaning and positive force behind creation, and the perfect communication and representation of God. This builds upon Old Testament notions of the divine personification of wisdom, such as in Prov 8:22-31 (cf. Sir 1:4-8; 24:9).

The Greek philosophers understood *logos* in a cosmic sense as the universal and divine wisdom, the reason for everything and the force behind the universe. A prominent Jewish philosopher, Philo of Alexandria (20 B.C.-A.D. 50), utilized the concept of *logos* in making Judaism comprehensible in a Greek culture.

Parallels between Philo's and John's use of the term indicate that John was likewise seeking to bridge Hebrew biblical and Greek philosophical notions of word in describing Jesus and making him comprehensible to his contemporaries. Paul likewise drew upon Greek concepts of virtue (cf. Phil 4:8) in order to make the Gospel comprehensible to his audience.

PEAK PASSAGES

 When we read the Bible and are convinced of its intrinsic connections with life, we, too, will be able to link legitimate secular concepts with the Gospel, and, therefore, share the word with people in a language they can understand, so as not to be displeasing or confusing.

Pope Paul VI's 1964 encyclical *Ecclesiam Suam* (Paths of the Church) and 1975 apostolic exhortation *Evangelii Nuntiandi* (On Evangelization in the Modern World) laid out a Christian model of communication and evangelization rooted in biblical spirituality and sensitized to modernity. This embodies the spirit of the Second Vatican Council, and, in particular, the document *Gaudium et Spes* (Pastoral Constitution on the Church in the Modern World), in which the phrase "truly human" appears numerous times as an expression of the Church's solidarity with humankind in the footsteps of her master (cf. Jn 1:14; 3:17).

GOD'S WORD IN TRADITION AND THE CHURCH

Catholics believe that God's word is present in Church Tradition (essential teachings and practices handed down for posterity) and in the faith of the contemporary community. The Second Vatican Council document on the Bible, *Dei Verbum* (Dogmatic Constitution on Divine Revelation), teaches that Scripture and Tradition are not separate sources of revelation, but rather parallel streams from the same "divine wellspring."

Scripture began as oral tradition, so the two share the same essence and origin. Likewise, the faith of the living Church as officially taught by the magisterium is not opposed to Scripture or Tradition, but rather safeguards, ponders (cf. Lk 2:19), and applies it to contemporary life.

GOD'S WORD IN HUMAN WORDS

Catholics (and many other Christians) articulate the Bible's simultaneously divine and human authorship in the expression: "God's word in human words." The Bible's divine origins are recognized by stating that the Bible is inspired by the Holy Spirit. The term *inspiration* literally means "spirit-breathed."

The Bible is subject to all the ambiguities and challenges of human communications, spanning the process of the human author(s) interpreting the message and articulating it in writing, the communities copying it for distribution, and each receptor of the message comprehending it in a unique way.

This accounts for the variety of translations (see Chapter Four) and interpretations of the Bible, and the caution of the Church in definitively determining the meaning of a passage, which historically it has done only for doctrinal and disciplinary (to clarify or affirm Church practice and order) reasons. This gives individual believers latitude in interpreting the Bible's meaning providing that we use Church-approved interpretive guidelines such as discussed in this book and stay within the confines of Church teaching.

The Bible itself recognizes its interpretive difficulties:

"So also our beloved brother Paul wrote to you according to the wisdom given him, speaking of this as he does in all his letters. There are some things in them hard to understand, which the ignorant and unstable twist to their own destruction, as they do the other scriptures" (2 Pet 3:15-16).

The Incarnational Nature of the Bible

The mystery of the Incarnation (cf. Jn 1:14) is a good analogy for comprehending the mysterious paradox of perfection (inspiration/divine authorship) and imperfection (human participation) co-existing in the Bible. Such mysteries do not lend themselves to precise explanations, which is why the Bible often uses stories, symbols, metaphors, and analogies. Gen 1-11 is a classic example of this.

Familiar and concrete images engage the reader's/listener's emotions, mental associations, symbolic world, and experiences, and are typically more effective than abstract philosophical language in making profound truths comprehensible and relevant.

God's word, like Jesus, is both divine and human. Jesus was born of a woman and under the law (cf. Gal 4:4). All manifestations of God's word: Jesus, human beings, Tradition, the faith of the contemporary community, and the Bible, are subject to human conditions and limitations.

The Catholic understanding of biblical inspiration in the context of human freedom may be stated, however imprecisely, as follows: God communicated a message to individuals and faith communities who, guided by the inspiration of the Holy Spirit, used their capacities to convey it in a manner comprehensible in both a time-conditioned (historical) and timeless sense.

Jewish and Protestant denominations vary in their understanding of the degree to which the Bible is both human and divine in origin. Beliefs range from positions similar to

Catholicism to fundamentalism (the Bible contains the literal words of God mechanically transcribed by human authors) and rationalism (denial or de-emphasis of the divine dimension).

BIBLICAL INERRANCY AND PAPAL INFALLIBILITY

One of the words frequently used in reference to the Bible is "inerrancy." Though currently more frequently used by Protestants, particularly evangelicals, it is also part of the Catholic vocabulary. It has traditionally been understood to mean that the Bible contains no errors of any kind.

The word inerrancy, or its equivalent, is not found in the Bible, and is ill-suited to describe the type of truth presented by the Bible. Its rigidly literal connotations are foreign to the mentality of the biblical authors and communities.

A parallel exists with the doctrine of papal infallibility. Just as the Pope speaks infallibly only when he proclaims his teachings on faith and morals *ex cathedra* (Latin for "from the chair" [of St. Peter]), likewise the Bible's "inerrancy" is limited to its central objectives. The definitive Catholic document on divine revelation, the Second Vatican Council's *Dei Verbum*, defines the Bible's truthfulness as follows:

"Therefore, since everything asserted by the inspired authors or sacred writers must be held to be asserted by the Holy Spirit, it follows that the books of Scripture must be acknowledged as teaching solidly, faithfully and without error that truth which God wanted put into sacred writings for the sake of salvation."

Therefore, "all Scripture is divinely inspired and has its use for teaching the truth and refuting error, for reformation of manners and discipline in right living, so that the man who belongs to God may be efficient and equipped for good work of every kind" (2 Tim 3:16-17, Greek text).

The latter is the Bible's primary statement on its inspiration and purpose.

The presence of errors in the Bible was pointed out at the

Second Vatican Council in a historic speech by Austrian Cardinal Franz König (1905-2004) on October 2, 1964. As examples, he cited the incorrect name used in Mk 2:26 (Abiathar should be Abimelech), Mt 27:9's ascription of a prophecy to Jeremiah instead of Zechariah, and an incorrect date used in Dan 1:1.

However, such historical, literary, or scientific discrepancies are peripheral to the Bible's purpose, and do not detract from its efficacy. It is more accurate to describe the Bible's truthfulness in positive terms related to its objectives. As indicated by the *Dei Verbum* quotation, Catholics believe that the Bible is completely true with respect to its teaching on matters related to salvation, including morality (right and wrong), theology (about God), and spirituality (how moral and theological principles translate into practice, for example, in worship, prayer, devotions, and study).

THE BIBLE'S ORAL ORIGINS

The seeds of the Bible lay in orally transmitted stories, prayers, proverbs, instructions, and songs (e.g., the Psalms, Song of Songs) that were handed down and eventually transcribed. Much in the Bible is the final revision of layers of oral and written traditions edited and woven together. Neither Jesus nor the Bible dropped from heaven. Both were born through normal human processes, aided by the Holy Spirit.

DEVELOPMENTAL PARALLELS

Just as Jesus' immersion in the human condition enabled him to draw close to us and vice-versa (the New Testament letter to the Hebrews explores this in detail), likewise the Bible's subjection to human conditions resulted in its development in a manner similar to the way humans develop. This makes it easier to relate to and identify with. This is the incarnational principle discussed earlier with reference to God's word. We'll explore the evolution of the Bible from the perspective of both historical and human development in the next chapter.

Chapter Three

———— The Human Development ————
of the Bible

Contents of this Chapter

- Familiarize yourself with the progression of persons, groups, writings, and revelation in the Old Testament.
- Learn concepts of biblical theology, such as the development of revelation, retribution doctrine, primary and secondary causes, and divine providence.
- Recognize parallels between your development and the Bible's.
- Recognize the ongoing aspect of divine revelation.

Like human development, the Bible's evolution is varied and complex. Given its ancient origins, there is much we can only speculate on. Still, in order to know the Bible on an intimate basis, you must know something of its roots and development.

In this chapter, we'll reflect on the process by which God gradually revealed himself in various ways, culminating in the gift of his son (cf. Heb 1:1-2). We'll conclude our introduction to the Bible's divine and human nature by surveying the general pattern of the Bible's evolution and its parallels to our development. Because it is meant for humans, the Bible naturally evolved in ways paralleling our growth.

THE DEVELOPMENT OF THE OLD TESTAMENT

The Old Testament took shape through a long and complex process that exceeds the scope of this book. For introductory purposes, I will summarize it according to the major individuals and groups involved.

The Patriarchs and Matriarchs

God spoke to and was active in the lives of Abraham and Sarah, Isaac and Rebekah, and Jacob and Rachel (the patriarchs and matriarchs). He was also active in the lives of Jacob's sons, particularly Joseph. The accounts of their experiences and interactions with God were handed down for centuries within the Hebrew tribes (the descendants of Jacob's sons) and were refined and recorded in chapters 12-50 of Genesis.

The Tribes

The twelve tribes of Israel (cf. Gen 49:1-28) became a nation, albeit still a loose conglomeration of clans, under Moses, and settled throughout the promised land.

The Scribes and Storytellers

During the reigns of Kings David and Solomon, scribes (persons who recorded the Scriptures and other important records) refined and recorded stories and revelations that had been handed down. They also chronicled the activities of David and Solomon and their predecessor, Saul. These were handed down and edited and became part of the books of Samuel and Kings.

The tradition of storytelling would continue in Israel through the post-exilic period (short stories such as Ruth, Esther, and Jonah) down to Tobit and Judith in the second century B.C.

The Sages

Inspired by King Solomon, the Bible's consummate wise man (cf. 1 Kings 3:3-15; 4:29-34), the sages (wise men) taught and compiled instructional material on effective and wholesome/moral living, the Bible's version of today's "self-help" counsel. It was passed down within families and schools, and eventually became part of the wisdom books of the Old Testament.

The Psalmists

Although we lack details on the precise nature of Israel's public worship and liturgical rituals, we know that music was a big part of it. The Psalms likely began taking form under David — himself a composer of at least some of the Psalms attributed to him — and evolved for centuries afterward.

The psalmists brought poetry, history, praise, wisdom, morality, and lamentation together in a manner that was so respected by the early Christians that they did not try to duplicate their efforts. No separate category of Psalms exists in the New Testament, and only a few hymns (e.g., Phil 2:5-11, Col 1:15-20) are included.

The Prophets

When the Jewish people and leaders strayed and followed the way of the polytheists (Israel's neighbors and conquerors who believed in many gods), the prophets called them back.

Although Samuel and Moses were identified as prophets (they were more prominently known as judge and lawgiver respectively) and esteemed ones (cf. Jer 15:1), the most famous prophet (he represented the prophets during Jesus' transfiguration; cf. Mt 17:1-8) was Elijah, who lived during the ninth century B.C., and was succeeded by another prominent prophet, Elisha. Their exploits are detailed in 1 Kings 17:1-2 Kings 1:18 and 2 Kings 2:1-8:29, respectively. Unlike the later prophets, neither is credited with authorship of a biblical book.

The prophetic books came from the prophets and their disciples, beginning with Isaiah and Hosea in the eighth century and ending with Joel in the late fifth or early fourth century.

The Priests

When the Jewish temple in Jerusalem was destroyed and the people were exiled to Babylon (587 B.C.), the Jewish priests organized and refined the Torah (the first five books of the Old Testament) and the books chronicling the conquest of the promised land and the exploits of the Jewish kings (Joshua through 2 Kings). These were assembled from the oral and written materials that had been handed down. Biblical scholars now believe that most of the books of the Old Testament took their final form after the return from Babylon in 538 B.C.

The People

With their primary mode of religious expression eliminated (temple worship), and being surrounded by polytheists, the Jewish people turned to the biblical materials (first in oral form, then written) to preserve their faith. The word of God assumed greater prominence in Jewish spirituality than burnt offerings, which was the way God had intended it all along (cf. Hos 6:6; Mt 9:13).

The Politicians

In the mid-fifth century B.C., the priest and scribe Ezra and his disciples, empowered by Nehemiah, the governor of Jerusalem, chronicled the activities of Israel after the return from Babylon, and compiled something close to a final version of the Torah.

The Potpourri

A potpourri of wisdom books, inspiring short stories, and accounts of later Jewish history known as the deuterocanonical books became the final books included in the Old Testament.

THE DEVELOPMENT OF THE NEW TESTAMENT

Because the New Testament has fewer authors and was written over a period of less than eighty years, its canonization process (determining which books were inspired and should be included in the New Testament) was simpler. Still, the list of books in the New Testament wasn't stated definitively until a letter of St. Athanasius in A.D. 367, and later at the councils of Hippo in A.D. 393 and Carthage in A.D. 397 (both in Africa).

The earliest New Testament documents, the letters of St. Paul, were written between A.D. 50 and 64. Other letters written by Paul and mentioned in his letters (cf. 2 Cor 2) have not survived.

As discussed in Chapter Sixteen, some of the letters attributed to Paul give indications of being written or edited by others, in which case they were likely written later, probably between the A.D. 60s and the early 90s. Known as pseudonymity, this practice was common in the ancient near east and other oral cultures. While the Catholic Church discourages irresponsible scholarly speculation about pseudonymity, the latter has no bearing on the inspired status of the books.

The apostles spread the word about Jesus, initially through oral preaching and teaching, and healing. Eventually, four evangelists (authors of the Gospels) organized and edited oral and written materials that were based on the apostles' preaching and teaching. Beginning with Mark and ending with John, the Gospels were published between A.D. 60 and 100.

This process is described in the Pontifical Biblical Commission's 1964 document, *Instruction on the Historical Truth of the Gospels*, which helped set the stage for the Second Vatican Council's document on Scripture, *Dei Verbum*.

Leaders of the early Church, whether the apostles or their disciples or scribes (cf. 1 Pet 5:12), composed letters to unnamed communities. Known as the catholic (universal) or general letters, these eventually became regarded as inspired. The last of these, 2 Peter, was probably written between A.D. 100 and 125.

The Role of Councils

The list of books included in the Bible was determined based on the opinions of influential leaders and usage within the communities of believers. Final decisions were made at official gatherings known as ecumenical councils. Councils and synods (gatherings of bishops, clergy, and/or laypersons) continue to be a forum through which the Church gathers to resolve issues related to the Bible, Church practices and doctrine, and contemporary life.

DEVELOPMENT OF REVELATION

As the Bible evolved, so did its teachings. The evolution of doctrine and practices within the Bible is known as development of revelation. The earlier books of the Bible teach concepts and practices that later books modify or reject.

For example, the early books of the Old Testament present God as approving of severe violence to Israel's enemies. Jesus goes beyond the bounds of nationalism and shows that God wills peace and forgiveness, rather than judgment and strict retribution.

Perhaps the most obvious example of the development of revelation is contained in the Sermon on the Mount (cf. Mt 5-7), in which Jesus goes beyond surface interpretations of Old Testament moral principles and focuses on the intent rather than the letter of the law.

Retribution Doctrine

Recognizing the development of revelation alerts us to several prominent theological issues. One example is the principle that in this world you are rewarded strictly according to the morality of your deeds. This is known as retribution doctrine/theology, or the Deuteronomic principle because of its presence in that book (cf. Deut 30:14-18). Later Old Testament writings, such as the Psalms (e.g., Ps 22, 31, 44, 69, 73), Job, and Wisdom (cf. Wis 1-3) rejected this doctrine, as did Jesus himself (cf. Lk 13:1-5; Jn 9:1-3).

Such inner tension within the Bible is one reason Catholics interpret it in context and as a whole, and within a community environment in which subjective perspectives can be balanced. Like life, the Bible's many paradoxical elements must be maintained in a healthy tension in order to arrive at balanced, prudent, and inclusive interpretations.

God's communication with believers is dynamic and ongoing. It is suited to our individual and collective capacities to receive the message (cf. Heb 5:11-14). We can comprehend the evolving message of the Old Testament, in particular, by recognizing that the ancient Israelites were a primitive society that apparently was not ready to receive the fullness of divine revelation until the time of Jesus. Jesus' disciples likewise exhibited a dullness of heart (cf. Mt 28:17; Mk 16:14; Lk 24:25; Jn 20:24-29). Each of us exhibits a slowness to grasp God's message. We can be thankful that God works with us as we are, and is patient (cf. Lk 13:6-9).

Divine Providence Distinctions

Another concept that was to undergo modification in the Bible was that of divine providence. The ancient Hebrews saw God as the ultimate or primary cause of everything. Its classic expression is Is 45:7: "I form the light and I create the darkness, I make well–being, and I create disaster, I, Yahweh, do all these things" (New Jerusalem Bible).

Gradually, the biblical peoples began to recognize that events could be attributed to secondary (natural) causes, which operated in the context of divine providence (God's caring maintenance of creation, particularly human beings).

We now know that human error, irresponsibility, and sinfulness, rather than God's wrath or fundamental defects in nature, are the source of most human and natural problems, although tragedies such as natural disasters and the death of babies or mothers during childbirth remain mysteries beyond human comprehension.

Jas 1:13-17 attributes all evil to secondary causes (human sinfulness), and all good ultimately to primary causes (God). God is the source of the goodness brought about by humans and nature.

There is a related theological distinction between God's direct and permissive will. Gen 2-3 teaches that God gave human beings freedom of choice in regards to obeying his commandments. God permits, or allows, evil as a consequence of and out of respect for free will, but he always desires and works to bring about (directly wills) good. The interplay between divine providence and human free will remains a mystery that even Jesus or the Bible doesn't try to explain. The solution offered by Job (cf. Job 42:6) and Jesus (cf. Lk 13:1-5) is repentance, that is, letting God change us rather than trying to change God and things beyond our control.

Even as they came to recognize the existence of secondary causes, the biblical peoples still saw God as present and active in their world. God's benevolent initiative in human affairs (cf. Lk 12:22-34) is traditionally referred to as divine providence. God's initiative is a fundamental precept of biblical theology: "We love, because he first loved us" (1 Jn 4:19).

RELATING THE BIBLE'S DEVELOPMENT TO YOURS

After surveying just the surface of the Bible's complex evolution, you can still discover dynamic parallels between its development and yours:

The Bible begins with creation (cf. Gen 1-2), even though the Hebrews experienced God as deliverer (through the Exodus [from Egypt] experience) before they knew him as creator.

Likewise, you perceive God in your origins after the fact, as you look back on your life and note how God has frequently come to your rescue. Through faith and reason, you recognize that his providential initiative has extended to your very beginning.

When God acknowledged the goodness of creation in Gen 1, he was referring to each of us. What better inspiration for a healthy identity or self-image than to know that God knew what he was doing in creating us, and that we bring him delight?

Jewish stories began with the patriarchal clans. Our first experience of spiritual values, or their lack, comes through family, or those in surrogate roles.

Our most intense experiences of God are when he helps us through a crisis. The defining experience of the Jewish people in the Old Testament is the Exodus, in which God delivered his oppressed people. They "passed over" from a life of physical slavery to one of potential spiritual and political freedom, depending on their response to God's covenant with them.

As we mature, we come to a more formal understanding of right and wrong ways of living. This corresponds to the forty-year period in the desert in which Israel struggled to assimilate the divine instructions given to Moses. As with the Israelites, each of our steps forward seem to be followed by two backward. Further, each of us has our "golden calf" experiences (cf. Ex 32) in the sense of shameful behavior motivated by fear, selfishness, and insecurity that requires correction.

When we are young and sowing our oats, we feel like kings or queens. We explore different ways of thinking, communicating, and living, and expand our horizons. Likewise, the period of the united monarchy under David and Solomon (the tenth century B.C.) was one of two periods in biblical history (the other was during Josiah's reign in the last half of the seventh century B.C.) in which the Jewish people exercised significant political and economic power. It was also the period in which the written Scriptures began to take shape. Likewise, many people record in a journal their perspectives and experiences during significant stages of their lives.

When we are young and vibrant, we express our emotions and experiences through poetry and music. The Psalms and Song of Songs filled this need for the Hebrews.

We seek to develop our potential and lead a wholesome and prosperous life. Biblical wisdom literature guided the Hebrews, and can help us.

At various points in life, we lose our way and forget our roots. Hopefully, there are persons in our lives, such as the Hebrew prophets, who will point out our indiscretions, refresh our spiritual memory, and get us back on track. The Church provides support in this area through the Eucharist, confession, magisterial teachings, pastoral counsel, and the preaching of the word at liturgy.

As we grow older, we encounter many ups and downs. Sometimes things work out; other times we experience estrangement and loss, and either literally or figuratively go into exile (physical, emotional, and/or spiritual alienation).

When we are stripped of everything, particularly non-essentials, and God feels furthest away, we can be most open to him. We have less to distract and deter us. During and after the exile into Babylon, much of the Old Testament arose, and older parts took final form.

The cycle of death and resurrection finds sacred expression in the sacraments. The Sacrament of the Anointing of the Sick

---

WRESTLING WITH THE WORD

What parallels do I notice between the development of revelation and the Jewish people in the Bible and my own growth?

Have God's communications and actions unfolded in my life in stages, as in the Bible? What have been the key events and turning points, and how have I responded?

Who or what am I hoping and living for? What can I do today to be faithful to that vision and hope?

---

offers God's consolation to suffering persons and their loved ones. It reminds the community to pray for those who are suffering and dying, and presents their sufferings as a building up of the body of Christ through Jesus' salvific death and resurrection (cf. Jas 5:14-15; Col 1:24).

In our later years, we begin to put life's pieces together. We continue to grow as new influences arise and better ways of living are discovered. Correspondingly, Ezra and Nehemiah organized and promulgated much of the Old Testament (most of the wisdom books arose later), and composed, or were the source for, their namesake books.

When we realize that all of our efforts have fallen short, we acknowledge and accept our critical need for a redeemer. This leads us to join fellow believers (cf. Heb 11) in focusing on Jesus (cf. Heb 12:1-2), while heeding later prophets, such as Malachi, who address issues of sinfulness (e.g., divorce and idolatry; cf. Mal 2:13-16), while preparing for a redeemer (cf. Mal 3:1-5; Mt 25:1-30).

Chapter Four

—— How to Select a Bible Translation ——

┌───┐

Contents of this Chapter

- Develop a basic familiarity with the translation process so that you understand why translations differ and comprehend related comments in Bible footnotes and commentaries.
- Learn the objectives and usages of the two main approaches to translation, and which suits your Bible reading capacities and purposes.
- Encounter the most important Catholic and ecumenical English translations of the Bible, and learn how to choose among them.
- Overview supplemental Bible study resources and consider their utility in your circumstances.

└───┘

One of the first questions people ask when beginning to read the Bible concerns which translation they should use. In this chapter, we will explore the two main approaches to Bible translation, and how to decide which is appropriate for you. We will then survey contemporary Catholic and ecumenical translations and study editions, and consider criteria that will help you select an individual Bible. We will conclude by discussing learning aids included as part of study Bibles or as separate resources.

TRANSLATION IS A COMMUNITY AFFAIR

In the previous chapters, we saw that the compilation and interpretation of the Bible has always been a community affair. Acts 8:27-31 is the classic biblical testimony to this. In this chapter, we will see that translations and supplemental resources are likewise a collective undertaking.

By reading the Bible prayerfully and humbly, and putting our interpretations and applications at the service of the Church, we enter into a constructive dialogue with others and build up the body of Christ. Instead of judging others, God, or the Church, we let the Bible judge us, that is, reveal our hearts and the ways we need to grow. In the process, we are affirmed by God (and perhaps, others) for our openness, and experience consolation/inner peace (cf. Phil 4:7) rather than condemnation (cf. Rom 8:1).

Most Bible translations are the work of committees rather than an individual. In the twentieth century, the most prominent translations of the Bible by an individual were by Monsignor Ronald Knox (who worked from the Latin Vulgate) and Protestant scholar J.B. Phillips. Both are eminently readable, though less literal than the translations we will discuss here. They are fine for devotional or aesthetic reading, but not for study.

HOW A TRANSLATION COMES TO BE

The first line of guidance for persons unacquainted with biblical Hebrew and Greek is a translation. A basic understanding of the translation process will give you an insider's sense of how and why translations differ, and which ones are right for you. This compensates in part for not working from the original languages.

A translation originates in an individual's or group's decision to make the Bible more understandable and suitable to a particular constituency (e.g., Catholics, mainline Protestants, or Evangelicals) or sub-group (individuals needing a Bible that is easy to read rather than rigidly literal). Initiators of translations can be scholars, a religious foundation or association, or the hierarchy of one or more denominations. Scholars from different denominations commonly work together on translations and other projects.

We don't have one original-language Bible from which to translate. We have no original Bible books. The manuscripts we have are copies of copies. A technical branch of biblical studies known as textual (lower) criticism, is concerned with determining the most authentic reading (original-language text) for translators to work with.

Textual criticism is known as lower criticism because it is closer to the source — it deals with the make-up of the text itself. Higher criticism seeks to interpret the text as determined by lower criticism. While lower criticism is beyond the scope of this book, in Chapter Nine we will encounter various methods of higher criticism that are accessible to beginners.

WHAT DOES IT MEAN?

 Use of the word "criticism" with respect to biblical studies is not meant negatively. Linguistically, the word means to seek the essence of something. Undertaken properly, biblical criticism is a scientific and reverential attempt to discover the essential meaning of the Bible. Applying this understanding to personal relationships, this would mean that when I criticize someone, including myself, I should focus on the underlying truth involved rather than the negative dimensions.

The most interesting and accessible introduction to textual criticism and other background issues relevant to beginners is the late Richard T.A. Murphy, O.P.'s *Background to the Bible* (Servant Books). Published in 1980, it is a little-known classic in its field.

Because of this and many other good resources available, readers without formal theological training can learn to read the Bible competently in a relatively short period of time. In few other disciplines can beginners so quickly gain a grasp of essential issues.

MANUSCRIPT VARIANCES AND AMBIGUITIES

Places where manuscripts differ are called variants. The vast majority of these are insignificant transposition or other transcription errors. Most of the remaining discrepancies can be attributed to scribal or community theological or literary concerns that can be identified by the text critic.

Translations vary both because of the ambiguities of the original-language text as well as the differences in how each of us interpret language. Many words or expressions in the Bible have multiple or ambiguous meanings. Some words appear only once in the Old or New Testament. The technical term for these is *hapax* (*legomena*).

To our knowledge, we do not have any surviving documents outside the Bible that are written by biblical authors. If such documents existed, they would give us additional insights into the authors' vocabulary, style, historical context, and theological perspective.

WHAT WAS THE BIBLE WRITTEN ON?

When the Hebrews migrated from oral to written communications, and individual books of the Bible were first put into writing, they were transcribed on animal skins, a refined leather known as parchment, or rolls and sheets manufactured from papyrus, an aquatic plant that grew in the delta of the Nile and in parts of Italy. Papyrus was used before parchment, and after co-existing with it for centuries, was replaced by it. Egypt's dry climate enabled many ancient *papyri* to survive until modern times.

Though these terms are occasionally mentioned in commentaries and footnotes, the more common and inclusive/generic term is manuscript (abbreviated ms or mss [plural]).

IMPORTANT ANCIENT VERSIONS

If you use a study Bible or commentary, you will encounter references to the following ancient translations of the Bible:

Septuagint: A Greek translation of the Old Testament undertaken in Alexandria, Egypt, beginning around 280 B.C. and concluding between 200 B.C. and 150 B.C.

Vulgate: St. Jerome's translation of the entire Bible into Latin. It was undertaken approximately between A.D. 382 and 418. It is abbreviated as Vulg.

Targums: Free (that is, not always literal) translations of some books of the Hebrew Bible into Aramaic (a related Semitic language that in the last few centuries before Jesus had displaced Hebrew as the language of the Jewish people), accompanied by commentary. These were undertaken from around 250 B.C until A.D. 300. Abbreviated Targ for the Targums as a whole, or Tg for individual Targums (e.g., on Job, Genesis, Deuteronomy, etc.).

Dead Sea Scrolls (DSS): The most important biblical manuscript discovery of the twentieth century, the Dead Sea Scrolls are scrolls and fragments of biblical and other ancient religious documents discovered between 1947 and 1956 in eleven caves near where the wadi Qumran empties into the northwest corner of the Dead Sea, approximately ten miles south of Jericho. One scroll contains the entire text of Isaiah. Our oldest Hebrew manuscripts, they shed light on how the Old Testament was interpreted and applied in the two centuries before Jesus.

TWO TRANSLATION APPROACHES

Translations fall somewhere in the spectrum between two approaches known as functional (formerly called dynamic) equivalence and formal equivalence.

Under the functional-equivalence approach, translators render the original language into an equivalent expression in the receptor language (e.g., English, Spanish). The layman's term for functional equivalent translations is "the Bible in plain English (or everyday language)." Of course, the communication theories underlying this method involve more than just a simplification of the language.

Under the formal-equivalence approach, translators stick as much as possible to a literal, word-for-word, rendering.

Most Bibles explain their translation philosophy in their introduction.

Functional Equivalence

All languages have idioms (unique, provincial expressions) that can be difficult to communicate accurately in another language and context. Some expressions are meant figuratively rather than literally.

In such cases, a rigidly literal rendering doesn't convey the meaning comprehensibly. Here the functional-equivalent translator opts for an equivalent expression that conveys the perceived meaning rather than the literal word(s). Because this adds subjectivity as well as clarity, it requires the translator to exercise good judgment and restraint, and to balance many factors.

The less acquainted you are with the Bible, the more you will appreciate the extra step taken by functional-equivalent translators to make the Bible's meaning comprehensible. The negative side effects — the translator bias that is injected and the loss of literal accuracy — are acceptable tradeoffs for most beginners. A nice middle ground is a study Bible (discussed below), containing a functional equivalent translation.

Functional-equivalent translations work well for beginners, for devotional reading, and in group settings where the members vary in reading competence. Functional-equivalent translations can be a nice break from the less fluid formal-equivalent translations.

Many readers find it helpful to have both types of translations available, for comparison purposes and to accommodate the varying ways they use the Bible (that is, study, prayer, group reading, etc.).

Formal Equivalence

The formal-equivalence approach does not rely on a translator's ability to render meaning for meaning. Its literal, roughly word-for-word approach (some departures are necessary for comprehension purposes and to avoid distracting repetitions) entrusts the reader to interpret the text as is, aided by footnotes and commentaries. Formal-equivalent translations are often used in academic settings, as well as for private and group study.

The formal-equivalent translations discussed in this chapter read smoothly enough for aesthetic, meditative, and prayerful Bible reading. Only folks who prefer simple vocabulary and grammar would find formal-equivalent translations rough going, and in such cases the extra degree of explanation provided by a functional-equivalent translation would also be helpful.

NO ONE-SIZE-FITS-ALL TRANSLATION

The subjective nature and different usage of translations rules out having a universally applicable version. All translations try to balance accuracy (fidelity to the biblical text and writer) with comprehensible expression (fidelity to the reader). All translations contain functional- and formal-equivalent renderings, but lean in varying degrees toward either approach in accordance with their translation philosophy and anticipated audience and usage. As you become familiar with some of the translations discussed in this chapter, you'll discover your preferences not only with regard to translation style, but content (number of footnotes and background articles), print size, and layout.

SHOULD I STICK TO CATHOLIC TRANSLATIONS?

Most individuals prefer translations made by those who share their religious affiliation or perspective. The study aids included in most Bibles are influenced by denominational perspectives. Spirituality is so intimate a topic that we naturally feel more comfortable with those who share our views and values. Accordingly, it seems prudent to stick to either Catholic translations or ecumenical translations with Catholic involvement and hierarchical approval.

WHAT ABOUT OLDER BIBLES?

Most of us have Bibles lying around on shelves, coffee tables, and bookcases. If you've had them awhile, you may be wondering if they are sufficiently up-to-date.

At least at the beginning, a Bible in your hand is worth two on the shelf. If you already have a copy, it is probably best not to buy another one until you know what you're looking for; the one you have may suffice. You may also wish to see to what degree you are able to maintain a Bible-reading habit. If you have one of the following, consider its contents, layout, and print size, along with my advice, and use that as a criterion for purchasing a new one, if you should so decide.

Pre- or early twentieth-century translations, such as the Douay-Rheims (translated from the Latin Vulgate rather than the original languages) and the King James Version and its successor, the American Standard Version (published in 1901) are inadequate, as many discoveries and advances have subsequently occurred, and the language itself has changed.

The Word of God: A Guide to English Versions of the Bible, edited by Lloyd R. Bailey and published by John Knox Press in

1982, is a splendid guide to older translations. John R. Kohlenberger III's *Words About the Word: A Guide to Choosing and Using Your Bible* (Zondervan Publishing House, 1987) discusses the more recent versions.

BIBLE BARGAINS

Before you buy a new Bible, you might consider the following sources of inexpensive or (practically) free Bibles:

- The local library. Most libraries have a good selection of modern translations. Try before you buy.
- Used-book stores and library and church book sales.

Recently Updated Translations

Let's now consider Catholic and ecumenical translations that have recently been updated. Each is adequate for beginners or readers with some familiarity with the Bible. If you are primarily doing devotional, casual, or aesthetic reading, you can stick with these indefinitely. However, the newer translations are more accurate and readable, so at some point you should think about upgrading. After you have read the Bible awhile, you'll get a better sense of your needs and objectives, and can return to this chapter for guidance.

The Revised Standard Version (RSV)

Originally published in 1952, and with a revised New Testament issued in 1973, the *RSV* was the long-awaited, broadly accepted successor to the *King James Version*. Much praised for its literal accuracy, its retention of King's English expressions such as "thee" and "thou" is distracting. It is still used by formal equivalence enthusiasts and in biblical studies courses.

ECUMENICAL/COMMON BIBLES

In 1966, the RSV became the first "Common Bible," that is, a translation sponsored and commonly used by Protestants and

Catholic Church approval of an ecumenical Bible translation does not imply that it disapproves of Catholics using other translations. Rather, it means that the deuterocanonical books are included, and that Catholic biblical scholars and a representative(s) of the hierarchy have reviewed the translation, made (usually few and minor) changes as appropriate, and footnoted them.

approved for use by Catholics. The *New Revised Standard Version* and the *Today's English Version/Good News Bible* also have Catholic/ecumenical editions.

The Living Bible has also been approved for use by Catholics. It is passable as devotional reading, but the functional-equivalent translations discussed below are equally readable, and are more accurate and less theologically slanted. If you use *The Living Bible*, supplement it with a translation.

Biblical scholars are rightfully cautious about paraphrases. They know the amount of interpretation already present in the translation process. When you interpret so much that it becomes a paraphrase, you mix commentary with text and risk losing the literal sense.

Today's English Version (TEV) / Good News Bible (GNB)

This pioneer functional-equivalent version was sponsored by the American Bible Society. Originally published in 1966 as *Good News for Modern Man*, and also known as *Today's English Version of the New Testament* or the *Good News Bible*, the New Testament was revised in 1971 and 1976. The Old Testament was published in 1976, and the deuterocanonical books in 1979. Children respond well to the *TEV*. The original edition's line drawings enhanced its appeal.

New English Bible (NEB)

The New Testament of the functional equivalent *NEB* was published in 1961, followed by the Old Testament (including the deuterocanonical books) and a limited New Testament revision in 1970. The Old Testament translation was diverse and insufficiently literal, but the New Testament was more consistent and literal. Bishop Fulton Sheen recommended this translation.

Jerusalem Bible (JB)

This 1966 functional-equivalent translation is overly dependent on its base translation, the French *la Bible de Jerusalem*. Its study aids were very good for its time, but are now outdated. Very literate and readable, it is acceptable for devotional reading and casual or aesthetic use.

JEWISH TRANSLATIONS

The more you get into the Bible, the more its Jewish roots become apparent. Because many Jewish cultural practices have biblical roots, observant Jews often have insiders' insights into the Bible and its translation. Catholics should feel free to access the following Jewish translations, and pay attention to the helpful footnotes provided.

Jewish Publication Society Version (JPS)

Published in 1985, the *JPS* is a formal-equivalent translation of the Hebrew Bible that conveys the fluidity and nuances of the original languages. Its footnotes are helpful but not obtrusive. It is the standard version used by American Jews.

The Schocken Bible (SB)

Everett Fox's translation of the first five books of the Bible helps you experience them as its original audience did. His translation is a synthesis of formal equivalence and the rhetorical (spoken and heard) dimension of the Bible. It is ideal for reading aloud. The background articles and footnotes are first-rate, though a bit advanced for beginners.

RECENT ECUMENICAL TRANSLATIONS

The following translations were undertaken by scholars from Protestant denominations and with Catholic participation.

New Revised Standard Version (NRSV)

Published to great anticipation in 1989, the *NRSV* retains the formal equivalent approach of the *RSV* while dispensing with the King's English. It is slightly less literal than the *RSV*, and uses inclusive language more pervasively than the other major contemporary translations. From an ecumenical standpoint, it is probably the most all-around (adequate for most purposes) and broadly accepted English translation.

Revised English Bible (REB)

The 1989 functional-equivalent *REB* is more literal and consistent than its predecessor (*NEB*), and is most appropriate for beginners and devotional use. It uses inclusive language moderately.

Contemporary English Version (CEV)

The functional-equivalent *CEV* uses simpler vocabulary and grammar than its predecessor, the *TEV*, and the other translations discussed in this chapter. It shares with the *Schocken Bible* a sensitivity to the way the Bible sounds when read aloud.

The introduction to the *Learning Bible,* a colorful, *CEV* study Bible published by the American Bible Society, points out two important facts. First, languages are spoken before being written. Second, more people hear the Bible read aloud than read it for themselves.

CATHOLIC TRANSLATIONS

Following are the two most recent Catholic translations of the Bible into English. Both include excellent footnotes and background articles as part of their regular editions. Though appropriate in ecumenical contexts, they are rarely used by Protestants.

New American Bible (NAB)

The *New American Bible* was the first official Catholic translation into modern English from the original languages. Since the Council of Trent, the Latin Vulgate had been the standard text. In America, the Bible readings at Mass are taken from the *NAB*, while in Canada the *NRSV* is commonly used.

After many years in the works, the *NAB* Old Testament was published in 1970. It balances formal and functional equivalence, and is amazingly up-to-date. It lacks inclusive language. The functional-equivalent *NAB* New Testament published in 1970 was replaced in 1986 by the formal equivalent Revised New Testament, which contains a moderate amount of inclusive language.

The 1970 edition of the New Testament received a post-translation level of editing (primarily for liturgical purposes) that detracted from its literalness and necessitated its revision. The title page of your *NAB* Bible will indicate whether it contains the 1970 or 1986 edition.

In 1990, the Revised Psalms with extensive inclusive language and updated footnotes were published. The translation strikes a nice balance between formal and functional equivalence.

New Jerusalem Bible (NJB)

The 1985 *NJB* is considerably more literal and consistent than its predecessor (*JB*). The updated background articles and footnotes are extensive and accessible. The *NJB* ranges between functional and formal equivalence, but leans toward the former. Its use of inclusive language is moderate.

You practically need a program to keep track of the various versions of the *NJB*. The most common are the Regular, Reader's, and Standard editions:

The Regular Edition contains the entire set of footnotes and introductory articles. The footnotes are in very small print.

The Reader's Edition contains an abridged version of the study aids.

The Standard Edition contains few footnotes and does not offer a brief introduction to each biblical book.

AUTHOR'S RECOMMENDATION

I believe the *New American Bible* is the best all-around English translation for Catholics because it is used in the liturgy, its helpful footnotes and introductions to the individual biblical books come standard with almost all editions, and it strikes a good balance between literal accuracy and readability.

For Bible study, a very close second would be the Catholic edition of the *Revised Standard Version* or *New Revised Standard Version*, depending on your taste for inclusive language. For devotional or aesthetic reading, the *New Jerusalem Bible Regular Edition* integrates a fluid translation with copious footnotes and cross-references.

SUPPLEMENTAL RESOURCES

It is not necessary that you start out with anything more than a Bible. An acceptable translation supplemented by footnotes and introductions to the individual books, and perhaps some background articles, is sufficient.

It is more important that you incorporate a community dimension into your Bible reading. This includes reflection on the Sunday or weekday readings in the lectionary or participation in Bible study or sharing groups, classes, or retreats. Above all, pay attention to the readings at Mass and reflect on them beforehand when possible. The Bible is in its natural and supernatural element in the community and the Eucharist. Jesus illustrates this in his interactions with disciples on the road to Emmaus (cf. Lk 24:13-35).

As the Bible grows on you, you may want to learn about its background and interpretation in greater depth. For such purposes, the following resources can be helpful.

Special Edition Bibles

There are Bibles with study aids and in some cases translations targeted to women, men, children, youths, the elderly, African Americans, Native Americans, Hispanics, and so on. Some special editions include the entire Bible, others selected passages of interest to the intended audience.

Wide-Margin Bibles

Some Bible readers like to highlight words or passages and record insights and questions in their Bibles. Wide-margin Bibles accommodate this by providing extra space on the outer and inner margins. This white space is restful to the eyes and encourages written interaction with God's word.

Just as God inspired the biblical writers, he can inspire you to write meaningful reflections, whether in your Bible, your journal, or in communications with others.

Parallel Bibles

Parallel Bibles present translations in parallel columns. This makes comparison of translations convenient, and is helpful for studying the Bible when you don't know the biblical languages. The Parallel Bible best suited for Catholics is Oxford University Press' *The Complete Parallel Bible*. It contains the *New Revised Standard Version*, *Revised English Bible*, *New American Bible*, and *New Jerusalem Bible* translations.

Study Bibles

If you want more background on the Bible, begin with a study Bible. Everything you need will be at your fingertips, and for only $10-$30 more.

The background articles included in study Bibles are usually written by articulate and prominent biblical scholars. The biblical cross-references included in study Bibles encourage you to consult related passages and arrive at a contextual interpretation. This enables the Bible to interpret itself. Cross-referencing helps you assimilate the variety of perspectives within the Bible, including the Old Testament roots of New Testament passages.

DO YOU NEED A STUDY BIBLE?

Not right away, unless you are particularly enthusiastic about learning more background on the Bible. If you want to build your Bible-reading habit slowly and surely, a study Bible may be overload. Further, you don't want to get into the habit of reading footnotes before you try to interpret the passage yourself. Footnotes should be a supplement rather than a first option.

If you're reading the Bible for casual, devotional, or aesthetic/literary purposes, you don't need a study Bible.

If you are exploring the Bible from a historical or literal/study perspective, a study Bible will be invaluable. Study Bibles include most or all of the following resources: extensive footnotes and background articles, maps, a glossary of biblical terms, and a concordance (an index) or listing of biblical passages by theme.

Catholic and Ecumenical Study Editions

The most popular ecumenical study Bible has been *The (New) Oxford Annotated Bible.* It originally came with the *RSV* or *NEB*, and now includes the *NRSV.* The *HarperCollins Study Bible* contains the *NRSV*, and was produced by the Society of Biblical Literature (a leading ecumenical association of biblical scholars).

Standard editions of the *NAB* translation come with extensive footnotes and explanatory articles, and thus can function as a beginner's study Bible. The *Catholic Study Bible* contains extensive background articles and reading guides, but its footnotes are less comprehensive than those in the *NJB Regular Edition.* The *Catholic Bible: Personal Study Edition* does not provide as in-depth scholarly guidance and background as the aforementioned, and its study aids are written at a more basic level.

Biblical Commentaries

Biblical commentaries range in scope from an individual or series commentary on one or more books or sections of the Bible, to a commentary on the entire Bible. Commentaries also vary according to target audience (beginners, advanced readers, scholars) and denominational perspective.

The best one-volume Catholic commentary is the *New Jerome Biblical Commentary*, published in 1988. Featuring contributions by a "who's who" of late twentieth-century American Catholic biblical scholars, it is appropriate for eager beginners and intermediate or advanced readers.

Beginners should consult a commentary only after initially encountering the text, and for specific needs (e.g., help on a difficult passage, detailed guidance on a particular biblical book, or general study purposes). A commentary can distract you from wrestling with the text yourself. You're tempted to let an expert do it for you. However, the expert can't determine what the Bible means to you and how it applies to your life. Further, experts don't have a monopoly on correct interpretations of the Bible, nor are they infallible. They have their blind spots, technical shortcomings, and prejudices, like everyone else.

One of history's greatest theologians and commentators on the Bible, St. Augustine, observed that the more he interacted with the Bible, the more he realized how much he didn't know.

Isn't that true of any intimate relationship? The closer we get, the more curious, confused, and sometimes consternated, we become. Ultimately, love, prudence, maturity, and humility pull us through. Under the guidance of the Holy Spirit and the Church, and in cooperation with fellow believers, you are capable of reading the Bible and arriving at appropriate interpretations and personal applications.

Synopsis of the Gospels

Because of their shared sources, the Gospels of Matthew, Mark, and Luke have become known as the Synoptic (from the

Greek words for similar view/perspective) Gospels. A synopsis presents related passages in the Synoptic Gospels (and sometimes the Gospel of John) in parallel columns so that you can see how the Gospel writers interpreted and communicated the events and teachings in the life of Jesus differently.

As discussed in Chapter Nine, this facilitates redaction/editorial criticism (study) of the Gospels: that is, observing how the evangelists' different presentations of shared sources reveal their theological perspectives and pastoral objectives. By making logical deductions, non-scholars can use a synopsis to arrive at competent literal interpretations of Gospel texts.

Synopses were popularized by various editions of Burton H. Throckmorton Jr.'s *Gospel Parallels* (Thomas Nelson Press). The most comprehensive and affordable is the American Bible Society's *Synopsis of the Four Gospels*.

Concordances

A concordance gives a biblical reference for each occurrence of a key word or phrase in English or the original languages. It is helpful for doing word and thematic studies. To some extent, it has been made obsolete by Bible software, which performs word or phrase searches quickly and flexibly. However, as in most disciplines, manual or hard-copy resources still have much and often specialized utility.

Bible Dictionaries

Because the Bible introduces you to a new world, newcomers often benefit from a dictionary. A Bible dictionary explains key concepts, persons, and places. When you come across an unfamiliar word or expression, an explanation can be moments away. Most study Bibles incorporate a small dictionary or glossary of key terms in an appendix. Like most of the resources discussed in this section, it is available in software format.

Bible Maps

Because of the many eras in biblical history, multiple maps are necessary to portray the changing geography and political climates of the ancient Near East. Study Bibles include several maps.

Bible Audiotapes and Videotapes

There is an abundance of audio-visual material explaining the Bible. If you have a mobile lifestyle, audiotapes or CD's containing either the text of the Bible or explanations of individual biblical books or themes are highly recommended. Listening to the Bible simulates the original oral transmission of the Bible.

Bible lessons on video vary widely in production and presentation quality. If possible, preview before you buy. Group viewing of videos integrated with Bible reading and discussion can be an effective way of learning and applying the Bible.

Bible Software

Bible software is an invaluable aid for scholars, teachers, and students, but it can also help casual readers. If you want to look up a verse, but only remember one or more key words, you can use a software program's search function to find not only that passage, but related passages you may have forgotten or been unaware of. If you want to print out an excerpt from the Bible or a collection of discontinuous verses or passages, Bible software automates the cut-and-paste process. If you have multiple versions of the Bible on software, you can compare them as if you had a parallel Bible. Advanced students can link to the original languages and scholarly resource materials (e.g., commentaries, synopses, and Bible dictionaries) through the use of key words.

Two premier ecumenical resources for Bible and reference software are Nelson Electronic (TM) Publishing (800-251-4000) and Logos Research Systems (800-875-6467).

A word of caution is in order. The Bible is meant to be read and heard in a reflective environment. No matter how interesting and convenient Bible software or Web sites are, they should not replace quiet and community time (i.e., Mass, retreats, and group or family Bible-sharing discussions) with the Bible.

Bible Internet Sites

Internet sites on the Bible or other religious topics can provide helpful information for persons at all levels of familiarity with the Bible. However, unlike books and except for sources communicated verbatim (such as the Vatican Web site, www.vatican.va, or the U.S. Catholic Conference Web site, nccbuscc.org), there is no guarantee that the information has gone through a substantial and independent editing process. Further, for all except the most computer-inclined persons, it is not the place for learning how to read the Bible. The next four chapters will show why.

Begin by using the Bible's natural mode: reading and listening to the word of God, both privately and communally. Why dwell in cyberspace when you can meet God directly in his word and community?

Building on our familiarity with translations and supplemental resources, in the next chapter we will explore various reading plans for exploring the Bible.

Chapter Five

How to Develop a Bible-Reading Plan

┌─ **Contents of this Chapter** ─────────────────────┐

• Learn where to begin reading the Bible and why.
• Encounter formal and informal approaches to sustaining a consistent Bible-reading habit.
• Explore Catholic liturgical-reading plans.

└──┘

The best way to begin reading the Bible is simply to get started. If you are able to adopt one of the structured approaches discussed in this chapter, great. If not, that's fine, too, as long as you get into the habit of reading the Bible. This chapter will review and critique both formal and informal reading plans and offer guidelines for effective implementation. This will help you decide which approach suits you, and how you wish to begin. Since experience often is the best teacher, I'll begin by sharing what worked for me.

AN INFORMAL PATH THROUGH THE BIBLE

I began reading the Bible seriously when I was a freshman in college. I did not follow a specific plan or consult a book for guidance. I wanted to explore the Bible and discover its message first hand.

I began, as you should, with the New Testament, and in particular, the Gospels. I then moved to St. Paul and the other New Testament letters. Eventually, I began reading the Psalms, Genesis, Exodus, Job, Proverbs, Sirach, Ecclesiastes, and parts of Isaiah. Out of curiosity, I read sections of Samuel and Kings relating to David and Solomon, but found the rest of the Old Testament too cryptic, so I stayed mostly in the New Testament.

This approach worked because I had the natural enthusiasm of someone new to an undertaking, and the only structure I needed was the discipline of reading the Bible for at least a few minutes each day.

READING DIRECTIVES

Permit me to share my informal plan more precisely. The order I suggest approximates the order in which the biblical books are discussed in this book.

In the early Church, Gentile converts were first exposed to the Gospels and Acts, then the epistles, particularly those of Paul, and the Psalms. Accordingly, begin with the Gospels, preferably in the order in which they have traditionally been read in the Church: Mark is ideal for beginners and converts. It puts them face-to-face with Jesus and the central reality of the cross. Matthew systematically translates this to daily morality. Luke cautions against a legalistic approach to the Christian life by emphasizing Jesus' mercy and pastoral sensitivity. Read John last because he builds on the others, and his spiritual profundity requires a more mature theological and interpretive foundation.

There are several caveats to the above. First, Mark is intense and lacks the teachings of Jesus, so you may wish to balance your initial reading of Mark with some of Jesus' teachings from Matthew and Luke. Despite its theological complexity, many parts of John are straightforward and uplifting. As long as you don't take John out of context and construct your own theology independent of Church teaching, you can benefit from reading him as a beginner. When you encounter passages you don't understand, consult a commentary, discuss it with a priest or an informed Catholic layperson, or move to another passage.

Within the Gospels, you can go directly to the stories of Jesus' passion, death, and resurrection in order to get to the heart of the Gospel message. This is where the early Christians started, as it is the foundation of Christian faith.

After reading the Gospels, go to Acts for a theological history of the early Church. You'll encounter the triumphs and tribulations of Peter and Paul and their associates. Acts is particularly appropriate after reading Luke, since they share the same author and are essentially one story in two volumes. Acts describes the new beginning that Jesus' mysterious end inaugurates.

Next move to Paul's letters, perhaps reading them in the approximate order in which they were written:

1 Thessalonians, Galatians, Philippians, 1 and 2 Corinthians, Romans, Philemon, Colossians, Ephesians, 2 Thessalonians, 1 and 2 Timothy, Titus. Many people find 1 and 2 Corinthians a good place to encounter Paul, as he discusses practical issues relevant to persons of all eras: sex, love, marriage, money, rivalries, and death.

While you certainly don't need to stick to this order, reading any author chronologically (as best we can determine with Paul) gives you insight into the development of his thought. It's also

---

SAINTS AND SAGES ON THE BIBLE

We want to approach reading the Bible as a discipline rather than a chore. As St. Gregory the Great noted in one of his personal letters, it is a privilege and honor to read the Bible; God thought enough of us to communicate it personally. St. Gregory uses the example of how his friend would respond if he received a letter from the emperor: he'd read it right away, and with enthusiasm and respect.

fine to jump around a bit, as getting to know someone or their works is not simply a linear process. We must make some allowance for spontaneity, particularly given the involvement of the Spirit, which blows where it wills (cf. Jn 3:8).

After reading Paul, our next stop would be the other New Testament letters. I view these as motivational letters because they are profound exhortations to act morally and persevere in the face of significant opposition from the world. They remind us that Christians have always been morally out of step with the secular world.

Begin the letters with 1 John, which bears great similarity in style and theology to the Gospel of John. Then proceed to James, because he is practical, straightforward, and succinct. For contrast, go to the other end of the spectrum, the letter to the Hebrews, which while theologically profound and one of the finest literary works in the New Testament, uses rabbinical argumentation and rhetorical devices that may be difficult for a beginner to follow. It is rich in insights and consolation for those who patiently follow its logic.

Peter's letters can be read at any point, as they are moral exhortations typical of what you would expect of a devoted, well-schooled leader. Begin with 1 Peter, which is easier to understand than 2 Peter. The latter was written considerably later and has more of an apocalyptic (referring to the end of the world) tone.

After reading 2 Peter, try Jude, a short work with apocalyptic overtones and similarities to 2 Peter.

Revelation (also known as the Apocalypse) is the last book in the New Testament, and it should be last on your reading list as well. While some parts are accessible to the beginner, most are cryptic and require the deciphering available in footnotes and a commentary. For this reason, survey Revelation for acquaintance purposes after you have gotten through the rest of the New Testament, and then return to it after you have more experience reading the Bible.

WHAT ABOUT THE OLD TESTAMENT?

My silence regarding the Old Testament's place in your reading plan does not mean that it should be excluded from your initial explorations. Rather, it should be integrated in a modest, coherent manner.

To begin with, stick to the basics: The Psalms (the Bible's prayer book, also referred to as the Bible in miniature), Genesis, and Exodus. Then move to 1 and 2 Samuel and 1 Kings in order to (re)acquaint yourself with the Jewish monarchy. Most of us read these stories as children, and as great literature and events, they will likely come back to us.

For practical guidance on getting along in life and with others, read Proverbs and Sirach, the Bible's version of self-help counsel. If you are suffering, read Job; if questioning God and the meaning of life, read Ecclesiastes. Both remind us that faith is a wrestling match as well as a journey. There is no better forum for questioning God than the Bible and the Church, for both are filled with folks who have undergone similar experiences.

When you are ready for the prophetic books, begin by sampling accessible and important passages. This will give you a feel for their style and help you determine which books you would like to read in greater depth.

It is good to get a taste of the diversity of the Bible in our reading diet. In an individual reading period, time permitting, I'd suggest the following. Begin with a few lines from a psalm, supplement a Gospel passage with an exhortation or counsel from a New Testament letter, and for context include a brief excerpt from the Old Testament. This variety is similar to what we get from the lectionary at Mass.

An advantage of one of the formal methods discussed below, the lectionary cycle, is that experts sanctioned by the Church carefully select these passages. Even if you spread these readings out over several sittings, you will still be following a balanced reading program. The Church interprets the Bible as a whole, rather than as isolated individual parts, so it makes sense to emulate this in our reading patterns.

The reading progression I have suggested is a framework rather than a straitjacket. You can integrate some of its aspects with the following reading plans and arrive at your own hybrid/customized program.

READING THE BIBLE THEMATICALLY

Reading the Bible by theme is appropriate for intermediate and advanced readers. Sample themes include forgiveness, prayer, salvation, justice, and mercy. Because thematic study presumes a basic theological and biblical background, it is generally not the terrain of beginners. Even intermediate or advanced readers find this approach most helpful when done in conjunction with a mentor, class, or book. It is helpful for beginners to be aware of it for future reference.

READING THE BIBLE IN ORDER

People often wonder about or experiment with reading the Bible or the Old or New Testament in order. Another name for this is its canonical order (canon is the sequential list of books in the Bible).

Reading the Bible in order respects the purposeful way it was laid out. However, since the books are not in chronological order, this approach does not give a precise sense of its development. Further, since you are not exercising selectivity in your reading, you are susceptible to getting bogged down in some of the Bible's more difficult parts.

Readers familiar with the Bible are more capable of coping with difficult passages and determining which to explore and which to skim or defer. I have talked to people who have read the Bible straight through, and my impression is that their retention rate is good, but not outstanding. Many important characters and passages are familiar to them, but because of the massive amount of material they have worked through, they often get things confused: they experience information overload in a context meant more for formation (personal and spiritual development). Unless you are an avid and disciplined reader, I'd recommend the other approaches discussed in this chapter.

READING THE BIBLE IN ONE YEAR

Books are available that take you through the Bible in one year. Sometimes the biblical texts are provided, other times just the passages are referenced.

These books typically suggest a time commitment of twenty to thirty minutes a day, which means you will read at a vigorous pace. "Bible speed-reading" is the opposite of the contemplative approach discussed in the next chapter, and is less suited to the nature of the Bible. However, if you prefer reading large sections of text at a brisk pace, and your goal is to become familiar with most of the Bible, following a one-year reading plan may be feasible and beneficial.

Unless you need the self-discipline, do not feel bound to hold yourself to the recommended time and reading schedule. Allow for the spontaneity of the Spirit and work within your circumstances and capacities. God has his own timetable, and spiritual growth is not a mechanical process.

The biggest advantage of this and the prior approach is that you become familiar with most of the Bible. If later you wish to concentrate on a particular book or section, such familiarity will come in handy, particularly when you look up cross references. Another advantage is that you can't get too bogged down or frustrated over not understanding a particular passage, because you have to keep moving to stay on track. Still, bear in mind that more is not necessarily better with respect to Scripture, where quality matters more than quantity.

BEGINNING AT THE END

We discussed the canonical approach that starts at the beginning of the Old or New Testament. There is also merit to starting at the end, with the stories of Jesus' suffering, death, and resurrection. These are known as the passion and resurrection narratives.

What seems like starting at the end is really starting at the beginning. Scholars believe that the Gospels were written backward, that is, beginning with the accounts of the death and resurrection of Jesus, the pivotal events of the Bible and history. These are the prisms through which the Gospels and Catholics view Jesus' life and teaching. They make an excellent preface to the rest of the Gospels and the Bible. Since Christian faith is based on the death and resurrection of Jesus, it makes sense to begin reading the New Testament there.

TAKING A CHANCE ON BIBLE ROULETTE

Bible roulette is the term used for the practice of randomly opening your Bible, pointing to a spot, and reading from there. Supplement this with common sense and prudence and it may have a niche in your Bible-reading repertoire, providing you don't become superstitious about it.

Be wary of reflexively imputing divine inspiration to the selection. What if you open up to a passage that describes the sacrificing of animals? Does that mean that Rover has to go?

When I am tired, I sometimes open the Bible and read from there. It's my way of relaxing with a friend without excessive structure. However, I don't feel bound to stay with the initial passage. I might try two or three before one touches me.

God can bring you to a suitable passage when you are too tired and discouraged to read the Bible in a structured manner. However, don't put him to the test (cf. Mt 4:5-7) by not doing your part. Reserve the roulette method for when you lack the energy for another approach.

FORMAL BIBLE-READING PLANS

For Catholics, there are two optimal ways of reading the Bible: following the lectionary or the Liturgy of the Hours. Both are liturgical, that is, formal ways of worshiping God as a community, and are structured according to the seasons of Advent, Christmas, Lent, Easter, and Ordinary Time (what doesn't fit into the first four).

The passages were selected by a commission composed of biblical scholars, liturgists, and theologians working under the supervision of the magisterium. These have not only stood the test of time, but have been adapted by other Christian denominations.

Both approaches help you integrate sacred and secular time. The Liturgy of the Hours in particular helps you experience restful and reflective Sabbath moments during your busy day.

When I follow either of the two programs, I do so in unison with Catholics (and other Christians) all over the world. God is not bound by time or space, so Jesus is present among us (cf. Mt 18:20). This universality and solidarity is an essential part of what makes a Catholic.

READING THE LECTIONARY

The lectionary is connected to the Eucharist. The ideal is to receive Jesus in God's word and under the form of bread and wine and in the person of ourselves and our neighbor through words and works of love. If you are unable or do not feel called to attend daily Mass, reading the lectionary selections or praying the Liturgy of the Hours is a good alternative.

The lectionary contains the biblical readings read at Mass on Sundays, holy days, and during the week. The Sunday readings occur over a three-year cycle, denominated by A, B, and C. Most of the Gospel readings from year A are taken from Matthew, B from Mark (with the option of using readings from John during several consecutive weeks in "Ordinary Time"), and C from Luke.

John is prominent during Lent of all three years and is used on feast days on which passages from his Gospel are particularly appropriate.

The Old Testament readings and Psalms are chosen for their correspondence to the Gospel selection, while the readings from the New Testament letters sometimes correspond to the Gospel, but almost always are presented sequentially; that is, for several weeks we read from the same letter.

The Liturgy of the Hours contains readings from the Bible, particularly the Psalms, and also includes prayers, intercessions, and readings from the writings of the Church Fathers and saints. As pointed out by Pope Paul VI in *Marialis Cultus*, his 1974 apostolic exhortation on devotion to Mary, the Liturgy of the Hours is actually a higher priority for family spirituality than even the Rosary. An excellent guide to the Liturgy of the Hours is *Together in Prayer: Learning to Love the Liturgy of the Hours,* by Charles E. Miller, C.M.

ADVANTAGES OF THE FORMAL APPROACHES

These formal or liturgical approaches incorporate the benefits of the informal approaches discussed above, and with advantages they don't have, such as passage selections made by a discerning, multi-disciplinary collection of experts working under the auspices of the hierarchy.

Both formal approaches survey the Bible and include the most significant texts. They offer structure, continuity, and a balanced perspective on the Bible without being overwhelming. Such exposure to a wisely selected array of texts gives you the Bible's big picture, which is helpful for interpreting individual passages in context.

There is another advantage to following this carefully constructed regimen. I have found that on down days I would providentially encounter texts that comforted me, while on good days I would come across sober and challenging texts. Of course, there were also down days when I would encounter unfamiliar or obtuse passages, at which point I would discern whether I had the energy to work through them. Mature Bible readers seek to develop a healthy tension between discipline and structure, and spontaneity and recognition of limitations.

If you only expose yourself to comfortable passages, you will limit your growth. Healthy living and Bible reading seek a balance between affirming and challenging experiences and passages.

REASONABLE EXPECTATIONS

If you can start out by following either of these programs, thank God and go for it. However, most likely they are something that you will have to build up to, and perhaps return to over and over again until they become a habit.

It is not necessary to follow these programs rigidly. Some days you may only have the time and energy to do one of the readings or prayers. One is better than none, and given your circumstances, may be quite generous.

Some days God may be taking the initiative in your life just as he did in the Bible, so pay attention to "the signs of your times." The key is to hold God's initiative in the Bible and in life in a healthy tension, so that you don't neglect his call in either place.

If you feel called to follow either the lectionary or the Liturgy of the Hours, but are unsuccessful in your efforts, try an abridged or customized version. Just read part of the day's readings, accompanied by prayer, intercessions (prayers are often requested of us, and we should comply), and reflection. We need not be slaves to formality or scrupulosity: the Sabbath (spiritual observance) was made for man, not man for the Sabbath (cf. Mk 2:27).

If you stick to this "partial compliance" approach, you will gradually witness your Bible-reading stamina and enthusiasm increase. Even on down days when the last thing you want to do is offer praise, you will anyways because deep down your heart is

God's. Like Jeremiah and the reluctant son in Jesus' parable (cf. Mt 21:28-32), your initial resistance to God turns to obedience because, as Peter proclaimed, to whom else will you go (cf. Jn 6:66-69)?

As discussed throughout the book, the closest human analogy to our relationship with the Bible and God is that of marriage and family life. Amid the ups and downs of life, sometimes all we can give our loved ones are little gestures that nonetheless speak volumes. Remember the monastic dictum, "Pray as you can, not as you can't."

If these formal practices don't suit you at the moment, or seem overwhelming, don't get discouraged; you don't have to start out with them. Further, you may be like me and never get to the point of being able to follow these approaches consistently. That is why I presented the informal approaches.

DIVINE CHECK-IN POINTS

Proactively "touching base" with God, the Bible, and yourself at different times of the day as programmed in the Liturgy of the Hours and adapted to your schedule helps you live the Bible and draw nourishment from it. Your communications need not be elaborate. Intentions and actions are what count.

The same approach nourishes a romantic relationship. Some partners call each other several times a day to touch base. Each couple has their own approach and rhythm. Experiment and develop your own daily "check-in" pattern.

You'll gradually want to spend more time with God, and you'll find a hidden reserve of energy and devotion to facilitate such. God loves the attention — as the Old Testament asserts, he is a jealous God, desiring to be first and without competition for our spiritual affections. He will help you find and make good use of time for dialogue with him if you want it bad enough.

SUMMARY

The difference between formal and informal Bible-reading plans is that the former are liturgical and more defined and have been approved by the Catholic hierarchy. The latter offer flexibility and their own form of discipline at the expense of expert guidance, community solidarity, and programmed cohesiveness. As with translations, there is no one-size-fits-all approach.

From an ideal and Catholic standpoint, the formal approaches are preferable because of their inherent community dimension and the helpful structure provided to readers. However, if the informal approaches work better for you, by all means go with them. You may end up with a combination of the above approaches adapted to your situation.

The best way to determine which approach suits you is to try them and pray for guidance. Don't be afraid to ask for help from fellow believers when you get stuck. You'll gradually find a comfortable approach and rhythm, but that does not eliminate the necessity of discipline and perseverance. There are many alternatives more tantalizing than God's word, but none as fulfilling. Keep in mind the counsel with which we began this chapter: Simply get started.

In the next chapter, you'll encounter an ancient model designed to optimize your reading and living experience. It is suitable for all the approaches discussed in this chapter, but is tailor-made for the formal plans.

Chapter Six

—— How to Read the Bible Holistically ——

Contents of this Chapter

- Experience western civilization's oldest and most powerful spiritual growth model.
- Discover how the rabbis, monks, and sages experienced the Bible.
- Learn how to practice *lectio divina*, the Church's official model for prayerfully and holistically encountering the Scriptures.
- Discover that you've already experienced the fundamental activities in Bible reading.

Within the Catholic tradition exists western civilization's oldest and most natural, universal, flexible, and holistic model of personal growth and biblical spirituality. You've already experienced it in some form and degree. When you encounter a process that people of all perspectives and backgrounds engage in naturally, you're onto something.

(RE)INTRODUCING LECTIO DIVINA

Lectio (lek-see-oh) *divina* (di-veen-a) means divine or sacred reading. Because of traditional usage and the difficulty of translating *lectio divina* precisely, the Latin expression (often abbreviated to *lectio*) is commonly used.

In biblical times, books were rare and expensive, and most people couldn't read. Because communal listening rather than individual reading was the most common way our ancestors encountered the Bible, it is also accurate to refer to *lectio divina* as "listening" to the Bible.

THE EVOLUTION OF LECTIO DIVINA

Like most things within Christianity, *lectio divina* has its roots in Judaism. The ancient Hebrews developed the principles and practices underlying *lectio divina* when the biblical material was in its oral stage, and gradually refined it through the centuries. The early church and later the monastic communities drew upon this inheritance in developing what they would refer to as *lectio divina*. The Benedictines and Cistercians (Trappists) have been major influences in *lectio divina's* development and popularization.

When the early Christians read or heard the New Testament writings, they processed them holistically the same way they had the Old Testament writings. *Lectio* was applied pre-eminently to the Bible, but also to the writings of the Church Fathers (e.g., Augustine, Gregory the Great, Ambrose, Jerome). Today its application to life is becoming increasingly emphasized. My books on time management, stress management, journaling, suffering, and care-giving explore the applications of *lectio* to each.

The Eastern Orthodox tradition has a parallel practice called the *Jesus Prayer*, taught in the anonymous spiritual classic *Way of a Pilgrim*, which involves repeating the expression "Lord Jesus Christ, have mercy on me."

THE STAGES OF LECTIO DIVINA IN MODERN TERMS

Lectio divina consists of activities that typically unfold in stages, though not necessarily sequentially. Not only does each person process the Bible and life experiences uniquely, but such changes with the circumstances and the person's development.

Traditionally, *lectio's* stages have been identified as reading, meditation, prayer, contemplation, and action. The following alliterative parallels in laymen's terms serves as a starting and reference point for the discussion of the traditional stages that follows.

- **Retreat (Refresh/Restore/Renew):** Step back from hustle-bustle. Carve out time for daily Sabbath moments.
- **Relax:** Come in to God's presence and get settled in, as you would with a friend.
- **Release:** Let God free you of unnecessary anxiety and concerns.
- **Read** ... slowly, aloud, using all the senses, perhaps following the words with your finger to slow down. This naturally heightens your awareness of the grammatical elements of the text, which also communicate meaning. Select a word, phrase, image, or verse(s) from the passage that touches or teaches you. This "word" can serve as your bridge to the day, a centering point to return to amid the day's activities.
- **Rhythm:** Enter into the flow of God's word and the Spirit through gentle oscillation (ranging back and forth) between the various activities. Don't cultivate rigid expectations of what the rhythm should feel like, or worry that you don't have it. It comes naturally with practice and grace, and it is unique to each person.
- **Repeat/Recite:** Gently murmur or recite your "word" repeatedly. This ingrains it in your conscious and subconscious mind as an inspired affirmation.
- **Reflect:** Consider what actions or attitudes your "word" is calling you to. What does it mean to you?
- **Reminisce:** Your "word" may trigger memories of other biblical or life passages. The Hebrew word "*pesach,*" from which comes the word "paschal" (i.e., mystery, lamb), refers to the Passover and means passage, which is the essence of Christian life: a journey home. Reminiscence (the word coined by medieval monks to describe this practice) helps

you connect the various passages, biblical and experiential, in your life. Passages, like reminiscences, link things.

- **Re-create:** Use your imagination to envision the biblical scene and character(s). Our objective is to interact with and imaginatively participate in the text holistically, that is, with all our faculties. To use St. Ignatius of Loyola's terminology, "consider the persons," meaning identify and perhaps dialogue with them.
- **React:** Share your thoughts and feelings with God, others, or your journal.
- **Receive:** Be present to God in silence. Listen. Experience divine consolation.
- **Rest:** Cool down as preparation for resuming your activities.
- **Respond:** Don't just pray there, do something. Put into practice what you have received.
- **Realize:** Enjoy the fruits of your labor. Discover God's initiative in your life. Experience your "word" bearing fruit in your life in various degrees as described in the parable of the sower (cf. Mk 4:2-20).

THE FLUIDITY OF LECTIO DIVINA

Lectio divina is an adaptable, flexible model rather than a rigid method. It isn't a mechanical, linear process. It is fluid and personal. You oscillate between its stages according to your capacities, circumstances, and the movement of the Spirit.

Because the activities of *lectio divina* overlap, it is artificial to distinguish between them rigidly. For example, reading and meditation are essentially two aspects of the same activity of taking in and responding to a biblical or life passage. Prayer and contemplation are the active and receptive aspects of dialogue with God. The early Church originally described this process in terms of reading and prayer. Meditation was considered part of reading, and contemplation was part of prayer.

The final stage, action, initially was assumed. In the Middle Ages, it was articulated as the consummating stage. *Lectio divina* continues to evolve with its environment: Cardinal Martini of Milan has shown how the principles of discernment, decision, and consolation, particularly as understood within the Jesuit tradition, are operative in *lectio divina*.

LECTIO IN ACTION

How does the *lectio* process unfold? Naturally, albeit with effort.

You might begin by reading and then be led by the Spirit to the silence of contemplation. Or perhaps you'll begin by praying your feelings and then move to meditation on your current situation in light of the biblical passage you are reading or reminded of (reminiscence).

You might also begin and stay awhile in the silence of contemplation, soaking up God's presence. When you're weary, just being with a loved one is what you need most.

The key is to follow where your faculties and the prompting of the Spirit take you, while eventually integrating all (in some degree) of the stages/activities. You thereby balance spontaneity and self-discipline, and avoid being too rigid or scrupulous (over-conscientious) or too lax. Catholicism is a religion of balance, integration, and moderation, attributes that characterize the Bible and human development as well.

LECTIO DIVINA IN HOLISTIC PRACTICE

Just as it is artificial to distinguish precisely between the stages of *lectio divina*, so the various faculties engaged (sensate, mental, affective/emotional, spiritual, and in a group, social/relational) are likewise intertwined and not readily divisible. This integration brings a side benefit: using all our faculties during *lectio* translates to using them more spontaneously in daily life.

A different faculty comes to the forefront in each stage of *lectio divina*. Let us now consider how *lectio* models the way we practice love of God, self, and neighbor with our whole heart, mind, and strength (cf. Mk 12:28-34), and how it forms us as whole persons according to Jesus' command (cf. Mt 5:48).

RETREAT

Both the verb and the noun! A retreat is a traditional spiritual practice of getting away for a day, a weekend, or more, to reflect on God's word and evaluate his activity in your life. You can call it an expanded Sabbath or a spiritual vacation.

"Retreat" is more of a description of the purpose and mentality underlying *lectio* than a specific stage or activity. *Lectio* is meant to be a periodic Sabbath moment bridged to our activities through application of the "word" we have received. It is a retreat from our hustle-bustle existence for purposes of slowing down, taking stock of life, and discerning God's will and initiative. Even a few minutes can be a regenerating oasis of calm. View *lectio* as a retreat rather than a burden. It is time to be refreshed and renewed by God's word.

RELAXING

Traditionally, relaxing has not been articulated as a stage of *lectio divina*. However, given the hectic nature of modern life and cultural pressures working against the *shalom* (peace/wholeness) that God offers us, it seems prudent to articulate relaxing as a preparatory stage.

As with a couple who have been away from each other for awhile, we need time to get used to a more intense experience of God's presence, and temporarily let go of anxieties and distractions. Otherwise, we will not be able to tune in to God's subtle *modus operandi*, the still, small voice (cf. 1 Kings 19:12).

To use a Eucharistic image, when you share a special meal with someone, you usually don't jump right into an intense discussion (at Mass we build up to the consecration). You get an initial reading on yourself, your counterpart, and the situation, and then enter into a mode of interaction conducive to a deeper engagement of minds and hearts.

Our ancestors knew how to relax and slow down. They didn't live in a secular, materialistic, productivity-oriented culture like ours. They didn't need to articulate relaxation as a stage because they did it naturally. We need to remind ourselves and take steps to facilitate relaxation. Examples of such include deep breathing, guided imagery, and awareness exercises. Physical exercise is also helpful for getting emotional toxins out of our system and clearing our mind.

Give yourself a few moments to relax in God's presence and prepare for the divine encounter. Temporarily place your swirling anxieties in the Lord's lap so that you can be more present to him. He will help you view your challenges in the proper perspective and proportion. Since God is present, *lectio* is a happening, a special event, even if it doesn't feel that way. Faith, hope, and love have an affective dimension, but fundamentally they are decisions and actions rather than feelings.

Relaxing is neither an escape nor a shirking of responsibilities. It is a spiritual form of leisure that is not akin to "wasting time." By giving ourselves time to relax and become conscious of God's welcome, we're more disposed to hear his word and receive his graces.

READING/LISTENING/SENSING

Lectio divina is unlike most styles of reading you have experienced. You read slowly and rhythmically, almost the antithesis of speed reading. You'll eventually settle into a rhythm that facilitates internalization of God's word.

Read using your voice, whether aloud or in an almost imperceptible whisper or undertone. Sometimes your energy level or the circumstances dictate that you read silently, but if at all possible, try speaking or whispering the word. Ancient physicians prescribed reading as a form of exercise. When you try reading aloud, you'll know why. It takes energy!

When you read aloud, you use all your senses. Yes, even taste and smell. The medieval monks who practiced *lectio divina* spoke of tasting the word by savoring its sweetness and mouthing or speaking the words in a careful, reverential way.

Can you smell God's word? Literally, no, but metaphorically, yes. Beginning with St. Paul, spiritual writers have spoken of spirituality in terms of an aroma (cf. 2 Cor 2:15). We can whiff the dusty roads on which Jesus walked, the sweet smell of the flowers he admired, and the stench of farm animals and laborers and sweaty travelers and fishermen.

This engagement of the senses is one reason I emphasized relaxing as a necessary preparation. The more relaxed and present you are, the less impaired your senses will be, and the more readily you will engage them.

As a holistic side effect, using all of your senses naturally engages your imagination. With greater familiarity with *lectio divina* and the Bible, you will have a fuller experience of the sensate dimensions of the text and life.

NIBBLING ON GOD'S WORD

In practicing *lectio divina*, we're not concerned with covering a certain amount of the Bible in one sitting. Just as a brief interpersonal encounter can have significant repercussions, so a small portion of the Bible can go a long way.

We typically begin with a small passage of Scripture. Precisely how much is not important. We read until some word, verse, image, theme, or perhaps a related personal experience or biblical text strikes us. We then take in and reflect on that stimulus.

Good things come in small passages. One of the side effects of sampling a small portion of Scripture is the humility it instills. We lose any pretense of being a master of the word or the world. In the spirit of Psalm 131, we don't set our eyes on the heights of personal gratification. Rather, we satisfy ourselves to be nurtured by the Lord. A small portion of Scripture, taken to heart, is more than enough to nourish and challenge us.

In giving our whole selves to a small portion of Scripture, we buck the consumption mentality of our times. Instead of mechanically devouring God's word and hurriedly going on to the next activity or stimulus, we savor it and let it permeate our being and influence our attitudes and actions.

What if no word stands out and we feel unmoved by the biblical passage? Don't worry about it. Accept what comes, even if it's only the slightest of inspirations or consolations (peaceful sensations). *Lectio divina* isn't a results-oriented competition in which we are judged by how much Scripture speaks to us. God will provide what we need. Our job is to make time for God, offer ourselves as we are, and keep at it (cf. Mt 24:46; Lk 8:15; 21:19).

MEDITATION

Once we have identified a portion of Scripture that speaks to us, our next step is to experience that text in all its richness. Savor and internalize it through repetitive recitation or murmuring.

In biblical and patristic times, the most frequent image associated with meditation was of a cow or goat ruminating (chewing its cud). Psalm 1:2 advocates murmuring or reciting God's word repeatedly.

Our memories are not as active or developed as were those of our ancestors. Without the benefit of communication-storage media, they had more practice. Most people can remember only a small portion of Scripture. Repetitively reciting Scripture enlarges our capacity for God's word, just as it did for our ancestors. Not only do we remember it better, but we internalize and assimilate it, making it a part of us.

INSPIRED PROGRAMMING

What else happens when we repeat God's word? Like a computer, we feed our mind and heart positive input. The better the data or programming we receive, the greater the likelihood of positive output. This is why we spend time during the reading stage seeking a personally meaningful word. Unlike a motivational tape containing subliminal (subconscious) messages, we chose this word, its personal meaning and energy heightened by its divine imprint. God's input/initiative helps us assimilate and live our resolutions.

What happens when we internalize God's word? We open ourselves to God's healing touch. We enable God to penetrate our subconscious and reform the negative programming (thoughts, images, and memories) that have been with us from childhood. (See Father Thomas Keating's *Open Mind, Open Heart* and other works for a detailed discussion of what he terms divine therapy). He replaces them with words and images of consolation and encouragement. Through spiritual osmosis (the seepage of fluid through a membrane), inspired attitudes, values, and behavior patterns gradually replace negative ones.

APPLYING THE WORD

The other dimension of meditation is personal application. What bearing does the word have on our lives? To what concrete actions and attitudes are God and the passage calling us?

Most of the time, the Spirit inspires us to make little improvements that we can implement in daily life. This keeps us humble and busy. If we wait for grandiose change, we might not handle it properly, presuming we even get around to it.

When we make the word personal and practical by applying it to our lives, we enable it to take root and transform us, day by day. It grows like the mustard seed (cf. Mk 4:30-32), imperceptible except to the eyes of faith, and dependent upon the virtues of patience and perseverance.

ACCESSING OUR MEMORY AND IMAGINATION

Meditation involves time/historical and creative elements as well. The Bible takes on another dimension when we engage our memory and imagination. We broaden our horizons both chronologically and mentally.

Reminiscence, the phenomena of one biblical text evoking recollection of another, also applies to life experiences: a biblical text can remind us of a personal experience, and vice-versa. Our memory helps us integrate the text with life and the rest of the Bible.

Our imagination can engage our senses and transport us to the biblical scene, or project it to our circumstances. In this way, we participate personally in the text, rather than as an observer.

PRAYER

Suppose you have read God's word sensitively, internalized it through repetition and reflection, and made it practical through application. These stimuli naturally evoke an emotional and spiritual reaction known as prayer, or the active dimension of spiritual dialogue. Its tone and thrust varies with the person and circumstance. You might lament, ask God for something, praise him, engage him in conversation, or simply be with him. All of this is prayer.

A traditional term used to describe the emotional content of prayer is the affective dimension: How am I affected by this biblical or life passage/event?

If you don't share your emotions with God and others, they are liable to be released in potentially destructive ways, such as inappropriate behavior, addictions, projections onto others, or physical ailments such as ulcers.

PERSEVERANCE CAN BE A PRAYER

The ideal is to include some element, however small, of praise, even if you're feeling low. If you don't feel capable of praising God at the moment, you can pray for the desire to praise him. Similarly, if you are having trouble forgiving others who have hurt you, you can pray for the desire to forgive them. By persevering in prayer and good works, God can break down the walls around your heart.

Affirming your faith in God and not resorting to bitterness or immorality when you have negative or ambivalent feelings toward him, and your life situation, is infinitely pleasing to God, even if you don't feel good about it. The late theologian Karl Rahner observed that a sign of the Holy Spirit's presence is when you do something good, yet don't have a positive, tingly feeling about it. This means that God deems you capable of doing good for its own sake, independent of the reward that might accompany it. This was the subject of the debate in Job (cf. Job 1:9; 2:3-6).

Saints such as Paul of the Cross, John of the Cross, and Thèrése of Lisieux went through extreme experiences of abandonment and depression. When we experience desolation amid prayer, and have not been lax about our faith or morality, we should recognize that we are in good company and invite their and the Spirit's intercession (cf. Rom 8:26-27).

CONTEMPLATION

Prayer is the active side of our dialogue. The receptive side is contemplation. At the risk of oversimplification, prayer is offering ourselves to God, while contemplation is receiving him. Together they result in a consecration of the person to God similar to that which occurs at the Eucharist. The traditional and popular term for contemplation, "simple presence," recalls our disposition toward the real presence of Jesus in the Eucharist. *Dei Verbum,* the Second Vatican Council document on the Bible, speaks of receiving the bread of life at the table both of God's word and Christ's body.

CONTEMPLATION AS BEING AND LISTENING/RECEIVING

Contemplation is a time for being and listening. When we are still and quiet, we are better able to hear God.

Contemplation is like sitting with a member of the opposite sex whom you care about. After sharing words and affections, you bask in each other's presence. Words are no longer necessary. Your goal is not achievement or activity, but intimacy and presence. To use popular jargon, you chill/mellow out with God, and rest from the energy-requiring activities in the *lectio* process. The strenuous part of your exercise completed, you cool down in God's presence.

DAILY SABBATH MOMENTS

Contemplation is the epitome and consummation of the Sabbath experience that is *lectio divina.* We rest and spend time with God. We need to recharge and re-center ourselves more than just weekly. Sabbath moments fill us with divine wisdom and peace/consolation. They energize us to live the word we have received.

Lest you get discouraged when you have difficulty sitting still with God, recognize that I (and many others) have the same problem. Slowing down and resting in God is difficult for persons in Western cultures, where hustle and bustle is the norm and autonomy (rugged individualism) is glorified. The idea of letting God take over for a few moments is a shock to our system and society. We can overcome both internal and external obstacles through a commitment to quiet time and trust in God's fidelity.

CONSOLATION

Consolation is not an activity of *lectio*. It is a fruit of the Spirit (cf. Gal 5:22-23) induced by *lectio* and other graced spiritual exercises. It can occur at any point in the *lectio* process, but often comes during contemplation, when we cease activities and move into receptive mode.

Consolation is essential for maintaining our enthusiasm for reading and living the Bible. It is essential that we go to the Bible expecting God to nourish us spiritually: "And without faith it is impossible to please him. For whoever would draw near to God must believe that he exists and that he rewards those who seek him" (Heb 11:6; cf. Lk 11:13).

── WRESTLING WITH THE WORD ──

 The nourishment and response we receive from God's word is not always to our liking. As articulated by Jesus in the Lord's Prayer and as exemplified in his response to the devil's temptations (cf. Mt 4:4) and in the Garden of Gethsemane, fidelity to God's word must take precedence even over our legitimate needs.

Only through the spiritual gift of consolation is human compliance possible (even Jesus received help from an angel; cf. Mk 1:13; Lk 22:43). We need consolation when we fall, become confused or discouraged, or perceive God as not holding up his end.

Amid such desolation, the speeches of Job can be a comfort, reminding us that we join the Lord and the saints as we offer "loud cries and tears" (cf. Heb 5:7) to God.

THE ESSENCE OF CONSOLATION

Consolation is not an ethereal feeling of well-being and contentment. It rarely includes an extra-sensory experience of God's presence, like Moses at the burning bush (cf. Ex 3:2-4) or

Elijah in the desert (cf. 1 Kings 19:11-18). Usually it is much more subtle and ordinary.

Consolation is a graced (freely given by God) state of "the shalom (peace and wholeness) that surpasses all understanding" (cf. Phil 4:7). It is better experienced than described: "Likewise the Spirit helps us in our weakness; for we do not know how to pray as we ought, but the Spirit himself intercedes for us with sighs too deep for words" (Rom 8:26).

Consolation has traditionally been understood as the comfort and peace that is a gift of the Spirit to those who love God and do as he commands (cf. Jn 14-16). The Bible's most thorough discussion of the gifts of the Spirit is 1 Cor 12-14. Discernment of spirits is mentioned in 1 Cor 12:10, 1 Jn 4:1-6, Jas 1:12-18, and 1 Thess 5:19-22, and discernment in general in Heb 5:11-14, 1 Cor 2:6-16, and 1 Pet 2:1-2.

ACTION

Despite the consoling reassurances that often accompany contemplation, we can't depend on God for everything: We have to do our part and cooperate with him. We must share and practice what we have received.

Action, the consummating stage of *lectio*, is the way we bear witness to the word and give it life. It is implicit in the other stages, as each requires us to engage in some sort of action. Even the most receptive stage, contemplation, requires us to make a conscious effort to sit still.

Action is the most exciting, beneficial, and difficult aspect of *lectio divina*. We encounter the strongest resistance from ourselves and others when we try to implement God's word. Talking about or conceptualizing the word does not threaten the world, the flesh, and the devil nearly as much as living it.

Even Moses was susceptible to the tendency to tell other people to trust in God, while he himself was slow to take action:

"And Moses said to the people, 'Fear not, stand firm, and see the salvation of the LORD, which he will work for you today; for the Egyptians whom you see today, you shall never see again. The LORD will fight for you, and you have only to be still.' The LORD said to Moses, 'Why do you cry to me? Tell the people of Israel to go forward'" (Ex 14:13-15).

Note in this text the integration of acting and stillness representative of *lectio divina*, and in particular, the activities of prayer and contemplation.

THE CONTINUITY OF LECTIO DIVINA

Lectio divina is ongoing and organic. It is the process through which God's word becomes the seed that bears fruit in abundance (cf. Mk 4:8). Many other spiritual exercises have their roots in or are related to *lectio*. As we apply the wisdom and directives we experience in *lectio*, we understand God's word and ourselves in a deeper way.

Lectio isn't a static, mechanical process that ends with the completion of our quiet time. Rather, it is a dynamic, evolving experience of living God's word amid human resistance and limitations. Life is the cauldron where God's word mixes with human responses to add chapters to personal and collective salvation history. In the next chapter, we will consider *lectio's* application to such chapters as relationships, group Bible sharing, and religious art.

Chapter Seven

———— How to Apply *Lectio Divina* to ———— Life, Groups, and Art

LECTIO ON LIFE

There is no dichotomy between practicing *lectio divina* on the Bible and life. Life and the Bible are in a continuous, inseparable dialogue. Life is the Bible's context (cf. Gen 2-11), and God's word is life's source and foundation (cf. Gen 1).

A biblical phrase may touch off recollection of a life experience, which may then become the focus of our *lectio divina*. One of the purposes of reading the Bible is to shed light on life experiences and help us understand how God may be communicating to us through them.

As discussed in Chapter Two, God's word manifests itself in ways other than through the Bible. The fundamental theme of biblical revelation and salvation history is the divine initiative, which when manifested in our lives is a natural subject for *lectio divina*.

Whether you begin your *lectio* with a life circumstance or experience, or the Bible leads you there, the process is fundamentally the same.

LECTIO ON A RELATIONSHIP

Perhaps you are having difficulty in a relationship, and you wish to bring it before God in a holistic manner. Your first step is to relax and enter into God's presence. Then, you use your senses to recall the relevant aspect(s) of that relationship or circumstance, and go over it in your mind (meditation).

If you are practicing *lectio* on a circumstance such as the birth of a child, a joyful or wounded memory, or an aspect of nature (e.g., a waterfall or stream), you use your imagination and senses to bring that entity into consciousness. This constitutes the reading/listening/sensing stage of *lectio*.

You meditate by repeating the words, emotions, or images associated with that experience or circumstance, and then discern how the Spirit is inviting you to respond. You then share your feelings and concerns with God as part of the prayer or active dialogue stage.

After getting everything out of your system, you sit quietly with God, and open yourself to his healing presence and wisdom (the contemplation stage and the consolation dimension). To use the language of the Psalms (cf. Ps 25; 37; 38:15;130:5), you wait on God in a posture of simple presence. When you are calm and inspired, you are in a better state to decide and act prudently and lovingly. Finally, you act upon the word/message that you have received.

Fundamentally, most of this is a review for you. You've already undergone this process in response to various stimuli sent by God and life; now you're encountering traditional names, concepts, and guidelines associated with it, and putting it all together.

GROUP OR FAMILY LECTIO DIVINA

Given its community origins, *lectio* is natural in a group setting. I have found it more helpful for participants in parish or family Bible-sharing discussions to follow the *lectio* approach than to engage in serious study. The latter requires a skilled and informed group leader and a serious commitment from group members. We need to wade before diving in.

Following are guidelines for conducting a Bible-sharing session using the *lectio divina* model:

- Begin by greeting one another and exchanging news and pleasantries (retreat, relax).
- Each person is given the opportunity to share what he wishes to pray for (prayer).
- The group leader reads a few lines from the Bible, preferably a Psalm, perhaps from the upcoming Sunday liturgy (reading).
- A group member or the leader follows the Psalm by entrusting the petitions to God and concluding with a formal (e.g., the Lord's Prayer) or informal prayer (prayer).
- If the passage is more than a few verses, divide it into several sections and have one or more members of each sex read it aloud. The passage should be read slowly and in an appropriate tone, that is, dramatic for a narrative or a lament, reflective for a meditation, didactic for proverbs or wisdom counsel (reading).
- After three or four minutes of quiet reflection, each person shares whatever word, phrase, verse, or image touched him, without explaining it (meditation in the sense of

rumination). Initially, a member of the group may forget the instructions and begin to comment on his "word." The leader should use discretion as to how long to let him go on before gently reminding him of the guidelines.

- Different members of both sexes (if feasible) read the passage aloud for the second time (reading).
- After three or four minutes of quiet reflection, each person shares why he chose his word, phrase, verse, or image (meditation in the sense of application or reminiscence).
- Each person has the option of sharing how he will implement his word (action).
- Ideally, each person will get a chance to share his application before others comment and the discussion takes off. Participants thereby practice listening, and observe the diversity and common elements of their responses. In some situations, direct feedback and immediate discussion may be acceptable, providing that everyone eventually gets the opportunity to share their application.
- After the discussion winds down, the group closes with a brief period of silence, a prayer, and perhaps one of the Sunday readings (contemplation, prayer).

GROUP-LEADER SECRET

Twenty-five years of participating in and leading Bible-sharing groups have taught me not to preempt the Spirit and the participants' insightfulness by explaining the passage up-front. If questions arise, I usually offer a brief response and defer the details until after participants have shared their reflections.

Empowered by Jesus' presence (cf. Mt 18:19-20), participants invariably arrive at insights found in biblical commentaries, and discover their capacity for making competent interpretations and applications of Scripture. This builds confidence in oneself and trust in the Spirit. Personal experience and capacities are a viable frame of reference for comprehending Scripture, particularly as it relates to one's own life.

Just as each person has a contribution to make in the interpretation and application of the Bible, so is each person's life a work of art. I wish to close this chapter by focusing on an oft-overlooked medium through which the Bible has made a unique aesthetic and spiritual contribution to western civilization. Much of the great religious art and literature of antiquity, the Middle Ages, and the Renaissance was produced and preserved by the same monks who faithfully practiced *lectio divina*. Let us now consider the edifying possibilities inherent in biblically inspired art.

LECTIO ON ART AND ICONS

One of the great treasures of Catholicism and Orthodoxy is the art it has commissioned, collected, and conserved throughout the ages. Arguably, the most beautiful specimens come from the Renaissance and Baroque periods, beginning with the pioneering work of Giotto.

The holistic nature of *lectio divina* is ideally suited to appreciation of art, which is designed to stimulate the mind, senses, emotions, and spirit. When we contemplate religious art, we often gain insights into the psychological and contextual dimensions of biblical passages. The various artistic elements (e.g., landscapes, colors, contrasts, materials, details) speak volumes.

Biblically based art is of its nature primarily *eisegetical*, that is, it projects the artist's/viewer's perspective onto the biblical passage. It is as much a reflection of the artist and viewer as of the subject. Thus, it is a medium for learning about ourselves as well.

All forms of creative expression, be it music, art, literature, or drama, have both a literal or intended meaning and an applied or received meaning. The expression itself takes on a meaning independent of the artist. Sometimes we communicate unconsciously, or God works through us in ways beyond our comprehension.

Many a speaker or homilist has been credited with something that they don't recall saying. This independent meaning interacts with the subjective perspective of its audience, thereby resulting in a wide array of perceptions and interpretations.

Thus, it is a legitimate aspect of interpretation to appropriate the text/artwork into our world and experience a subjective personal meaning that may not correspond exactly to the literal sense (which itself always has some degree of subjectivity). The key is to recognize these subjectivities and not impose our interpretations or perceptions on others, while maintaining a healthy connection with the literal/intended meaning of the work so as to avoid arbitrariness.

An example from the art world may be instructive. Art critics share their opinions about the quality of a piece of art, without requiring that their audience perceive the same value and meaning.

Art (and other forms of entertainment or cultural expression) tells us much about a society. For example, the countless "Madonna and child" and Holy Family paintings and sculptures from pre-Enlightenment times (the eighteenth century) communicate reverence for the incarnation and family relationships. The rarity of such images in modern art reflects the diminishment of those values.

Developing our awareness of the heritage of biblically inspired art contributes to the process of holistic personal growth and spirituality evoked by *lectio divina*. It adds an aesthetic pleasure and refinement to life that fulfills our creative and sensual needs in a superior way to the carnal entertainments and pursuits that permeate modern Western cultures.

Both the Bible (cf. Mt 12:43-45; Lk 11:24-26) and psychology tell us that it is not enough to "just say no" to enticing temptations. We need a positive alternative. The Bible, in conjunction with the sacraments and Christian community and culture (art, music, literature, drama), constitute a first and privileged choice.

HIDDEN MASTER(PIECE)S

I recently had the opportunity to view an exhibit of the Spanish artist El Greco's work at the Metropolitan Museum of Art in New York. I came across an English art dealer and his curator friend who were very knowledgeable about religious art, and who interacted with some of the most knowledgeable curators in the world.

I mentioned my interest in biblical art, and asked who he thought did particularly fine religious art. He mentioned Giovanni Bellini, whose father, brother, and brother-in-law (Mantegna) were outstanding painters, and who mentored such masters as Titian and Giorgione. Neither of the latter ever received a public commission for a large oil painting while Bellini was alive. On a trip to Venice in 1506, the greatest German Artist, Albrecht Dürer, observed that while Bellini was very old (around seventy-five), he was still the finest artist in Venice.

The art dealer pointed out that each of Bellini's "Madonna and child" paintings had their own nuances and special qualities,

---

SACRED HUMOR

Although many people claim that the grocery store is a place to meet someone of the opposite sex, in my opinion a religious exhibit at an art museum is as good a place as any. At one such venue, I saw two women standing mesmerized before a Sandro Botticelli painting and commenting profusely on its exquisite quality. It was one of the easiest female conversations I have ever broken into. Art can lower people's defenses, if only for a moment.

reflecting his evolving understanding of the mystery and his craft. Both of us had the opportunity to view some of Bellini's finest works at the *Gallerie dell' Accademia* in Venice.

While well-known to art enthusiasts, Bellini's work is unfamiliar to the casual observer. He is an example of an artisan who does not have the reputation of the most familiar names in his field, yet whose work rivals theirs in quality, if not necessarily in quantity or breadth.

If you choose to explore the world of religious art, you may discover other comparatively unheralded geniuses who shared their *lectio divina* on the divine mysteries in an artistic manner, thereby enriching generations to come. Likewise, if you persist in Bible reading, you will find many unheralded masterpieces of biblical literature that touch you.

PAPAL PATRONAGE

Pope Paul VI was an admirer of art and classical music. His profound address and meeting with Roman artists in the Sistine Chapel on May 7, 1964, was followed up by an international effort coordinated by his secretary, Monsignor Pasquale Macchi, to both gather modern religious art and foster a better understanding between the Church and artists.

These initiatives resulted in the opening of the exquisite modern religious art section of the Vatican Museum on June 23,

---

SAINTS AND SAGES ON THE BIBLE

"In approaching artistic masterpieces from whatever era, the mind is prompted to open itself to the mysterious fascination of the Transcendent, because a mysterious and unexpected spark of the Divine is present in every genuine artistic expression." This articulation of the effects of *lectio divina* on art was excerpted from Pope John Paul II's address for the Jubilee Celebration for Artists, Friday, February 18, 2000.

1973. On a tour of the Vatican Museum in 2001, a guard who worked there for more than forty years and had witnessed the development of this section gave me a private tour of closed modern art galleries, including an impressive bronze statue of Pope Paul. He told me that in response to Pope Paul's initiative, art poured into the Vatican from all over the world, far more than they could ever display.

So significant was Pope Paul's promotion of religious art (and other forms of Christian culture) that in April 1999, a special exhibit, entitled *Paul VI, a Light for Art*, was hosted by the Cathedral Museum of Milan and the Charlemagne Wing of the Vatican Museums.

In the same year, Pope John Paul II wrote a pastoral letter to artists that should be required reading for art and Bible enthusiasts. It is available on the Vatican website www.vatican.va.

In his letter, Pope John Paul points out the role art can have in the transformation of culture, the enjoyment of life, and our appreciation and application of the Bible. Referring to sacred music, he noted that many of the great composers (he lists Handel, Bach, Mozart, Schubert, Beethoven, Berlioz, Liszt, and Verdi) "have given us works of the highest inspiration in this field."

MEET THE MASTERS

Following is a list of artists whose works (as depicted in readily available books) can be a pleasant supplement and stimulant to your Bible reading:

Giovanni (and also Jacopo) Bellini

Tintoretto

El Greco

Michelangelo

Raphael

Botticelli

Titian

Castagno
Veneziano
Filippino Lippi
Rembrandt
Ghirlandaio
Dürer
Rubens
Piero della Francesca
Fra Angelico
Fra Bartolomeo
Giambattista Tiepolo
Giotto
Donatello
Chagall (An outstanding twentieth-century Jewish artist with
    a museum in Nice, France, which features much of his
    biblical art. He referred to Scripture as an "iconographic
    atlas.")
Masaccio
Mantegna
Ghiberti
Rogier van der Weyden
Bernini
Caravaggio
Correggio
Hubert and Jan van Eyck
Grünewald

In the next chapter, we will meet Jewish and Christian models
for deepening our experience of the Bible and life through
consciousness of their different levels of meaning.

Chapter Eight

How to Recognize Levels of Meaning in the Bible and Life

Contents of this Chapter

- Experience a rabbinical companion to the monastic model of *lectio divina.*
- Expand your capacity for interpreting the Bible according to its multiple levels of meaning.
- Discover similarities between Jewish and Christian models of the Bible's levels of meaning.
- Apply the levels of meaning in the Bible to life.

In this chapter, we will learn about the different levels of meaning found in the Bible according to both Jewish and Catholic tradition. The names associated with this material throughout Jewish (e.g., Rabbi Akiba, Rashi, Moses Mendelssohn, and Max Kadushin) and Christian (e.g., Origen, Augustine, Jerome, John Cassian, Gregory the Great, Thomas Aquinas, Richard of St. Victor, and Richard Simon [a French priest who anticipated the modern Catholic approach to Scripture by three centuries]) history communicate volumes about its importance.

I will use the rabbinical model as our starting point because it is easier to remember (it has a memorable acronym and story associated with it), and provides a starting point for assimilating the various Catholic models that have evolved over the centuries.

Since the Second Vatican Council, the Church has consistently emphasized the importance not only of relationships with the Jews, but of learning from them, particularly in areas that overlap with Christianity. Contemplative reading and application of the Bible certainly fit that bill.

THE PATH TO PARADISE

A model developed by the rabbis in the Middle Ages for interpreting the Torah was known by its acronym *pardes*. As Hebrew originally had no vowels, its four components begin with the consonants P, R, D, and S.

Pardes is actually a Persian word meaning an enclosed, paradise-like park, garden (such as Eden), or orchard. In the arid Near East, it is easy to understand why these would be associated with paradise. In Lk 23:43, Jesus promises *paradeisos* (the Greek translation of *pardes*) to the repentant criminal. The word is used in two other important passages in the New Testament (cf. 2 Cor 12:3; Rev 2:7).

LEVELS OF MEANING IN THE BIBLE AND LIFE

In rabbinical tradition, the *pardes* acronym stands for the four levels of meaning (also referred to as "senses") in the Torah (the Pentateuch), the most important part of the Bible for Jews. It also applies to the rest of the Bible. These levels are:

- *Peshat* (pe-shaht): The simple (i.e., straightforward), plain, literal meaning.
- *Remez* (re-mez): The hinted or clued, allegorical/symbolic meaning.
- *Derash* (de-rahsh): The applied meaning, such as used in homilies. The rabbis often used stories called *midrashim* (which has *derash* as its root) to make the Bible relevant to

their audience. Similarly, a good homilist uses stories or anecdotes to illustrate his point.

The word *derash* means "draw out." A homilist or any interpreter draws out a biblical passage's meaning and implications. Thus, *derash* is what the Bible means to its audience. This level of meaning or "sense" of Scripture is based upon and complementary to the literal meaning, or *peshat*. Using familiar concepts and examples, we draw out lessons from the Bible in relation to our lives.

- *Sod* (sahd): The mystical or infused (given by God) meaning.

PARDES AS A DESCRIPTION OF LIFE

Pardes also describes the levels of meanings that we experience in life. Our general pattern is to:

1. Experience things initially on the straightforward or literal level. This encompasses what we sense, think, and feel, based on what is readily apparent.
2. Discover and respond to clues, hints, or symbols. A subtle level of perception.
3. Translate our experiences and insights into conclusions or applications. We draw parallels and make connections.
4. Consider how God may be speaking to us through these stimuli: the providential or transcendent dimension.

THE STORY OF PARADISE

In the Talmud (the transcription of the Jewish oral law, with rabbinical commentary), there is a classic Jewish midrash entitled *The Four Who Entered Paradise* (*Pardes*). Four rabbis enter paradise, but only the Torah scholar Rabbi Akiba (d. A.D. 135), known for his advocacy of the literal sense of Scripture, ascends and descends in peace. The three other rabbis met unfortunate fates because they did not approach paradise with the proper motivation and grounding. For a popular fictional adaptation of this story, see *The Four Who Entered Paradise* by Howard Schwartz (published by Jason Aronson, Inc.).

MYSTICAL CAUTIONS

The midrash can be interpreted as a caution against pursuing esoteric spiritual knowledge or ecstasy for reasons of personal aggrandizement and independent of the literal or straightforward meaning of the Bible.

In New Testament times, both Christians and Jews faced this challenge in the form of mystery religions, such as gnosticism, which emphasized secret/privileged knowledge of God and spiritual truths. Both the Gospel and first letter of John refute such spiritual elitism.

Both the rabbis and Church Fathers recommend that persons use caution before indulging in mystical interpretations of the Bible. It is best to begin with the straightforward/literal and applied levels of interpretation at first, and as you develop your interpretive skills, the clued/hinted/symbolic level.

INTEGRATING LECTIO DIVINA AND PARDES

Permit me to share my synthesis of the monastic and rabbinical models. I have italicized key words from the *lectio divina* and *pardes* models.

I preface my Bible reading with a prayer, perhaps a line or two from a psalm or another part of Scripture, while offering any petitions or concerns to God.

I always start by trying to ascertain the simple, straightforward meaning of either a biblical passage or a personal encounter or experience. Usually, these manifest themselves at the sensory level, similar to what I pick up in the reading/listening/sensing stage of *lectio divina*.

I also look for subtle clues or hints as to its meaning. Going over the passage or experience several times, as per the ancient understanding of meditation, helps me discover these. Sometimes the passage or experience brings another passage or experience to mind. These hints or clues are an example of the *lectio divina* practice of reminiscence.

The first two levels/senses of *pardes* come together when I pay attention to the grammar of the passage. The literal presentation gives me hints or clues as to its meaning. I look for repeated words or phrases, a sure sign of biblical emphasis. If I really want to penetrate the literal meaning, I notice whether the sentence is declarative (factual), imperative (motivational), or interrogative (posing a question), and consider the verbs, nouns, and modifiers used. (This is one reason I favor a formal equivalent [literal] translation). You don't have to engage in this intense level of analysis on every passage, but it helps to be aware of vocabulary and grammar.

I then draw parallels and connections between the biblical passage and my own situation and experiences. This drawing out (*derash*) of the meaning corresponds to the application aspect of meditation given particular emphasis during the Middle Ages.

Although during the prayer and contemplation stage of *lectio divina* I hope to experience consolation or peace, for purposes of avoiding pride or false humility I am hesitant to ascribe mystical connotations to my experiences. Analogously, the Catholic Church only attributes mystical meanings to persons and events after considerable discernment and investigation. The canonization process and the substantiation of apparitions are two examples of such.

Mystical insights or revelations occur at God's discretion, typically at trying times when we are in need of encouragement, and are not an end in themselves. The mark of an authentic mystical experience is not what you feel or say, but how you respond: "Not every one who says to me, 'Lord, Lord,' shall enter the kingdom of heaven, but he who does the will of my Father who is in heaven" (Mt 7:21).

PARDES AS A MODEL FOR PERSONAL ENCOUNTERS

As pointed out throughout this book, marriage is the primary biblical metaphor for God's relationship with his people. The following exemplifies how *pardes* models the progression of a significant personal encounter. I will use a scenario that most people can relate to.

I met a special person. Based on her (literal) appearance, there was an attraction. As we gazed and talked (sensate level), we engaged in gestures and body language symbolic of our mutual interest.

We also received hints of our compatibility through our discovery of common interests and values. Now that we were getting comfortable with each other, we began exchanging stories and making connections, that is, drawing out the meaning of our encounter.

The special person commented on how our meeting seemed almost mystical or meant to be. (Indicative of the fragility of premature spiritual attributions, a substantially different interpretation can emerge as the relationship unfolds!)

We consummated our encounter by mellowing out together through simple presence to each other (contemplation), while thanking God (prayer) for bringing us together. God, of course, is the ultimate matchmaker and father of the bride, performing those functions first in the story of the creation of Eve (cf. Gen 2:18-25).

Our experience of a synthesis of *pardes* and *lectio divina* continued as we got to know each other better. In accordance with our personalities, capacities, and circumstances, we oscillated between the various activities and senses as is natural in a meaningful encounter. We kept discovering basic (straight-forward) information about each other, our likes and dislikes, and so on. We exchanged growing symbols of our mutual affections and continued to infer a mystical/providential dimension. We soon began building shared stories, applications, and connections. Like *lectio divina* and *pardes*, our lives were becoming intertwined.

Only after interacting on the first three levels of *pardes* did the mystical intuition acquire real, rather than romantic/idealized/projected, substance. Both Jewish and Christian tradition view the first three levels of meaning as a foundation for the fourth. Likewise, the contemplation stage of *lectio divina*, whereby we dispose ourselves for a deeper encounter with God, is given substance by the other activities of *lectio*.

THE HOLISTIC NATURE OF PARDES

Using an example from daily life, note how the whole person is involved in *pardes*, just as in *lectio divina*. You first encounter someone with your senses in a simple manner. You then use your intuitions and deductive reasoning to discern symbols (hints and clues), and pay attention to your emotions to gauge if you want to exchange stories and draw out applications/connections. Finally, you listen to the Spirit to discern how God is mystically present and communicating with you.

These descriptions are not intended to convey an overly rational and mechanical approach to interactions that should be natural, spontaneous, and fluid. They are guidelines describing flow rather than blueprints with rigid boundaries. As with the stages of *lectio divina*, the distinctions between the *pardes* levels of meaning are somewhat artificial. There is much overlap and fluid interaction between them. Each level is present in the other levels.

Lectio divina and *pardes* have an instinctual and natural quality. You don't have to intellectualize everything while you're doing it. You flow. I have referred to these as models rather than methods in order to avoid any mechanical, compulsive connotations.

Should we be conscious of these stages and levels as we go through the process? An analogy from the world of sports may shed light on the question. When athletes train and practice, their consciousness of the intricacies of their sport prepares them to do their best. When it becomes time to perform, they have to trust their preparations and reactive instincts and avoid thinking too much. Otherwise they'll be mechanical and lack fluidity. Consciousness is not the same as compulsion.

Awareness of the components and progression of these models helps us determine whether overall we are using all our faculties and processing the Bible and our experiences in a holistic and balanced manner. If we notice certain activities or senses (levels of meaning) consistently missing or out of proportion, we may have an indication that something is amiss. It is helpful to occasionally review our Bible-reading practices for reasonable compliance with these models' flexible guidelines.

The time and energy we expend practicing these models is more than offset by the resources conserved by spurning hyped, secular personal-growth programs and resources that are inferior to what God, nature, and the Judeo-Christian tradition offer for free.

LEVELS OF INTERPRETATION IN THE CHRISTIAN TRADITION

Similar models describing the multiple levels of meaning of a biblical text have been developed within Christianity. In the early Church, the two great Near Eastern centers of Christianity, Antioch and Alexandria, emphasized the literal and allegorical (symbolic, i.e., spiritual) senses respectively. This corresponded to the Antiochene community's emphasis of Jesus' humanity, and the Alexandrian community's emphasis of his divinity.

John Cassian, an early desert father, developed a model quite similar to *pardes* that became the model for medieval exegesis. His categories were the literal/historical, the allegorical or Christological (that is, how passages in the Old Testament in particular refer to Christ in a symbolic sense), the moral or anthropological (man's meaning, what he is urged to do by

Scripture), and the anagogical (leading) or eschatological (end-times) — where the Bible leads us (toward God and heaven). The last three senses are traditionally grouped together as the spiritual senses. Both the Pontifical Biblical Commission's 1993 document *On the Interpretation of the Bible in the Church* (II, B) and the Catechism of the Catholic Church (115-118) present the above model and the following medieval couplet:

"The Letter speaks of deeds; Allegory to faith; The moral, how to act; Anagogy our destiny."

In his *Morals on the book of Job*, one of the most influential and profound Christian expositions of a biblical book, Pope Gregory the Great organizes his comments according to the historical, allegorical, and moral senses. In his *Summa Theologica*, St. Thomas Aquinas affirms the traditional distinction between the literal and spiritual senses, and divides the latter into the symbolic (allegorical) and moral.

THE PRIMACY OF THE LITERAL SENSE

The fundamental principle underlying these senses was articulated by St. Thomas and affirmed by Pope Pius XII in his landmark 1943 encyclical *Divino Spiritu Afflante* (which approved the use of modern interpretive methods within the bounds of Tradition and the magisterium): "All other senses of Sacred Scripture are based on the literal." St. Thomas also points out, "Nothing necessary to faith is contained in the spiritual sense that Scripture does not put forward elsewhere in the literal sense."

EQUATING THE JEWISH AND CHRISTIAN MODELS

The mystical sense in *pardes* would roughly correspond to the *anagogical* in the Christian models, and the applied/homiletic sense to the moral sense, while the hinted or clued sense would be approximately equivalent to the Christian allegorical sense, except that the former obviously does not incorporate a Christological sense.

Though essential for Christians, the latter should be applied judiciously so as not to lose the literal/historical sense of Scripture, particularly the Old Testament. Zealous interpreters of Scripture sometimes prematurely move to the spiritual level and infer that texts prefigure (anticipate) or speak symbolically about Christ when attentiveness to the literal meaning would present a more direct link to Christ and his teachings. If we choose to use the *pardes* model, we should bear in mind its differences from the Christian model, and integrate the latter when necessary (e.g., when encountering a text with Christological meaning).

ACCESSING OUR HEBREW HERITAGE

I have exposed you to the *pardes* model not only for its accessible, complementary, and memorable qualities, but because it exemplifies Christianity's Hebrew heritage. It is a good starting point for learning the slightly more complex Christian models. A personal anecdote illustrates the wisdom of incorporating a Hebrew mentality in our exploration of the Bible.

The importance of land in the Bible became clear to me when I was the only Gentile in a Jewish Bible class. They began talking passionately about the land of Israel, when suddenly I realized how many parables and teachings of Jesus involved land (cf. Mt 5:5). I recognized how little consideration I gave to the many biblical references to land.

When I shared this insight with the group, one of the individuals looked at me point blank and declared, "Where do you think you guys get most of your stuff?" He underscored the importance of Christians learning from Jews, and respecting them as elder brothers and sisters in the biblical tradition.

CONTINUING OUR TOUR OF PARADISE

Throughout this book, you have been immersed in the first and third levels of *pardes*, the literal and applied levels. You have also been exposed to the second level, hints or clues, through the subtle interpretation insights I have shared, and occasional Christological comments (e.g., on Is 7:14 in Chapter Twenty-Five).

When it comes, the mystical level ensues primarily from the prayer and contemplation stage of *lectio divina*. It should not be feared, trivialized, ambitiously courted, or made into an elite experience. It happens on God's timetable according to our readiness. The writings of Christian mystics and the discernment principles developed by St. Ignatius and incorporated in his spiritual exercises, along with competent spiritual direction, can help us discern God's mystical messages.

THE HUMAN MODEL OF LECTIO DIVINA AND PARDES

The *Magnificat* (cf. Lk 1:46-55) exemplifies the proper attitude for *lectio* and *pardes* (or the Christian models discussed above). Mary takes God's word to heart, ponders his initiative in personal and salvation history, and responds obediently and perseveringly. She encountered the ultimate mystical dimension of life (the Incarnation) in the most humble way, through maternal and spousal love and submission to God's will. She received God in his most vulnerable form, through the baby Jesus, thereby fulfilling the Last Judgment criteria for salvation (cf. Mt 25:34-40). She inspires and prays for us as we join Rabbi Akiba and countless others in ascending and descending from paradise (communicating with God while loving ourselves and neighbor, and being stewards of creation).

THE COMPLEMENTARITY OF LECTIO DIVINA AND PARDES

In *lectio divina, pardes,* and its Christian parallels, we experience an interwoven and complementary dimension of Jewish and Christian biblical spirituality. As you become more aware of the levels of meaning in biblical texts, you will arrive at a synthesis of these that enables you to receive the message God intends for you. You will develop a personal rhythm and system for encountering the Bible and life according to your capacities. The ensuing continuity brings to mind the seamless-garment imagery (cf. Jn 19:23) used by the late Cardinal Joseph Bernardin to describe inclusive and balanced C/catholic spirituality.

In reviewing the context and development of the Bible, translations, and Bible reading plans and models, we laid the groundwork for encountering the Bible directly. The New Testament is next.

Section Two

—— How to Read the New Testament ——

Chapter Nine

—— Introducing the New Testament ——

— Contents of this Chapter —

- Learn the basic contents and background of the New Testament, and how to read it in context.
- Survey the Jewish factions at the time of Jesus.
- Learn accessible interpretive methods that will help you discern the Bible's literal meaning.
- Discover how the Gospels developed and the purpose they served.
- Discover the overlooked and beneficial gender dimension of the Gospels.

COMPONENTS OF THE NEW TESTAMENT

The New Testament consists of 27 books that can be divided into the following sections:

- The Gospels (Matthew, Mark, Luke, and John).
- Acts of the Apostles ("Acts" chronicles the activities of the apostles, and is written by the evangelist Luke. Luke and Acts are a two-volume work).
- The Epistles (pastoral and personal letters). These can be further divided into the following categories.

- The letters of St. Paul (Romans, 1 and 2 Corinthians, Galatians, Ephesians, Philippians, Colossians, 1 and 2 Thessalonians, 1 and 2 Timothy, Titus, and Philemon).
- The Catholic (i.e., universal) Epistles (James, 1 and 2 Peter, 1, 2, and 3 John, and Jude).
- Hebrews and Revelation (also known as the Apocalypse). Their authorship has always been shrouded in mystery, though tradition has at times ascribed them to Paul and John respectively.

THE HISTORICAL CONTEXT OF THE NEW TESTAMENT

The oldest New Testament book is Paul's first letter to the Thessalonians. It was written around A.D. 50. The last letter to be

---

WHAT DOES IT MEAN?

 The word "Gospel" derives from the Greek word *euangelion* and means good news. It is a unique literary form designed to proclaim "the good news of Jesus Christ, the son of God" (Mk 1:1, New Revised Standard Version).

The Gospels relate Jesus' life, teachings, and identity, and what it means to be a disciple. Historical data is presented to tell the story and convey theological and moral truths, rather than for its own sake. The writers of the Gospels are evangelists (heralds of the good news) rather than biographers. For example, they do not provide such typical biographical details as physical appearance and personality characteristics (other than what can be inferred from the text).

BIBLE VOCABULARY

St. Paul's letters are often referred to as epistles. This derives from the Greek *epistole*, which was used in New Testament times to refer to all types of letters. With the exception of the letter to Philemon, St. Paul's epistles were designed to circulate and be read aloud in public assemblies.

---

written was the second letter of Peter, which scholars date between A.D. 100 and 125. The New Testament's writing span of between 50 and 75 years is dwarfed by the Old Testament's.

Even in the New Testament's short time span, the social and religious scene changed considerably. In A.D. 70, the Romans crushed a Jewish revolt and destroyed the second temple at Jerusalem (the first was destroyed by the Babylonians in 587 B.C.). The promised land was under oppressive Roman rule during the entire New Testament period. When Jesus preached love of enemies, there were tangible and painful applications right in front of his audience.

Through a gradual process probably formalized (historical records are ambiguous) at the Jewish Council of Jamnia around 90 B.C., Christians were excluded from the synagogue and became distinct from Judaism. The Gospel of John, written in the nineties, alludes to the expulsion from the synagogue (cf. Jn 9:22; 12:42). The Gospel of Matthew, written to a Jewish Christian community approximately a decade before, likewise reflects these tensions.

THE BIBLE SAYS WHAT?

 Though Jesus and his disciples spoke Aramaic, the New Testament is written in what is called *koine* (common) Greek, as distinguished from classical or modern Greek.

JESUS AND THE OLD TESTAMENT

Jesus, his disciples, and the writers and communities of the New Testament revered the Old Testament and viewed it as inspired Scripture (cf. 2 Tim 3:14-17; 2 Pet 1:20-21). While the entire New Testament draws upon the Old Testament, the Gospels of Matthew and John, Paul's letters, and the letter to the Hebrews do so most frequently and explicitly.

Jesus viewed himself and his teachings as fulfilling the Old Testament (cf. Mt 5:17-20; 7:12; Lk 24:44-45). He got into trouble with the religious leaders for giving himself authority over the Torah: "You have heard it said (that is, in the Torah) . . . but I say to you. . . ." (cf. Mt 5:21-48). Jn 5-8 contains a lengthy dispute between them.

Heb 1:1-3 contains the New Testament's most eloquent expression of Jesus' fulfillment of the Old Testament:

"In many and various ways God spoke of old to our fathers by the prophets; but in these last days he has spoken to us by a Son, whom he appointed the heir of all things, through whom also he created the world. He reflects the glory of God and bears the very stamp of his nature, upholding the universe by his word of power."

Chapters 7-10 of Hebrews reveal how the priesthood, covenant, and sacrifice of Jesus supersede that of the Old Testament. Chapter 11 of Hebrews showcases Old Testament heroes who were the forerunner of Jesus and remain inspiring models for Christians.

The more familiar you are with the Old Testament, the more you will understand the New Testament. It is the foundation for the ministry and message of Jesus. He was a Jew who followed, interpreted, and fulfilled the Old Testament.

JEWISH FACTIONS AT THE TIME OF JESUS

There was much political and religious unrest in first-century Palestine. The Romans exerted a heavy hand, and there was tension among Judaism's religious factions. John the Baptist and Jesus preached to a discouraged crowd. There were five main religious and political groups:

The Pharisees — The Pharisees were the spiritual teachers of the people. They instructed and influenced Jesus as well. They tried to help the people conform to the law by "building a hedge around it." (Most structured religions at times operate according to this mode, which can lead to scrupulosity and hypocrisy as well as piety and self-discipline). Many of Jesus' disputes with the scribes and Pharisees involved these over-enthusiastic appendages to the law (cf. Mk 7:9-11). John the Baptist's criticisms of their legalism and hypocrisy (cf. Mt 3:7) foreshadowed Jesus' (cf. Mt 23).

In order to avoid letting these hostilities evoke anti-Semitic sentiments, we must remember that the Gospels' portrait of the Pharisees likely reflects the times of both Jesus and the early Church. First-century tensions between the Jewish and Christian communities undoubtedly affected how the evangelists told the story and how the people heard it.

The Pharisees were the sole group to survive the destruction of Jerusalem in A.D. 70, and were responsible for the preservation of Judaism.

The Scribes — These experts in the law and copyists of the Scriptures were part of the Pharisees. Scribes are also described as lawyers in Mt 22:35 and Lk 10:25. The scribes in Mk 12:28-34 and Lk 20:39, Nicodemus (cf. Jn 3; 19), and Joseph of Arimathea (who buried Jesus) are among the few Jewish leaders presented favorably in the Gospels.

The Sadducees — Conservative, aristocratic priests who tried to preserve temple worship from external (Roman) and internal (the Pharisees) interference. Because they recognized only the Torah (the first five books of the Old Testament) as Scripture, they did not believe in the resurrection of the dead (cf. Mt 22:23-33; Mk 12:18–27; Lk 20:27-38). The latter became a part of Jewish belief only gradually, and is found only in the later books of the Old Testament. This was an example of how revelation develops over time, as discussed in Chapter Three.

The Zealots — Anti-Roman political activists and rebels. One of Jesus' disciples, Simon (not Peter), was called "the Zealot." The Zealots instigated the ill-fated A.D. 66-70 rebellion against Rome. They are only mentioned in reference to Simon (cf. Lk 6:15; Acts 1:13).

The Essenes — The ascetic Essenes are known historically from the mid-second century B.C. to the destruction of the temple in A.D. 70. They practiced celibacy and congregated in out-of-the way places to preserve their purity. They came to modern consciousness as the Qumran community that preserved the Dead Sea Scrolls. They are not mentioned in the Bible.

WHAT DOES IT MEAN?

"Christ" is the Greek (*Christos*) translation of the Hebrew Messiah (*mashiach*), which means "anointed." Initially, it was a term used to refer to a king or a person designated with a divinely decreed function, such as a priest (cf. Lev 4:3,5), but gradually it developed connotations of savior (cf. Dan 9:25).

The Old Testament does not clearly reflect an expectation that the Messiah would be divine. This helps us understand why the intensely monotheistic Jews would have such difficulty with Jesus' assertion of his divine Sonship (cf. Jn 16:1-4). Misunderstandings and misguided zeal as well as malice and jealousy underlie the religious leaders' opposition to Jesus.

INTERPRETING THE NEW TESTAMENT

The following interpretive methods, a key hypothesis, and vocabulary, will help you interpret the New Testament's historical/literal meaning using the insights of modern biblical scholarship. As discussed in the previous chapter, the literal meaning of Scripture is the basis for its applied/personal meaning.

If you are new to the New Testament, you might take these one at a time and read through them gradually. Even a basic awareness of these will help you understand biblical footnotes and commentaries. The real excitement comes when you apply these principles and discover that you can interpret the New Testament for yourself.

CRITICIZING THE BIBLE

As discussed in Chapter Four, the Greek word for criticize means to identify the essence of something. It was used in reference to evaluating drama. Thus, it is an honor and a sacred responsibility to criticize the Bible. Otherwise, you won't know what it means.

Following are the interpretive (critical) methods most relevant to non-scholars. I discuss these in the context of the New Testament because for folks new to the Bible, becoming familiar with the Old Testament and its background is challenge enough.

- **Exegesis** means "reading out of" the Scriptures, that is, determining their literal meaning. Another name for a biblical scholar is exegete.

- **Eisegesis** means "reading into" the Scriptures, that is, projecting your experiences, values, and perspectives onto the biblical text. This is a necessary aspect of the interpretive process, for it facilitates application.

  Exegesis and eisegesis are interdependent. Exegesis alone is stale and lifeless, while eisegesis divorced from exegesis lacks substance and context. As observed by Bassanio in Act 3, Scene 2, of the Merchant of Venice, by William Shakespeare, bereft of a respect for the literal sense of Scripture, anyone can make Scripture out to mean almost anything: "In religion, what damned error, but some sober brow will bless it and approve it with a text, hiding the grossness with fair ornament?"

- **Hermeneutics** is the technical term for the science of interpretation (or conveying a message). It derives from the name of the Greek messenger god, Hermes. St. Paul was compared to Hermes in Lystra (a town in Asia Minor) because he was the lead speaker (cf. Acts 14:12).

- **Biblical criticism** is the catch-all name for modern interpretive methods.

- **Text (lower) criticism** seeks to determine the correct biblical text among the varying manuscripts. It is the foundation for translation and interpretation (e.g., the application of the higher criticism methods discussed below).

- **Historical criticism** explores the Bible's historical and cultural context. Used interchangeably with the term "the historico-critical method," it is the collective term for the "higher criticism" methods discussed below.

- **Source criticism** seeks to identify oral and written sources influential in the composition of the biblical text. You can identify what a text or person means to say more accurately when you know where they're coming from, that is, when you consider the source(s).

  Source criticism is primarily used in reference to the Old Testament, where the texts underwent a long process of transmission and adaptation. The documentary hypothesis discussed in Chapter Twenty-One is an example of source criticism.

- **Redaction (editorial) criticism** is a form of source criticism applied to the Gospels. It analyzes how the writers of the Gospels edited and wove together their oral and written sources with their own material in order to express their theological viewpoint and pastoral message.

- **Form criticism** identifies the literary form of a passage and how this bears on the passage's interpretation. Examples of literary forms include proverbs, parables, myths, narratives, and hymns. You inherently apply form criticism when you enjoy a story, sing a psalm, heed a proverb, personalize a parable, or decipher a myth.

- A complement to historical criticism, **literary criticism** applies to the Bible principles and methods used by literary critics. It includes elements of communications theory, that is, how individuals interact with and derive meaning from a text, and the text's independent aspect (it contains meaning of itself, in addition to reflecting the perspectives of both author and audience).

THE SEQUENCE OF THE GOSPELS

Though neither the biblical manuscripts nor other early Church documents explain the order in which books appear in the New Testament, we can draw reasonable conclusions. The Gospel of Matthew probably comes first because it was the most heavily utilized (it's great for catechesis), was initially believed to have been written first, albeit in Aramaic (which we have no direct evidence of), and was attributed to an apostle, whereas Mark and Luke were not.

Mark follows Matthew probably because more than 80 percent of his material is found in Matthew. Luke comes next probably because it has much of the material found in Mark, but has more affinities with John than do the others. John is the last Gospel because it was the last one written, is quite different from the others, and received more resistance to inclusion in the Bible than the other Gospels.

THE FORMATION OF THE GOSPELS

Tradition means "handed on." The contents of the Gospel message, like the Old Testament, was initially shared orally, thus making it oral tradition. In 1964, the Pontifical Biblical Commission (the Pope's biblical advisory team) issued a document entitled *Instruction on the Historical Truth of the Gospels,* which corroborated the prevailing scholarly hypothesis that the Gospels reflect three stages of development:

- **Historical stage:** The life and ministry of Jesus: his words and deeds and the events surrounding him.
- **Apostolic stage:** The early Church's oral proclamation of Jesus' suffering, death, resurrection, and imminent return ("the second coming"), and his words and deeds.

- **Evangelist stage:** The recording of orderly accounts (cf. Lk 1:1-4) of the oral traditions and apostolic teaching both for posterity and to address community issues.

THE BIBLE SAYS WHAT?

 One current of modern biblical scholarship has been the quest to assess the stage represented by Jesus' words and deeds. In other words, how historical and literal is a given text?

Because the Gospels were written thirty to seventy years after Jesus' death, and that society did not have the recording devices we possess, they relied on excellent and collective memories. Further, their objectives were not biographical or historical but religious: to share their faith and testify to the truth about Jesus.

Truth is not always expressed in literal form: for example, the parables of Jesus convey truths, but they are meant symbolically. The evangelists relate Jesus' story truthfully, which particularly in their culture does not necessarily mean literally. They communicated its spirit and essence, and the message the Holy Spirit intended. The Church has always affirmed the historical basis of the Gospels even while recognizing the literary, cultural, and theological filters through which it is communicated.

HARMONIZING THE GOSPELS

Believers unaware of the pastoral objectives of the Gospels (to affirm the faith of the evangelists' communities) may become disconcerted by the differences between the Gospels. Since the third century A.D., believers have tried to reconcile these in order to develop a unified portrait. Such efforts are known as "harmonizing the Gospels." This reflects a concern with literal correspondence that was foreign to the biblical writers and their communities. It is akin to treating siblings as one unit rather than individuals who share a common heritage.

THE COMPLEMENTARITY OF THE GOSPELS

The Gospels complement one another nicely. Mark is a story-teller who emphasizes the role of the cross (suffering) in the life of Jesus and his followers. Matthew is a teacher and Church

WHAT DOES IT MEAN?

Following are terms you will encounter in Bible footnotes and commentaries:

The synoptic Gospels are Matthew, Mark, and Luke. They are called synoptic because their similarities are such that they can be viewed (optic) along side one another (syn means with or together). As discussed in Chapter Four, a synopsis is a study resource that presents similar passages in the Gospels in parallel columns.

The synoptic question/problem concerns the dating and interdependence of the synoptic Gospels, as discussed below.

Q (from *Quelle*, the German word for source) is the name given to the hypothetical collection of Jesus' sayings/teachings underlying such passages found only in Matthew and Luke. Since Matthew and Luke give no indication of direct knowledge of each other, to explain these parallels scholars hypothesize the existence of a composite source accessed by both Gospels. Q was likely oral at first, then written. It is also referred to as the "Sayings Source."

Special material refers to biblical passages unique to Matthew (designated as "M") or Luke ("L"). One of the few teachings of Jesus in Mark that is in neither Matthew nor Luke is the parable known as "the seed growing secretly" (cf. Mk 4:26-29).

The most widely accepted explanation of the synoptic problem is known as the Two-Source Theory/Hypothesis. Based on the presumption of Markan priority (i.e., that it was the earliest Gospel), it assumes Matthew and Luke drew from both Mark and Q. Scholars discern Matthew's and Luke's theological and pastoral message both from their special material and the way they edit Mark and Q.

leader who focuses on morality and solidarity. John is a contemplative who emphasizes dynamic faith expressed through love and intimacy with Jesus and fellow believers. Luke is a crafter of memorable portraits and images, who emphasizes mercy. His pastoral sensitivity and subtlety is a wonderful balance to the rabbinical brilliance of Matthew, the homiletic intensity of Mark, and the spiritual genius of John.

Mark is the Gospel of Christian initiation and Matthew of teaching and Church order. Luke's pastoral sense addresses areas left unresolved by the former, while contemplative John helps us plunge the depths of the mystery of Christ amid the suffering and even persecution that is the Christian's lot. John ends with Jesus' prediction of a violent death for the leader of the apostles, Peter.

Were we to associate the Gospels with the spirituality or apostolic focus of particular religious orders, we could identify Matthew's orderliness, teaching orientation, and strident penchant for social justice with the Jesuits, Mark's focus on preaching and the passion as reflective of the Order of Preachers (the Dominicans) and the Passionists, Luke's pastoral and feminine sensitivity as Franciscan, and John's contemplative tone as reflective of the Carmelites and other contemplative orders.

Were we to continue in our associations, we might link the letters of Paul with the various missionary orders, the suffering-centered, pastorally sensitive letters of Peter with diocesan priests, and the practical books of Proverbs and Sirach and the letter of James with laypeople and the lay-oriented Salesians. Who else could we associate with the Psalms than the Benedictines and Trappists/Cistercians, the longtime custodians of the Liturgy of the Hours?

Obviously, these associations are debatable generalizations that oversimplify both the biblical books and the charisms of the religious orders. However, it serves the purpose of showing that the diverse spiritual traditions and ministries in the Bible continue to flourish today.

THE GENDER DIMENSIONS OF THE GOSPELS

While we are highlighting the uniqueness, diversity, and complementarity of the Gospels, we should note their oft-misunderstood gender dimensions that have practical implications for our gender identity and relationships as well.

Masculine Matthew and Mark

The Gospels of Matthew and Mark are the most similar of the Gospels, and they convey an intense, masculine tone: Matthew with his rabbinical orderliness, precise pedagogy, and unyielding moral demands, and Mark with his coarse Greek and blunt witness to the cross and the apostles' lack of faith. Neither has the literary elegance of Luke or John, yet their message is just as powerful.

Only Matthew and Mark present Jesus reciting Ps 22:1 ("My God, my God, why hast thou forsaken me?") at the moment of his death. They were less concerned with upsetting believers than with faithfully handing on the accounts they received and letting their audience come to terms with them and hopefully reach a deeper level of faith. Luke and John reflect a feminine tendency to soften or adapt harsh realities to the sensibilities of their audience. They present Jesus' death in a more uplifting manner (cf. Lk 23:39-46; Jn 19:25-30).

Intimate Luke and John

Reflecting the feminine desire for intimacy and solidarity, John emphasizes abiding in Jesus (cf. Jn 15:1-11), while Luke alone presents Jesus as affirming the apostles for standing by him amid his trials (cf. Lk 22:28).

While all four Gospels highlight Jesus' compassion and sensitivity to persons in pain, Luke and John spend more time on Jesus' dialogue with them, and inject a more dramatic tone: for example, Jesus' long discussion with the Samaritan woman in Jn 4, and Jesus' outreach to the sinful woman in Lk 7:36-50 and Jn 7:53-8:1.

The latter, the story of the woman caught in adultery and brutally humiliated by the hypocritical men, is actually found in Luke's Gospel in various manuscripts and flows better there than in John.

Luke and John emphasize Mary's receptivity to Jesus and portray her as the model disciple. Women have a greater presence in Luke and John, perhaps in part because they are at a more mature stage of the development of the Christian community.

"The pastoral and contemplative message of Luke and John are brought to life in a special way by women, whose pastoral contributions (cf. Rom 15:1-6) and contemplative gifts (e.g., the many female mystics, recognized and anonymous) have enriched the Church since its inception.

The Relevance of the Bible's Gender Guidance

Identifying and drawing applications from gender-specific characteristics and teachings not only in the Gospels, but the entire Bible, facilitates three important components of spiritual and human development:

1. Responding to gender identity and differences as a gift from God.
2. Integrating our own male and female attributes.
3. Interacting harmoniously with the opposite sex.

Drawing upon gender models and counsel from the Bible and Church teaching helps us discern the integrity and value of messages we receive from secular sources.

The gender-specific dimension of human and spiritual development is often overshadowed by the universal human dimension and contemporary confusion over gender identities and roles, thereby leading to various moral, social, and economic difficulties. Conversely, the Church's and Bible's affirmation and applications of gender distinctiveness and complementarity help us become whole persons, families, and communities.

Without falling into sexism or excessive stereotyping, we can recognize gender-specific elements in the Bible and relate them to our life and relationships, asking the Holy Spirit to help us be the man or woman we are meant to be.

Is the Bible Sexist?

Many persons characterize the Bible as sexist. Clearly, cultural and Christian values have evolved since biblical times. Yet, there are nuances that merit reflection and application.

First, for its time, the Bible as a whole was remarkably egalitarian and cognizant of women's dignity. The literature and religions of Israel's neighbors were far more demeaning toward women.

Second, sexism is primarily interpreted in modern society through the perspective of radical feminism, which as it has become more ideological and powerful, has become less dialogical and representative of its constituency. Accordingly, it has not addressed compelling critiques and alternative, reconciliatory models by respected authors such as Warren Farrell, Cornelius F. Murphy Jr., Christina Hoff-Sommers, F. Carolyn Graglia, and Luigi Zoja.

The strident emotionalism and adversarialism of radical feminism coincides with modern social and media tendencies, and effectively drowns out or marginalizes alternative viewpoints. Consequently, those who emphasize the Bible's sexism typically have little exposure to these. This results in a decrease in dialogue, trust, and collaborative efforts. An objective assessment of biblical sexism is possible only if all sides are heard and respected.

The 1993 Pontifical Biblical Commission document *On the Interpretation of the Bible in the Church* offers balanced perspectives on feminist critiques of the Bible's sexism. It points out methodological limitations to such exegesis, particularly the imposition of a preconceived (feminist) ideology on a text and culture.

A balanced, contextual survey of both biblical and human history confirms the conclusions of common sense, tradition, and experience: oppression and discrimination, as well as advocacy and mutuality, is and always has been a joint affair. Moral issues ultimately are human and individual, and each sex, like each person, is its own worst enemy.

Finally, given the treatment of women as pleasure objects and men as disposable objects in contemporary society, it would seem presumptuous for modern persons to assail the Bible's sexist shortcomings. We would be better off using the Bible's insights on gender identity, vocations, and relationships to correct our own individual and collective chauvinism.

The Church's Adoption of Biblical Intuitions on Gender

The Church captures the spirit of the Bible's teaching on gender by affirming the equality of the sexes without blurring them by proclaiming their equivalence. Life itself testifies to the beauty of gender distinctiveness.

Paul's letters are identified as having a sexist dimension, but when viewed in context, their doctrines and directives reflect a refined sense of the equality and mutuality of the sexes. In 1 Cor 11:11-12, Paul points out that while Eve came from Adam, the order is now reversed, and all have their origins in Christ. Eph 5:21-33 shows how mutuality in marriage should flow from Christian spirituality and solidarity and the complementarity of the sexes in the natural order.

In contrast to his rabbinical peers, Paul counted women among his prominent friends and supporters (cf. Rom 16:3-16; Phil 4:2-3). He observed that in Christ there is neither male nor female (cf. Gal 3:28). Obviously, this has not been perfectly realized within the Church, but neither have the other ideals in the Bible.

Papal Perspectives

Pope John Paul has frequently pointed out that passages that reflect oppressive (not only toward women, but slaves and foreigners) cultural values and practices need to be interpreted with the concept of development of revelation in mind, without dispensing with essential values that transcend cultural limitations.

John Paul's exegesis of gender-related texts during his papal audiences from 1979-1984 reflects an innovative reciprocal ethic: he shows how what in the Bible is directed toward one sex has similar or complementary applications to the other. Both sexes have their work cut out for them, and need each other.

Like a caring parent, the Bible corrects both its sons and daughters. Both have their gifts, limitations, vulnerabilities, and shadow sides, and share a common humanity. By correcting for cultural limitations while acknowledging our own chauvinism, we can discover profound insights and inspirations, and develop a greater appreciation of and receptivity to the opposite sex.

BEGINNING THE GOSPELS

The beginning of each Gospel sets the tone for the rest of the Gospel, particularly its account of Jesus' suffering and death:

- Mark begins with John the Baptist to link the public ministry of Jesus to the Old Testament (Mark quotes Is 40:3). He emphasizes both the need for repentance and John the Baptist's deferral to Jesus. Some in the first century ranked John the Baptist above Jesus — Jesus' first disciples had previously been disciples of John (cf. Jn 1:35-40). Of all the Gospels, Mark narrates John's death in the greatest detail (cf. Mk 6:17-29), foreshadowing the similar fate of Jesus.
- Matthew's infancy narrative (story of Jesus' birth) casts Old Testament themes and events in a new light. Joseph's dreams and righteous, merciful actions are reminiscent of

his Old Testament namesake. Herod's paranoid slaughter of the infant boys recalls Pharaoh's actions in Ex 1, thus linking Jesus to Moses. Jesus' life begins with a death sentence by a hardened, fearful politician, and it ends the same way under Pontius Pilate.

- Luke's story of Jesus' humble beginning foreshadows the inclusiveness of Jesus' ministry. Jesus' birth is preceded by angelic announcements to not only the faithful of Israel, represented by Zechariah and Mary, but outcasts such as the poorly esteemed and often corrupt shepherds. In Luke's Gospel, Jesus suffers and dies as he was born: humbly, gently, and innocently, surrounded by both saints and sinners.

  Luke's infancy narrative concludes with an elderly observant Jew's (Simeon) prophesy that Jesus will be a sign that will be opposed, ultimately resulting in his death and the piercing of Mary's heart (cf. Lk 2:34-35). Simeon prophesies that the inner thoughts of many will be revealed — one striking example is Luke's account of the repentance of one of the thieves on the cross (cf. Lk 23:39-43).

- John's prologue (cf. Jn 1:1-18) previews the major themes of his Gospel, including Jesus' rejection by the world and the Jews and his manifestation of God's qualities (grace/kindness and truth/fidelity) and presence.

INTERPRETING THE PARABLES

Because the parables are not a familiar literary or pedagogical (teaching) mode, they merit a brief introduction. They are rooted in the Old Testament, and are also found in the literature of Israel's neighbors.

The key to interpreting the parables is to perceive the contradictions, ironies, essential values, and fundamental choices that they expose. They highlight the inconsistencies and foibles of human nature, as well as its possibilities.

The parables enable you to personalize teachings by identifying with the characters and circumstances. Wise teachers use stories because their symbols and motifs draw their audience in and circumvent their defenses. The parables are an invitation to repentance and a commentary on life and spiritual truths.

Nobody likes to be told directly that they are "missing the mark" (one of the biblical expressions for sin). Nathan used a parable to address David's sins of adultery and murder. How could the king dispute his own verdict? (cf. 2 Sam 12) The same applies to us when we accept Jesus' invitation to let the parables interpret and convert us.

If you want to get a sense of the parables, go to the longest sections of parables in the Gospels: Mt 13, Mt 25, and Lk 15-16.

JESUS' HUMOR

The parables and Jesus' verbal exchanges with others reveal his sense of humor and human nature. He frequently injected levity into intense situations. He engaged in by-play with a woman who persistently sought his help (cf. Mk 7:24-30). He commented that a dead boy and a friend were sleeping before he revived them (cf. Mk 5:39; Jn 11:11).

Jesus had his greatest difficulties with those who took themselves too seriously. Consider his main opponents in the Gospels: the stern religious leaders, the callous Pontius Pilate, the ruthless King Herod, and the demons whom Jesus casts out of possessed persons. All are humorless. Jesus needed a sense of humor to expose the pompous behavior of the religious leaders and to endure his apostles when they misunderstood him and pursued their own agenda.

The Gospels never portray Jesus as laughing or smiling. The eyewitness sources of the Gospels experienced Jesus' humor firsthand, and didn't feel the need to spell it out. For Jesus' contemporaries and their immediate descendants, his humanity was never in doubt, and thus there was no need to emphasize what was taken for granted: his humor. How else could he have survived his apostles, the incessant crowds, folks seeking special treatment (cf. Lk 12:13-15), and the stiff-necked religious leadership?

However, the Gospels clearly indicate that Jesus knew how to have a good time: he turned water into wine at the wedding at Cana (cf. Jn 2) and was criticized for dining with tax collectors and sinners — lively company, no doubt.

SACRED HUMOR

Humor comes from the disparity between what should be and what is. For example, a dressed-up animal makes us laugh because of its ridiculousness and incongruity. It requires humility to recognize the light side of imperfections and human nature. We are living an important dimension of the Bible and Catholic spirituality when at appropriate times we laugh at the lighter side of life, the Bible, and human nature, particularly our own behavior (e.g., on being burned at the stake, St. Lawrence reportedly said words to the effect of, "You can turn me over now, I'm done on this side"; and several books have been published on the humor of Pope John XXIII).

THE SALVIFIC DIMENSION OF BIBLICAL HUMOR

Of course, humor was not Jesus' main quality or priority. Salvation is no laughing matter. The only time God laughs in the Old Testament is at the folly/pride of human beings (cf. Ps 2:4; 37:13).

Both Jesus' humor and that of the Bible is subtle. St. Paul occasionally makes us laugh by his crude bluntness (cf. Gal 5:12), but he isn't laughing when his communities get off track.

Confronting the pain and alienation of humanity does not lend itself to frivolous humor or forced smiles. The truly humorous and joyful person knows the sorrows and trials of life, yet has found a way to endure them with hope. The model for such is Jesus, and his formula for joy is the Beatitudes.

Jesus bore the pain of human sinfulness and became a man of sorrows (cf. Is 53:3) so that God could laugh with rather than at us. We experience occasions of levity and celebration in this life, but the real feast comes when Jesus returns.

Foretold in the Old Testament (cf. Is 25:6), the messianic banquet consummates Jesus' return (cf. Mt 8:11; 22:1-14; Lk 12:37; 14:15-24). It is anticipated in the memorializing of the Last Supper. When Catholics celebrate the Eucharist, they anticipate the final meal shared with Jesus. This is explicitly stated in the Eucharistic prayers.

On this anticipatory, eucharistic note, let us now review the individual Gospels, beginning with Mark.

Chapter Ten

How to Read Mark, the Gospel of the Cross

> ### Contents of this Chapter
>
> - Learn the background and setting of Mark's Gospel.
> - Encounter the structure and style of Mark.
> - Discover the primary themes and highlights of Mark.
> - Review a representative passage as a preview of Mark's style and theology.

The Gospel of Mark was the first Gospel written, and according to tradition it was composed in Rome (contemporary scholars are questioning this, but no consensus has arisen) in the early to mid A.D. 60s, with Peter as its primary source. In this chapter, you'll encounter the background, structure, and main themes of Mark, and suggestions for experiencing its power. Since its inception, Mark has always been an excellent foundation for the other Gospels.

WHO WAS MARK?

The evangelist is traditionally identified as the John Mark of Acts 12:12, 25, cousin of Barnabas (cf. Col 4:10), and the Mark (described as Peter's son) of 1 Pet 5:13. His missionary presence was a point of contention between Paul and Barnabas in Acts 15, resulting in an unfortunate rift that would foreshadow subsequent Church divisions.

THE SETTING OF MARK'S GOSPEL

As evidenced by his explanation of Jewish terms, Mark's audience was largely Gentile. Converts from polytheism had to get accustomed to Mark's central message, the role of the cross in the life of Jesus and the Christian, while Jewish converts struggled with the transition from Judaism and potential rejection by their friends and families (cf. Mk 10:29; Lk 14:26-27).

THE GOSPEL OF THE CROSS

The Gospel of Mark was the first exposure of novice Christians and potential converts to an organized presentation of the Christian message. Mark's Gospel portrayed a God who could not be manipulated like the polytheistic deities, and whose son and messiah (anointed one, chief representative) underwent the severest of Roman punishments, the cross.

The Gospel's turning point is Peter's confession of Jesus as messiah, which is immediately followed by his attempt to sway Jesus from the cross (cf. Mk 8:27-38). From that point on, the Jewish religious leaders' resistance to Jesus crystallizes, and the cross looms on the horizon.

BEGINNING WITH THE BAPTIST

Unlike Matthew and Luke, Mark does not describe the birth of Jesus. True to his stark style, Mark begins with the jarring figure and preaching of John the Baptist, who like Jesus experienced a violent death.

John the Baptist symbolizes the transition from the Old Testament: his parents struggle with infertility, a frequent Old Testament theme (cf. Gen 15-30; 1 Sam 1), and his fiery manner and message of repentance is reminiscent of the prophets, particularly Elijah, whom the Jewish people expected to return as a forerunner to the Messiah. Jesus identified John as the fulfillment of this expectation (cf. Mt 11:14; Mk 9:13).

— THE BIBLE SAYS WHAT? —

In Mark more than in Matthew and Luke, Jesus often (sometimes sternly) counsels those he heals not to tell anyone. This is particularly noticeable in the first eight chapters of Mark, culminating in Peter's confession of Jesus' messiahship in Mk 8:27-30. Jesus' discreet approach is referred to as the messianic secret.

Jesus did not want to become associated with the political notions of messiah rampant in first-century Palestine. John reports that the people wanted to carry Jesus off and make him king (cf. Jn 6:15). Jesus revealed himself gradually, according to his disciples' capacity for understanding him and the role of suffering in his and his followers' mission. He wanted his teachings and ministry rather than the peoples' narrow expectations and hopes to define his mission.

THE STRUCTURE AND STYLE OF MARK

Until the middle of the twentieth century, Mark's coarse Greek, relative lack of Jesus' teachings, and seemingly simple structure and theology caused it to be considered the least sophisticated of the Gospels, and correspondingly it was infrequently featured in the lectionary.

Nowadays, biblical scholars and the magisterium are more aware of Mark's subtleties, powerful message, and distinct theology, and it receives equal billing in the lectionary.

Mark presents Jesus on the move; observe how often the adverb "immediately" is used in reference to Jesus. Mark is a master storyteller; his narration of Jesus' parables and miracles is the most detailed of the Gospels. In line with its emphasis on the cross, Mark's Gospel has been described as a passion narrative with a long introduction. It was a discipleship manual for the early Church, and remains so.

HIGHLIGHTS OF MARK

Mark is short and straightforward enough to be read in one or two extended sittings. Following are key events and sections in Mark:

- The ministry of John the Baptist (1:2-8).
- Jesus' baptism in water and by fire (the temptation in the desert) (1:9-13).
- Jesus' ministry in Capernaum (1:14-3:6).
- Jesus' expands his itinerant ministry (3:7-6:6a).
- Jesus teaches his disciples (6:6b-8:30).
- Jesus issues three predictions of his suffering and death, engages in personal encounters, and performs miracles (8:31-10:52).
- Jesus in Jerusalem (11:1-12:44).
- Jesus' discussion of the end-times (13:1-37).
- The passion and resurrection narrative (14:1-16:20).

SAMPLING MARK: THE COMMUNAL HEALING OF THE PARALYZED MAN

As is usually the case, Mark's narration of Jesus' healing of a paralyzed man (cf. Mk 2:1-12) is more detailed than Matthew's and Luke's (cf. Mt 9:2-8; Lk 5:17-26). Mark alone relates that the crowd overflowed to the door and that four persons carried in the paralyzed man.

The healing of the paralyzed man illuminates the therapeutic and reconciliatory power of communal faith (cf. Col 1:24). It is the only time in the Gospels where the faith of others is directly responsible not just for someone else's healing, but the forgiveness of that person's sins.

On this note of community solidarity, let us now proceed to the Gospel of Matthew, whose vision and structure of the Church has played a major role in its development.

Chapter Eleven

——— How to Read Matthew, ——— the Gospel of the Church

> ## Contents of this Chapter
>
> - Learn the background and setting of the Gospel of Matthew.
> - Recognize the significant influence Matthew has had on Church doctrine and practice.
> - Encounter the structure, style, and theology of Matthew.
> - Explore the message of Matthew's account of Jesus' birth.
> - Observe Matthew's frequent and formulaic use of the Old Testament.
> - Understand the purpose and literal meaning of the Beatitudes.
> - Discover the primary themes and highlights of Matthew.

Matthew is known as the "teaching Gospel" because of its organized presentation of Jesus' words and deeds, and as the "ecclesiastical Gospel" because of its discussion of Church order and discipline (cf. Mt 18). Of all the New Testament books, it has had the most influence on Church teaching and practices. Matthew's (rather than Luke's) versions of the Sermon on the Mount, the Beatitudes, and the Lord's Prayer are the ones most often accessed by the Church and individual Christians.

WHO WAS MATTHEW?

Christian tradition attributes the First Gospel to Matthew the apostle and former tax collector. (The name of the author of each Gospel was inserted as a heading into the manuscripts long after their composition). Matthew the apostle could be the source of the Gospel, but its probable date of composition (in the A.D. 80s) makes it unlikely that he was directly responsible for its final form.

As in the Old Testament, a New Testament book or letter could be attributed to a credible source whose teachings and/or reputation it reflected or was compatible with. The Hebrew and ancient Near Eastern cultures were not as literal-minded as we are. For Catholics and most Christian denominations, belief that the attributed author wrote the work is not necessary for acceptance of the work as inspired.

The Gospel of Matthew reflects the work of a scribe steeped in the Old Testament. His Greek is better than Mark's, but less stylish than Luke's.

MATTHEW'S AUDIENCE

Many scholars think that Matthew was written in Antioch (Syria), where the term "Christian" was first used (cf. Acts 11:26). Composed of a mixture of Jewish and Gentile Christians, the community at Antioch struggled with the relationship of the Jewish law to the teachings of Jesus (cf. Gal 2:11-14). Matthew addresses this by presenting Jesus as the new Moses and the fulfillment of the law. Also, Antioch was a wealthy community, and the monetary denominations used in Matthew are higher than in Mark and Luke. Only Matthew among the evangelists uses the highest monetary denomination, "talents" (cf. Mt 18:23-35; 25:14-30; Lk 19:11-27).

MATTHEW'S STYLE AND THEOLOGY

Matthew uses his words purposefully and sparingly. He condenses stories he borrows from Mark and is generally more concise than Luke. One of the most prominent Catholic biblical scholars, Father John Meier, who has published several works on Matthew, refers to him as a "verbal architect."

Using formulaic expressions such as "this was to fulfill," Matthew quotes the Old Testament more often than the other New Testament books do. Scholars refer to these as "fulfillment quotations." Matthew highlights Jesus' presence among us (cf. Mt 1:23, 18:20; 25:31-46; 28:20) and emphasizes practical expressions of love of neighbor.

WHAT DOES IT MEAN?

Matthew's and Luke's recounting of the events surrounding Jesus' birth are known as infancy narratives.

MATTHEW'S STRUCTURE

Matthew is the most structured Gospel. It is composed of five books (like the Pentateuch) linked by transitional phrases between sections (i.e., "when Jesus finished. . .", cf. Mt 7:28; 11:1; 13:53; 19:1; 26:1) and sandwiched between an infancy and passion and resurrection narrative:

- Prologue: Genealogy and infancy narrative (1:1-2:23).
- Book One: The proclamation of God's kingdom (3:1-7:29).
- Book Two: Jesus' ministry in Galilee (8:1-11:1).
- Book Three: Disputes and parables (11:2-13:52).
- Book Four: Formation (spiritual development) of the disciples and the Church (13:53-18:35).
- Book Five: The Judean ministry and the parables of the end-times (19:1-25:46).
- The passion and resurrection narrative (26:1-28:20).

MATTHEW'S BEGINNING

Matthew begins with a genealogy that extends back to David. The generations are grouped in three segments of fourteen (the numerical value of David's name in Hebrew).

Universal-minded Luke traces Jesus' lineage forward from Adam. Besides reflecting the evangelists' respective Jewish and Gentile orientations, this difference shows that while we have our ethnic and nuclear family roots, we are also part of one human family. When we lose sight of either, we lose an important part of our identity.

Genealogies were important to Jews for economic, legal, and personal identity/heritage reasons. From a theological perspective, they also reveal how God works out his plan amid all sorts of personalities and situations. Jesus' family tree was imperfect, but that did not impede him from fulfilling his vocation/potential and doing God's will. Accordingly, I should not use my imperfect background to justify my faults and misdeeds.

THE BIBLE SAYS WHAT?

 Readers often wonder about the differences between Matthew's and Luke's infancy narratives, but forget how much they agree on:

- Jesus' birth during the reign of Herod the Great.
- A virgin named Mary is in the first year of the betrothal process to Joseph, a descendant of David.
- An angel announces the birth of Jesus, and discloses his name and vocation.
- Jesus' conception occurs through the Holy Spirit.
- Mary and Joseph do not have sexual relations before the conception of Jesus.
- Jesus is born after the two-year engagement process is complete and Joseph takes Mary into his home.
- Jesus is born in Bethlehem and grows up in Nazareth.

Matthew's infancy narrative is filled with symbols and events that point to both the Old Testament and Jesus' suffering and death. Key events include Joseph's dreams, the visit of the Magi, the flight into Egypt, and Herod's paranoia resulting in the slaughter of the innocent children. The latter recalls Pharaoh's infanticide decree (cf. Ex 1:22), foreshadows the innocent Jesus' death, and exemplifies the innocent suffering that mysteriously occurs within God's providential plan.

The reference works on the infancy and passion and resurrection narratives are Raymond E. Brown, S.S.'s *Birth of the Messiah* (revised edition) and *Death of the Messiah*.

Jesus' public ministry begins with his baptism by John and concludes with his anointing by a woman at Bethany, which Jesus views as preparation for his burial. Because John mentions Jesus going up to Jerusalem for three different Passover feasts, we assume that his ministry lasted three years. Lk 3:23 reports that Jesus was thirty when he began his ministry.

WHAT DOES IT MEAN?

Mt 1:21 introduces Jesus' name through the angel's instructions to Joseph. In Hebrew, Jesus' name is *Yeshua*, which means "Yahweh, help!" and is an abbreviated form of *Yehoshua* (Joshua). Mt 1:21 explains *Yeshua* as meaning "Yahweh saves" because *Yeshua* sounded like the word for salvation, *yeshuah*, and thus the people commonly associated *Yeshua* with the verb for save. The name *Yeshua* became popular among Jews after the Babylonian exile (587-538 B.C.). Even Jesus' name and the popular misunderstanding of its meaning reveals his common roots.

READING MATTHEW

Matthew's purposeful structure, concise wording, and intense moral teachings influence prudent readers to slow down and savor each passage. Because Jesus' sayings (cf. Mt 5-7), parables (cf. Mt

13; 24-25), miracles (cf. Mt 8-9), and thematic teachings (cf. Mt 18) are grouped together, they are ideal for both private reading and instruction in the faith.

Keep in mind Matthew's concern with linking the Gospel to the Old Testament and his rabbinical promotion of morality through images and ideals (the Sermon on the Mount), examples (the Gospel characters whom Jesus praises, but particularly Jesus himself), and participative stories (Matthew's concise, pointed parables).

THE SERMON ON THE MOUNT

Matthew presents his primary collection of Jesus' sayings in what has become known as the Sermon on the Mount (cf. Mt 5-7). In Matthew, Jesus is portrayed as teaching on a mountain, evoking images of Moses at Mt. Sinai, while Luke presents Jesus giving his discourse on a plain, which would be more familiar to a Gentile audience.

Jesus uses hyperbole (exaggerated expressions not to be taken literally) such as cutting off one's hand or plucking out one's eye (cf. Mt 5:29-30; 18:8-9) to describe the serious consequences of sin. He wants you to pay attention. Obviously no one can impeccably sustain idealistic morality, but Jesus and Matthew want you to try, and when you or your neighbor fall, seek or render forgiveness, a major theme in Matthew's Gospel (cf. Mt 6:14-15; 18:21-35).

This blending of idealism and realism is one reason Matthew is the Gospel of human potential, the premier Christian document on the development of the whole person: moral, spiritual, social, familial, and psychological: "You, therefore, must be perfect, as your heavenly Father is perfect" (Mt 5:48). Jesus' and Matthew's introduction to Christian potential fulfillment is the Beatitudes, where paradoxically we meet conditions contrary to our normal perceptions of human fulfillment.

THE BEATITUDES

The Beatitudes (cf. Mt 5:3-12) are the heart of the Sermon on the Mount and of Christian spirituality. Their original context and literal connotations reveal how radically they are meant to transform our attitudes and actions.

A beatitude is a form of congratulations issued in response to a condition or achievement. "The Beatitudes" as popularly known are found in Mt 5 and Lk 6, but there are also beatitudes in the rest of the New Testament, the Old Testament (cf. Ps 1:1; 32:1-2; 144:15), and in Egyptian and Greek literature.

A beatitude assumes a right relationship with God, and thus implies happiness or blessedness from a spiritual rather than secular perspective. How else could being poor, heartbroken, or persecuted be cause for congratulations? A more precise and expressive translation than "blessed" would be "Oh, the happiness of the person who. . ."

— WHAT DOES IT MEAN? —

Scholars often refer to beatitudes as macarisms, from the Greek word *makarioi* (blessed/happy) that begins the beatitudes. The Latin translation, *beatus*, is the source of the expression "beatitude."

Distinguishing Beatitudes and Blessings

"Blessed" is an ambiguous translation for a beatitude because it does not precisely communicate congratulations. Further, "blessed" may imply that the speaker is calling down a blessing on the person, whereas in a beatitude the speaker is only describing and applauding their situation. There are different words in Hebrew, Greek, and Latin (i.e., *benedictus*) to designate a cultic or personal blessing.

Types and Time Frames of Beatitudes

The most ancient form of beatitude in the Old Testament appears in the wisdom books. It relates to this world, as in Sir 26:1: the husband of a good wife is called happy (cf. Prov 31:28). Wisdom beatitudes refer to a happy condition that the congratulated person has already achieved. For example, Psalm 1 congratulates the person who avoids evil company and behaviors and meditates on God's word day and night.

When beatitudes are used by the prophets (cf. Is 30:18; 56:2), they generally refer to future happiness in this world. When the prophets preached, Judaism did not have a clearly defined notion of an afterlife other than the shadowy netherworld called Sheol. Beatitudes in the New Testament and in the later books in the Old Testament (cf. Dan 12:12) typically refer to the next world as the context for their realization.

The Beatitudes summarize the spirituality of Jesus and the New Testament. They are the maturation of Old Testament spirituality, particularly that of the prophets. The Beatitudes capture life's and the New Testament's tension between the pain of the present and the joy of the future (cf. Rom 8:12-39; 1 Cor 15).

Matthew's Most Important Beatitude

Matthew's last Beatitude, Mt 5:11-12, expands upon Mt 5:10, and is the only one written in the second person (underscoring its personal relevance). Its acknowledgement of the rejection and persecution of God's servants links the Old and New Testament and life.

SAVING THE BEST FOR LAST

Wise teacher Matthew often saves the best for last. He ends his sections with important, summarizing points: for example, the command to practice God's will that ends the Sermon on the Mount (cf. Mt 7:21); the wise person who integrates the Old Testament and Jesus' teachings (cf. Mt 13:51); the Last Judgment criteria of compassionate deeds that ends the parables of preparation (cf. Mt 25); and the commission to bring Jesus and his teachings to the world (cf. Mt 28:18-20).

WRESTLING WITH THE WORD

When you encounter a beatitude in the Bible, consider whether you fit its criteria. If not, how might you better conform by changing your lifestyle, actions, and attitudes?

Which of Matthew's or Luke's Beatitudes (cf. Lk 6:20-23) touch you the most?

What are the beatitudes of secular society?

The Lord's Prayer

The Lord's Prayer is found in Mt 6:9-13 and Lk 11:1-4. Matthew's vocabulary differs from Luke's, and he adds the petitions "Your will be done, on earth as it is in heaven" and "But deliver us from evil." The first half of the Lord's Prayer petitions for the coming of God's kingdom, and the last half requests sustenance for believers. The Lord's Prayer communal mentality is underscored by its articulation in the plural.

The Protestant version of the Lord's Prayer includes an ending missing from most ancient manuscripts and often presented in biblical footnotes (cf. Mt 6:13): "For yours is the kingdom, and the power, and the glory, for ever. Amen." Resembling 1 Chron 29:11-12, this doxology was likely prayed during public worship, and is now recited following the Lord's Prayer during Mass.

MATTHEW'S DEFINING THEME AND PASSAGE

The distinctive theme in Matthew from beginning (cf. Mt 1:23) to end (cf. Mt 28:20) is God's presence with us in the person of Jesus. The last parable in Matthew (cf. Mt 25:31-46), known either as the parable of the sheep and the goats, or the Last Judgment, is placed right before the passion narrative for emphasis. It sums up Matthew's perspective on spirituality and salvation: The person who ministers to the person in need/pain is the one who loves Jesus and who will be welcomed by him in the next life.

Each person and act is literally a matter of life and death. At issue is our suitability for the kingdom, which hinges on our response to the king. As he does throughout the Gospels, in the footsteps of God in the Old Testament who demanded protection of the defenseless (cf. Ex 22:20-26; Ezek 22:7; Zech 7:10; Mal 3:5), Jesus identifies with each vulnerable person and therefore makes each human interaction a divine encounter as well (cf. Mt 25:40, 45). We either give life or foster death, born to others and ourselves. These daily choices actualize the morality of the Sermon on the Mount (cf. Mt 7:21).

As affirmed in two other books with a strong Hebrew flavor, the letter of James and the letter to the Hebrews, faith must not only be professed, but practiced. As a guide to such, Matthew is unsurpassed.

In the next chapter, we will encounter Luke's Gospel, where compassion receives equal emphasis.

Chapter Twelve

— How to Read the Gospel of the Spirit: — Luke and Acts of the Apostles

The Gospel of Luke and Acts of the Apostles form a two-volume work constituting more than one-fourth of the New Testament. Because of their continuity and common themes, they are often referred to jointly as Luke-Acts, and we will discuss them together. Both have been referred to as the Gospel of the Holy Spirit. Only John among the evangelists emphasizes the Holy Spirit as much as Luke.

WHO WAS LUKE?

Catholic tradition has consistently named Luke, the beloved physician and companion of Paul mentioned in Col 4:14, as the author of Luke-Acts. Since Luke was neither an apostle nor an eyewitness of Jesus' ministry, there would be little reason to attribute the Gospel to him were he not associated with it. As a physician, it is plausible that he would possess the education necessary to write the stylish literary Greek of this Gospel. His care-giving efforts could also shed light on the compassionate perspective that pervades the Gospel.

Some modern scholars dispute this traditional attribution. The best commentary on Luke, Father Joseph Fitzmyer, S.J.'s two-volume set in the Anchor Bible series, contains a balanced review of the evidence and concludes that the disputations are not overly convincing.

LUKE'S COMPOSITION DATE AND AUDIENCE

Luke's Gospel was written to predominantly Gentile churches affected by Paul's missions sometime between the late A.D. 70s and early 90s, approximately concurrent with Matthew. In sensitivity to his Gentile audience, Luke's usage of the Old Testament is less formulaic and explicit than Matthew's, and less controversial (with respect to Judaism) and symbolic than John's.

LUKE'S AGENDA

Luke is the evangelist most concerned with social justice and the dignity and spirituality of the poor. The wealthy coexisted insensitively and uncharitably alongside the poor in Luke's community, thus prompting numerous warnings about greed (cf. Lk 6:24; 11:39; 12:15). Only Luke has the parable known as The Rich Man and Lazarus (cf. Lk 16:19-31).

Jesus' birth in a manger among the poorly regarded and often corrupt shepherds links him with society's outcasts. Jesus begins (cf. Lk 4:18-19) and focuses his ministry on vulnerable persons, the spiritual descendants of the *anawim*, the poor of Yahweh in the Old Testament who await deliverance (cf. Zeph 2:3; 3:12-13; Is 51:12-15; 61:1-11).

LUKE'S LEGACY

More stories and images have come into popular consciousness from Luke than from the other Gospels: for example, the parables of the Prodigal Son and Good Samaritan, the angels and shepherds announcing the newborn Jesus, and the repentant thief on the cross. The Prodigal Son is probably the most beloved parable, closely followed by the Good Samaritan. The medieval poet Dante appreciated Luke's compassionate craftsmanship and called it the Gospel of God's loving kindness.

LUKE'S FEMININE TOUCH

A sensitive, nurturing, and reconciliatory tone pervades Luke's Gospel. He portrays the negative side of the apostles less than the other evangelists do, particularly compared to Mark, who does not hesitate to point out their (and particularly Peter's) shortcomings. Would Peter (presumably Mark's source) want it any other way? Luke presents the positive side of social outcasts such as the sinful woman in Lk 7:36-50, Zacchaeus in Lk 19:1-10, and the repentant thief in Lk 23:39-43. Even the enemies of Jesus, Pilate and Herod, are reconciled, a detail related only in Lk 23:12.

Women are more prominent in Luke's Gospel than in the other Gospels, though kindred spirit John spotlights the anonymous Samaritan woman at the well (cf. Jn 4), Jesus' mother, Mary and Martha of Bethany, and Mary Magdalene. Luke portrays women attending to Jesus' needs during his ministry and accompanying him along the way of the Cross. He presents Mary saying yes to God's word and contemplating it in her heart (cf. Lk 1:38; 2:19, 51). Jesus' loving gaze at the sinful woman while teaching Simon, the self-righteous Pharisee, about hospitality and love, is one of the most moving images in the Gospels (cf. Lk 7:44).

LUKE'S STRUCTURE

The turning point of Luke's Gospel is Jesus' journey to Jerusalem, which begins at Lk 9:51. Jerusalem, the holy city of the

Old Testament, plays a prominent role in both Luke and Acts of the Apostles.

Luke's Gospel is built around Jesus' ministry, while Mark centers on his passion, Matthew on his teachings, and John on his identity as manifested through dialogues, disputations, self-designations, discourses, and signs.

Among the evangelists, only Luke and John explain their purpose in writing (cf. Lk 1:1-4; Jn 20:30-31). Matthew and Mark implicitly reveal theirs: By ending with the great commission of Jesus (cf. Mt 28:20), Matthew reveals his evangelical and catechetical intentions, and Mark inaugurates the Gospel as a literary genre by beginning with his announcement of the good news of Jesus Christ (cf. Mk 1.1). Luke acknowledges the existence of other accounts of Jesus' life, and sets out to offer an orderly and truthful account. His Gospel is organized as follows:

- Prologue and stories of Jesus' birth and youth (1:1-2:52).
- Preparation for Jesus' public ministry (3:1-4:13).
- Jesus' ministry in Galilee (Galileans were regarded by Judeans as deficient culturally and religiously [cf. Jn 1:46]; their lowliness fits Luke's portrayal of Jesus reaching out to the poor and lowly regarded) (4:14-9:50).
- Material unique to Luke that chronicles Jesus' journey to Jerusalem (9:51-18:14).
- Material from Mark edited to fit Luke's theology and pastoral objectives (18:15-19:28).
- Jesus' ministry in Jerusalem (19:29-21:38).
- The passion and resurrection narrative (22:1-24:53).

LUKE'S THEMES

Luke's main themes are prayer, renunciation (detachment from worldly possessions), reconciliation, forgiveness, compassion, healing, and the universality of salvation.

In all the Gospels, but particularly in Luke, sinners engage Jesus in a close encounter at the most critical moments of their lives. The only believer to address Jesus as "Jesus" in the Gospel of Luke is the repentant thief on the cross (cf. Lk 23:43). This reveals the personal nature of their encounter in a most unlikely setting. The disciples and those who seek healing from Jesus address him as "Lord," Luke's favorite term for Jesus, and an Old Testament name for God. This underscores Jesus' divinity.

Luke and John emphasize Jesus' role as savior, while Mark and Matthew don't identify him as savior other than the latter explaining his name (cf. Mt 1:21). They implicitly acknowledge Jesus as savior, while emphasizing his other roles and titles (e.g., suffering servant, son of man, messiah, son of David, son of God).

Most Bible readers assume that Jesus is explicitly recognized as savior by all the Gospels. This is an example of how we unconsciously harmonize the Gospels at the expense of their individuality. The more you read the Bible, the more you will discover how many assumptions surrounding it are inaccurate or imprecise. One of the keys to interpreting the Bible properly from a Catholic perspective is to recognize each book's unique message in the context of the Bible's overall message. This integrated approach keeps us from arriving at extreme interpretations.

LUKE'S PREPARATION FOR JESUS

Luke sets the stage for Jesus by creating a parallel between the birth and mission of Jesus and that of John the Baptist. An angel announces the birth of a son to both Zechariah and Mary. Luke revives the Old Testament theme (cf. Gen 15-30; 1 Sam 1) of a previously infertile woman (Elizabeth) giving birth to someone who will play a pivotal role in God's plan, in this case, John the Baptist.

LUKE'S ACCOUNT OF PETER'S DENIALS

Among the most dramatic and revealing events in the Gospels is Peter's denials of Jesus (cf. Lk 22:31-34; 54-62). The memory of Peter's denials was so compelling for the early Church that all four Gospels narrate the event in detail, including Jesus' prediction of Peter's denials. If the Gospels were propaganda, they would hardly highlight and detail the lowest moment of the first leader of the Church.

Luke's portrayal differs in detail and tone from the other Gospels. Luke presents Peter's plight more sympathetically than the other Gospels. With great psychological insight, he perceptively narrates Peter's descent into confusion, doubt, and fear.

Luke depicts Peter's denials as the culmination of a series of events beginning at the Last Supper: the betrayal of Jesus, the agony in the garden, the abandoning of Jesus by the rest of the apostles, and the hostile environment into which an isolated and beleaguered Peter was thrust. Unlike Mark and Matthew, Luke and John do not report Peter's cursing and swearing, the latter specifically prohibited by Jesus (cf. Mt 5:33-36).

Other than the beloved disciple, Peter was the only disciple to follow Jesus after his arrest, albeit at a distance (cf. Lk 22:54), which in the Gospels means wavering discipleship. Though the other Apostles joined Peter in pledging to stand by Jesus (cf. Mk 14:31), only Peter had the courage to put himself in a position where his faith would be tested.

THE LOOK OF LOVE

A poignant look at a pivotal moment can communicate volumes. Only Luke mentions two penetrating stares, one by a servant girl and the other by Jesus. Different Greek words are used to distinguish the stares. The word used to describe Jesus' gaze at Peter literally means "look into." The New Jerusalem Bible translation reveals this nuance by stating that the Lord "looked straight at Peter" (Lk 22:61).

In contrast with the servant girl's look of accusation and condemnation, Jesus' look communicates compassion and concern. Jesus goes beyond the surface and looks into Peter's heart. Though separated by physical and spiritual distance, they share a profound moment of painful intimacy. Jesus' look pierces Peter's soul and reminds him of their earlier conversation. In the other Gospels, it is the cock crow that evokes Peter's recollection. As usual, Luke opts for a personal, relational touch.

PETER'S PASSION: A PARADIGM OF STRESS

As a physician, Luke knew fear, stress, and suffering firsthand. He deftly portrays Peter's rapid descent into crisis: Peter first denies his association with Jesus, then with the disciples, then his identity as a Galilean.

Isn't this the experience of a stressed person? Their religious identity and affiliations plunge into ambiguity and confusion. They feel isolated from God and loved ones. If pressures exacerbate, they potentially lose touch with themselves. Luke's dramatization of this progression constitutes a concise yet profound model of the spiritual, social, and psychological effects of stress.

Stress causes even persons who love one another to act in uncharacteristic ways. Even the leader of Jesus' followers can fall

---

WRESTLING WITH THE WORD

Only Luke reports that an hour passed between Peter's second and third denials (cf. Lk 22:59). What do you think went through Peter's mind? Recall how you felt when faced with a crisis or hour of (in)decision? What might have been going through Jesus' mind as he fixed his gaze on Peter, and by application, on you during your time of trial?

Transpose Jesus' compassionate, piercing/revealing, presence to a conflict you are having with a loved one. Imagine Jesus gazing at you and your loved one(s) during your crisis. What does his gaze communicate, and how does it make you feel? What kind of gaze do you give your loved one when they let you down, or vice-versa?

---

in the worst way: ". . . but he who denies me before men will be denied before the angels of God" (Lk 12:9). We should remember "Peter's passion" whenever we or our loved ones fall, and recall the Lord's admonition to strengthen one another (cf. Lk 22:32) in response.

Jesus demonstrates the ideal response to human weakness: a compassionate look (cf. Lk 22:61), affirming words (cf. Jn 21:15-19), and recollection and actualization of God's word (cf. Lk 22:61). Jesus models the compassionate framework for responding to life and God's word that characterizes Catholicism, and hopefully, this book and our lives.

ACTS: THE GOSPEL OF THE HOLY SPIRIT

Acts of the Apostles picks up where the Gospel of Luke leaves off. It highlights the apostles' and their peers' (e.g., Stephen) proclamation of the good news about Jesus in the context of significant events in the life of the growing Church. Faith in Jesus was handed down through the apostles, thus the book's title.

ACTS' STRUCTURE

Consider reading Acts straight through to get a sense of its unfolding events:

- The Ascension of Jesus (1:9-12).
- The selection of a replacement for Judas (1:13-26).
- The outpouring of the Holy Spirit and Peter's discourse (2:1-47).
- The first encounter of the Spirit-filled apostles with the Jewish authorities (4:1-22).
- The idealized portrait of Christian community and charity/sharing (4:32-5:16).
- Delegation of authority and duties in the community (6:1-7).

- The ministry and martyrdom of Stephen, and introduction to Paul (6:8-7:60).
- Stephen's last words (Acts 7:59-60) echo Jesus' (Lk 23:34, 46).
- Philip's evangelical and catechetical encounter with the Ethiopian eunuch (8:26-40).
- The call, Christian formation, and gradual assimilation (into the Christian community) of Paul (9:1-30).
- The conversion of Cornelius and the mission to the Gentiles (10:1-11:18).
- Barnabas's and Paul's mission to Antioch (11:19-30).
- James's death, Peter's imprisonment and escape, and Herod's death (12:1-23).
- Paul's first missionary journey (13:1-14:28).
- The applicability of circumcision (the Mosaic law) to Gentiles (15:1-34). *Judaizers* was the term used to refer to Jewish Christians who insisted on retaining observance of the Mosaic law, including for Gentile converts to Christianity.
- The break-up and separate missions of Paul and Barnabas (15:35-39).
- Paul's second missionary journey (15:40-18:22).
- Paul's third missionary journey (18:23-21:14).
- Paul's perilous return and imprisonment in Jerusalem (21:15-26:32).
- Paul's shipwreck in Malta and subsequent arrival and ministry in Rome (27:1-28:31).

SIMILARITIES BETWEEN LUKE AND ACTS OF THE APOSTLES

- Luke begins with preparations for Jesus, Acts with preparations for the Holy Spirit.
- Both books periodically recall Old Testament themes, but not as methodically as Matthew or as mystically as John.

- History's turning point is reached in Jesus' death and resurrection, which is described in Luke's Gospel and proclaimed in Acts. The ascension serves as a literary and spiritual transition between the two books.
- Just as Luke ends with the final days of Jesus' ministry, Acts concludes with the final days of Paul's ministry (neither his nor Peter's death is mentioned), thus forming a literary transition to Paul's letters, which follow in the Bible.

Acts' central theme is the dynamic presence of the Spirit guiding and consoling the Church. It is theological history, rather than a strictly literal recounting of events. Although Luke is an artful and conscientious historian, he is more concerned with theological and pastoral (community) issues.

The broad horizon of Jesus' and the Holy Spirit's actions in Luke-Acts sandwiches in the Bible the cosmic and focused/micro world of John, where single events and themes unfold in chapters, and Jesus' identity, signs, and teachings are explored in unparalleled depth.

Luke-Acts can be read in several sittings. John's profound symbolism and double meanings require more time and attention, as we will see in the next chapter.

Chapter Thirteen

How to Read the Contemplative Gospel and Letters of John

The Gospel of John is the most studied Gospel, the favorite of many experienced readers of Scripture. As with a new lover, it instantly attracts, makes for a pleasant courtship, flirts and confuses, then moves to a period of adjustment whereby the novelty of its striking statements and images wears off and its complexity and mysteriousness comes to the fore. If the reader perseveres, the relationship matures and a deeper appreciation is fostered.

John is the most profound and elusive Gospel. You can experience the richness of its poignant sayings and images by following the guidelines suggested in this chapter.

WHO IS JOHN? WHO KNOWS?

At the Last Supper, the Gospel of John introduces us to an unnamed follower of Jesus referred to as the beloved disciple. He is the source, if not the actual author, of the Gospel of John (cf. Jn 21:24).

Catholic tradition associates the beloved disciple with the Apostle John largely because, although prominent in the other Gospels, neither John nor his brother, James, are named in John (there is a reference to "the sons of Zebedee" in Jn 21:2), and the beloved disciple is not mentioned in the other Gospels.

Scholars debate whether the Apostle John wrote the Gospel and is the beloved disciple — for a detailed discussion, see the late Father Raymond E. Brown's commentary on John in the Anchor Bible series. However, these authorship issues have no bearing on the book's inspired status, as the books were included in the canon of the Bible not primarily because of perceived authorship, but because they reflected the faith of the Church.

When I refer to John in this chapter, I mean the evangelist, who is presumably the beloved disciple, who may or may not be the apostle.

JOHN'S EYEWITNESS ACCURACY

In the early 20th century, scholars considered John the least historical of the Gospels, but recent archaeological evidence has confirmed many of John's geographical details. As befitting an eyewitness (cf. Jn 21:24) who twice remarks that Jesus did many things not recorded in the Gospels (cf. Jn 20:30; 21:25), John is frequently more specific than the other Gospels. For example, only John reveals the name of the high priest's slave (Malchus) whose ear Peter cut off when Jesus was arrested, and that Malchus's relative prompted one of Peter's denials (cf. Jn 18:10, 26).

WHEN AND WHERE WAS JOHN WRITTEN?

Most scholars date John between A.D. 90 and 110, thus making it the last Gospel to be written. Ephesus (in modern day Turkey) or its surrounding area has been proposed as its place of composition, with Syria also a possibility.

The sources underlying John's Gospel are clearly different from the other Gospels'. It is likely that a school or community of disciples preserved the teachings and recollections of Jesus shared by the beloved disciple.

The standard popular resource on John's community is Raymond E. Brown's *The Community of the Beloved Disciple*. A complementary title by the same author is *Churches the Apostles Left Behind*.

JOHN'S STRUCTURE AND STYLE

John's structure is quite simple. It begins with a prologue (1:1-18) that previews the main themes of the Gospel. It continues with what is traditionally known as the *Book of Signs* (1:19-12:50). John substitutes the term "signs" for miracles. Then comes the *Book of Glory* (13:1-20:31), John's passion and resurrection narrative. John presents Jesus' suffering and death as his glorification and spiritual coronation, and omits many of the details of Jesus' physical and emotional suffering that are presented in the Synoptic Gospels. An appendix composed later contains a resurrection appearance in Galilee.

John's Gospel is heavily theological and mystical, and his writing style is repetitive (even more so in the original Greek).

Rather than cover the broad range of events reported in the other Gospels, which presumably he was familiar with, he describes at length crucial events, encounters, disputations, and discourses of Jesus.

John emphasizes the divinity of Jesus more than the other Gospels, partly in response to first-century "false teachers and heresies" (deviations from orthodox faith) that denied the divinity of Jesus.

As you will see in the next chapter, John often uses irony and misunderstanding as an entrée to communicate key teachings.

JOHN'S VOCABULARY AND THEMES

Though it may be wearying to modern ears at times, John is a master at using repetition to emphasize different aspects of a theme. In an oral culture, such repetition assists the audience in remembering the story. He uses familiar images such as vine, shepherd, gate, and light. This makes Jesus' sayings easier to relate

---

WHAT DOES IT MEAN?

 John often uses the expression "the Jews" to refer to the religious leaders or to the people as a whole. This is a pastoral and theological polemic rather than an anti-Semitic vendetta, as the apostles and Jesus were Jewish. It reflects the tensions experienced with the Jewish community both at the time of Jesus and of the early Church. Excommunication of Christians from synagogue worship in the late first century created a crisis for many Christians (cf. Jn 9:22; 12:42-43).

The expression "the world" is used by John positively in regards to creation, which God loves (cf. Jn 3:16-17), and negatively with respect to persons and beings (Satan, the prince of this world) opposed to Jesus (cf. Jn 7:7; 15:18). Worldly people live according to the flesh rather than the spirit (cf. Jn 6:63-71; Rom 8:1-11).

---

to, particularly for Jews, whose religion and language was concrete and practical.

The noun for faith is not found in the Fourth Gospel. The verb to believe or trust is used instead. For John, faith is dynamic, expressing itself through love.

SAVORING THE GOSPEL OF JOHN

John is the Gospel most responsive to slow, contemplative reading. It is like a drink made from choice fruits. I am personally stimulated and refreshed each time I taste it, with something different striking me each time. Its initial effect is strong and memorable, and requires getting used to, but with repeated exposure it becomes smooth and satisfying, without losing its effervescence.

JOHN'S PROLOGUE

Jn 1:1-18 is one of the most beautiful and revealing passages in the Bible. It has been described as a symphony in which the essential themes/notes of the Gospel are sounded in harmonious fashion, reaching a crescendo in Jn 1:16-18. However, it is so intense and theological that it does not immediately yield practical applications. Only with repeated exposure and reflection does its fullness sink in and reveal itself. Its main themes are:

- Jesus is the word, the ultimate communication and wisdom of God, the source and the meaning of life.
- 1:1-4: Creation occurred through Jesus. This teaching is not explicitly present in the other Gospels, where the humanity and Sonship of Christ is the main focus, though it does appear in Paul's letters (e.g., Eph 1; Col 1).
- 1:5: Jesus could not be comprehended or conquered by the forces of evil.
- 1:6-9, 15: John the Baptist is not the messiah (as some in the first century thought), but only a witness.

- 1:10-11: Jesus was rejected not only by the secular world but by his own, including relatives and townspeople (cf. Mk 6:1-6) and one of his apostles. Such will be the lot of Jesus' followers as well (cf. Jn 15:20). John discusses Judas more extensively and negatively than the other Gospels, perhaps due to the beloved disciple's great hurt over the treachery perpetrated on his dear friend Jesus.

  Matthew is similarly hard on the religious leaders (cf. Mt 23), whom he views as betraying Jesus and the Jewish people (a frequent theme in the Old Testament). His knowledge of the Old Testament indicates he may have been a scribe or at least dwelt in those circles, and thus he would have naturally expected more out of his peers. Only Matthew mentions Judas' regret over his actions and the religious leaders' callousness that precipitated his suicide (cf. Mt 27:3-10).
- 1:12-13: Jesus empowers believers to become children of God (cf. Jn 20:17).
- 1:14-16: Jesus manifests the covenantal kindness (*hesed*) and fidelity (*'emet*) of God, his primary characteristics in the Old Testament. In the New Testament, these qualities are translated as grace and truth, and their meaning is similar.
- 1:17-18: The law of Moses is consummated and superseded by Jesus, the "human face of God," who reveals the Father.

SHARED VOCABULARY AND THEMES WITH 1 JOHN

With its brief prologue, interwoven themes and images (light, darkness, truth, sin, repentance, life, water, peace, the Spirit, abiding in Jesus, love, service, fellowship, and the animosity of the world), and poetic and contemplative style, 1 John (the first letter of John) is mostly a pastoral application of the Fourth Gospel.

In John's Gospel, the enemies are misguided religious and political leaders who disregard the truth (cf. Jn 8:31-48; 18:37-38). In the letters of John, the enemies are false prophets (cf. 1 Jn 4:1) who are identified as antichrists in 1 Jn 2:18, 22; 4:3; and 2 Jn 7. Like the false prophets of the Old Testament, they distort God's word and mislead and dishearten the people, leading to scandal, division, and false hopes (which, as St. Augustine points out, do serious harm to the soul).

John's Emphasis of Fraternal Love

The Gospel and first two letters of John emphasize love of fellow believers because Jesus wants love to be the mark of his disciples (cf. Jn 13:34-35); otherwise their witness will lack credibility. John focuses on Jesus' great love for his followers (cf. Jn 13-17) and their vocation to share that love.

In John, Jesus also models love of enemies: he demonstrates how to turn the other cheek with dignity (cf. Jn 18:22-23). The commandment to love your enemies occurs in Mt 5:44-48, Lk 6:27-36; 23:34 and Rom 12:17-21. Only John, Paul (cf. Rom 12:10; 13:8; 1 Thess 4:9), and the author of 1 Peter (cf. 1 Pet 1:22) use the expression "love one another."

SAINTS AND SAGES ON THE BIBLE

"In his old age at Ephesus, Blessed John the Evangelist could barely be supported in church on the arms of his disciples nor could he say more than a few words when he got there. At each service he would only repeat: 'My little children, love one another' (cf. 1 Jn 3:18).

"Finally, the disciples and brothers who were present, wearied by such constant repetition, said to him: 'Master, why do you always say the same thing?' The reply was worthy of John: 'Because it is the LORD's command, and if you do only this, it suffices.' " (St. Jerome, *Commentary on the Epistle to the Galatians*).

"We know that we have passed out of death into life, because we love the brethren. He who does not love remains in death" (1 Jn 3:14).

"If any one says, 'I love God,' and hates his brother, he is a liar; for he who does not love his brother whom he has seen, cannot love God whom he has not seen. And this commandment we have from him, that he who loves God should love his brother also" (1 Jn 4:20-21).

READING 1, 2, AND 3 JOHN

The three letters of John are similar enough in style, vocabulary, and theology to have been written by the author of the Fourth Gospel.

1 John is easier to read than the Fourth Gospel. Consider reading 1 John first because it is shorter and more practical. You can read through the letter in one sitting, though some of the phrases and assertions are so poignant and inspiring that you may wish to linger on them.

2 John is a short letter (thirteen verses) that takes up the theme of love and, like 1 John, warns of false teachers who distort Jesus' message. For pastoral reasons, concern over false teachers is a frequent theme of later New Testament letters (e.g., Revelation, Jude, 2 Peter). 3 John is a mostly personal letter (fifteen verses) that affirms the link between faith and good works, and exhorts the community to practice hospitality.

HIGHLIGHTS OF JOHN: ENCOUNTERS WITH JESUS

John uses Jesus' interpersonal encounters to communicate his identity and teachings. The accounts of Jesus' encounters in the Synoptic Gospels are shorter and more narrow in scope; they focus on one or two attitudes or actions that the believer should embrace or avoid. John's narration of key encounters (cf. Jn 3; 4; 9;

11; 18-20) communicates key themes of his Gospel. Following are highlights of these encounters:

- **1:35-39:** The timeless invitation to "come and see" Jesus and stay with him.
- **1:43-51:** Jesus expresses admiration for Nathanael's sincerity. John may be hinting that such an attitude is necessary for encountering Jesus authentically.
- **2:1-11:** The mother of Jesus (like the beloved disciple, with whom she models discipleship for John's community, Mary's name is not disclosed in John's Gospel) perseveres in her faith in Jesus, despite an abrupt deferral. She tells the wedding reception servants to "do whatever he tells you" (Jn 2:5). This recalls Pharaoh's command regarding the instructions of Joseph (cf. Gen 41:55) and even more so the Israelites' promise of obedience upon being given the covenant at Mt. Sinai (cf. Ex 19:8). As discussed in Chapter Nine, one of the keys to deriving a proper literal interpretation of the New Testament is to recognize its Old Testament underpinnings.
- **3:1-21:** Nicodemus learns about baptism and Jesus.
- **3:25-30:** John the Baptist, like the mother of Jesus, fades to the background in deference to Jesus (cf. Jn 1:19-30). This affirms the prologue's identification of the Baptist as the messenger/witness rather than the messiah (cf. Jn 1:6-9).
- **4:1-41:** The woman at the well becomes an unexpected disciple. Jesus does not let social norms (a Samaritan woman who goes by herself to a well in the heat of mid-day would be viewed contemptuously by most Jews) deter him from reaching out to someone. Do I?
- **4:46-54:** The royal official and his household become believers after their son's healing.
- **5:1-18:** Jesus' healing of a man evokes persecution from the religious authorities. Sometimes the good I do brings opposition from others. Will this deter me?

- **6:60-71:** Jesus' proclamation of himself as the bread of life causes some of his disciples to leave him. Peter promises to stay. Am I willing to join Peter out on a limb for Jesus?
- **7:53-8:11:** The woman caught in adultery experiences forgiveness. Who are the anonymous yet exposed sinners in this passage?
- **9:1-41:** A blind man encounters Jesus in this superb drama of the progression of faith. From both a literary and theological standpoint, it is one of the finest stories in the Bible. Jesus rejects the popular notion, carried over from the Old Testament, that suffering is always due to sin (cf. Jn 9:1-3), and identifies God's redemptive purposes. The passage offers encouragement to Jewish Christians who were barred from the synagogue once Judaism and Christianity became distinct religions.
- **11:1-44:** The raising of Lazarus. Martha's proactive (reflecting her hyperactiveness) and Mary's receptive (corresponding to her passivity) response to Jesus model different ways of encountering and following him according to our personal characteristics and situations. Amid this life-and-death drama, the crowd is mixed in their response to Jesus. The shortest verse in the Bible, "Jesus wept" (Jn 11:35), is one of the most profound. What things in my life or about me would cause Jesus, myself, or others to weep? Do I believe God will wipe away all my tears (cf. Is 25:8; Rev 7:17; 21:24)?
- **12:1-8:** Mary of Bethany is generous and Judas is stingy in their response to Jesus. How am I like both characters in my response to Jesus and others?
- **13:1-20:** Through Jesus' example, Peter learns the importance of service.
- **18:19-24:** A sycophant guard is invited by Jesus to look into himself after slapping Jesus in a brusque attempt to curry his superiors' favor while invoking Ex 22:27, the injunction not to curse a high priest (who is interrogating Jesus).

Jesus provides a conflict-resolution model for maintaining the integrity of both parties. He responds to violence not with deference, as Paul did in a similar situation (cf. Acts 23:5), but through a direct question/challenge posed respectfully but firmly.

Note the psychological wisdom in Jesus' response: Rather than accuse and go on the offensive, he invites the offender to reflect on their motives and change their behavior. He retained his sense of dignity amid abuse, and did not submit to injustice in a masochistic manner.

Jesus practiced his teaching both about turning the other cheek and how to conduct ourselves (in a dignified, but not subservient or anxious manner) when cross-examined about our faith. The Holy Spirit will teach us what to say (cf. Mt 10:19-20; Mk 13:11), and Jesus has given us a living example.

Because of free will, there is no guarantee of a positive response on the part of aggressors, but even in the gravest of situations opportunities for healing, repentance, and reconciliation exist.

- **18:28-38; 19:1-16:** Pilate epitomizes politically correct persons who relativize morality for expediency purposes: "What is truth?" Pilate is attracted to Jesus/good, but he will not make the difficult choice and pay the price.
- **Jn 19:25-27:** The dying Jesus entrusts his mother to the beloved disciple. A thorough exegesis of the symbolic and pastoral import of this passage can be found in two books written by Father Ignace de la Potterie, S.J., and published by Alba House: *The Hour of Jesus* and *Mary in the Mystery of the Covenant.* The next chapter will further discuss this passage and the role of Mary.
- **20:11-18:** Jesus calls Mary Magdalene by name and tells her not to cling to him prior to his ascension. She must make the transition from the earthly to the ascended Jesus. She must focus on what is from above (cf. Col 3:1-3).
- The risen Jesus encounters his apostles (cf. Jn 20:19-23). Unlike Luke and Acts, in John, Jesus gives the Holy Spirit

prior to his ascension (Jn 20:22). Peace, the evangelical commission (to make disciples; cf. Mt 28:20; Jn 20:21), and the forgiveness of sins are signs of the presence of the Spirit. This passage highlights the amazing trust and powers Jesus bestows on the Church, including that of the forgiveness or retention of sins.

- **20:24-29:** Thomas, pessimistic and insecure throughout the Gospel (cf. Jn 11:16; 14:5), comes to faith through eyewitness, prompting a beatitude for those who believe without seeing. Despite his doubts, Thomas did not touch Jesus, yet made the most personal affirmation of Jesus' divinity in the Gospels: "My LORD and my God!" (Jn 20:28) Temporary unbelief can be redeemed by an obedient response to God's reconciliatory initiative.
- **21:15-23:** The rehabilitation of Peter. See commentary concluding this chapter.

WRESTLING WITH THE WORD

Put yourself in the shoes of those who encountered Jesus. What are the timeless challenges present? What parallels to these encounters occur in your life?

JESUS' IDENTITY ("I AM") STATEMENTS

In John, Jesus reveals himself through familiar terms and images, many with Old Testament overtones. Each is ripe for personal reflection:

- **6:35-59:** The bread of life. Jesus compares himself to the manna (dew-like flakes) that sustained the Israelites in the desert (cf. Ex 16:31-35; Num 11:4-9).
- **8:12:** The light of the world. The word "light" appears five times in Jn 1:1-18, the Gospel's prologue and overview.

The battle between light and darkness is a significant theme in John, and to a lesser extent in Luke (cf. Lk 16:8), who alone among the Gospels twice mentions the importance of not hiding the light of the Gospel under a vessel (cf. Lk 8:16; 11:33).

John's community was exposed to the heresy of Gnosticism, a mystery religion that claimed private/privileged knowledge of God and spiritual realities, and which used dualistic imagery, such as light and darkness. Jesus is the true light because he reveals God and the way to him.

In his instruction of Nicodemus, Jesus uses the themes of light and darkness (cf. Jn 3:19-21). Prior to giving a blind man sight, Jesus refers to himself as the light of the world (cf. Jn 9:4-5). See also Jn 11:9-10; 12:35-36, 46.

- **8:58; 13:19; 18:5, 8:** In using the expression "I am" without an adjective or direct object, Jesus associates himself with God's name as revealed to Moses in Ex 3:14.
- **9:35:** Son of man. This is Jesus' favorite self-designation in the synoptic Gospels.
- **10:7, 9:** The gate. This is a prelude to his declaration of being the way, the truth, and the life.
- **10:11, 14:** The good shepherd. This recalls the Old Testament passages, particularly Ezek 34, in which the evil shepherds (religious leaders) are denounced and God promises to shepherd the people himself.
- **10:24-25:** The messiah. In response to questions from the Jews, Jesus reminds them that he has testified to this title in word and deed.
- **11:25-26:** The resurrection and the life. Jesus says this prior to reviving Lazarus. Martha associates this expression with the titles messiah and Son of God (cf. Jn 11:27).
- **14:6-7:** The way, and the truth, and the life. Jesus is the path to the Father. This expression integrates his identity

as the gate and the resurrection and the life, and recalls his debate over truth with the Jewish leaders (cf. Jn 8) and Pilate (cf. Jn 19:37-38).

- **15:1, 5**: The true vine. Throughout the Fourth Gospel, particularly Jn 14-17, the theme of abiding in (intimacy with) Jesus is emphasized. The branches (believers) need to abide in Jesus in order to obey his commandment to love one another.

WRESTLING WITH THE WORD

Which of these identity statements resonates with you, and why? Which most describes your understanding of and relationship with Jesus?

CLASSIC JOHN: THE REHABILITATION OF PETER

John's appendix/epilogue (cf. Jn 21:15-23) contains an encounter between Peter and Jesus that is not reported in the other Gospels, but builds upon the affirming look of Jesus described in Lk 22:61 and discussed in the previous chapter. Following are essential aspects of the encounter and its exemplification of John's style and theology.

Healing of Memories

Jesus knew Peter's memory of his denials needed healing. He thrice asks Peter to affirm his love for him. Peter's last(ing) memory of a threefold repetition would be of an affirmation, not a denial. At Jesus' third repetition of the question, Peter recognizes the connection with his denials and expresses his hurt.

When love is wounded, fragile memories must be addressed at the proper time. This encounter occurred some time after Jesus' initial post-resurrection appearance, perhaps in order to give Peter time to reflect upon his denials in light of Jesus' resurrection. God often lets us twist in the wind momentarily in hopes that we will get a clearer perspective on our sins and God's mercy, and be more receptive to him in the future. Our response to this challenging situation can be as transformational as Peter's was.

Preparing for Death

Jesus' prophesy that someone would tie Peter's hands and take him against his will is a compelling description of aging, infirmity, and death. Peter thought that he could serve Jesus effectively through willpower and sincere intentions alone. He wanted to give his life for Jesus (cf. Jn 13:37), and would get his wish according to God's timing (cf. Jn 21:18).

Through his denials, Peter learned that he could only make this sacrifice through the gift of the Spirit, whom Jesus would send at Pentecost (cf. Acts 2; Jn 15:26; 16:7, 13). He also learned to be compassionate toward others who likewise fell short despite good intentions (cf. Lk 22:31-32; Rom 7:14-25; Prov 24:16).

I selected Peter's (com)passion to focus on in these two chapters because the events are repeated in each of our lives. When I fall, do I view it as an opportunity to respond to the Lord's piercing and reassuring gaze (cf. Lk 22:61) and strengthen my brothers and sisters (cf. Lk 22:32; Jn 21:15-17) through the lesson, character, and compassion I gain, or do I let it become an occasion for bitterness and despair?

Peter's restoration is representative of John in that it uses repetition, emphasizes love, shows Jesus' foreknowledge of events, and communicates a key message through someone's misunderstanding of Jesus.

Jesus' prophecy of Peter's suffering and death is a good transition to the next chapter, where we will see how the New Testament portrays Jesus' suffering.

Chapter Fourteen

How to Interpret and Apply the Passion Narratives

Contents of this Chapter

- Consider the events leading up to Jesus' suffering and death.
- Note the different emphases and nuances in the eucharistic accounts.
- Draw parallels between characters and choices in the passion and those in your life.
- Explore the progression of events in the passion and their different portrayals in the four Gospels.
- Explore the profound truths revealed in Jesus' encounter with Pontius Pilate.
- Recognize the fundamental meanings of the "seven words" from the cross.

The accounts of Jesus' passion (i.e., suffering), death, and resurrection are the most important part of the New Testament. They occupy a large portion of each Gospel and were probably the first part to be written. They were the foundation of the catechesis (religious education) and formation of the first Christians, and have remained so throughout the centuries. As discussed in Chapter Five, they are the prism through which we should interpret not only the Gospels, but the rest of the Bible and life. Accordingly, we will explore them in considerable detail.

Given the intensity and significance of the events, you may want to read this chapter piecemeal, reflecting on the ways the words, actions, and attitudes are re-enacted in your life.

These accounts are a composite of:

- Memories of the historical events handed down in the communities.
- References to Old Testament passages viewed as prophetically applicable to Jesus.
- Theological insights and pastoral (community-directed) messages from the evangelists.

WHAT DOES IT MEAN?

The Gospel accounts of the events leading to the death and resurrection of Jesus are known as the passion and resurrection narratives (PRN).

STAGES OF JESUS' PASSION AND DEATH

The Gospels' accounts of Jesus' suffering and death unfold in four stages:

- **Preparation:** Preparation for Jesus' suffering and death can be traced to his birth. Both Matthew's and Luke's infancy narratives point to the violence that will surround Jesus. John's prologue likewise anticipates his rejection.

  To the bewilderment of his apostles, during his public ministry Jesus thrice predicted his suffering, death, and resurrection. He continually emphasized the importance of carrying one's cross (persevering faithfully amid suffering) and going through the narrow gate and hard road that leads to life (cf. Mt 7:13-14).

  Closer to the passion itself, preparations begin at the anointing at Bethany, the Last Supper, and the Agony in the Garden, where the suffering begins to take on its most intimate dimension.

- **Trials:** In the Garden of Gethsemane and in the Lord's Prayer, Jesus told the Apostles to pray to be spared the kind of trials and testing of their faith that will occur at the end of the world. Such was foretold in Daniel and in Jesus' discussion of the end-times (cf. Mt 24; Mk 13; Lk 21). Such testing amounts to a shaking of the foundation of one's faith and identity/vocation.

  In the trials stage, we see Jesus moving from the private, interior trials of Gethsemane to the public trials before the Jewish leaders, the people, and Pontius Pilate. These trials included emotional (rejection and public humiliation), physical, and spiritual (the experience of progressive abandonment) suffering.

- **Death/Crucifixion:** The Gospels spare us most of the physical details, and focus on Jesus' seven comments from the cross and the behavior of those around him.

- **Burial:** Jesus' disciples and the Jewish leaders approach his burial differently. Joseph of Arimathea seeks his body, the women mourn him, and the Jewish leaders suspiciously seek a guard for the tomb.

THE SCANDALOUS NATURE OF JESUS' DEATH

Despite Jesus' warnings and preparatory events, Jesus' followers were unprepared for his death. Initially they were

---

WRESTLING WITH THE WORD

 The seventeenth-century mathematician and Christian philosopher Blaise Pascal observed that Jesus is in agony until the end of time. What does he mean by this, and do you agree with him? What bearing does this have on your suffering and your reading of the PRN?

---

scandalized by it. How could God be with someone who died so shamefully? Pre-eminent in their minds was this ominous Old Testament text: "And if a man has committed crime punishable by death and he is put to death, and you hang him on a tree, his body shall not remain all night upon the tree, for you shall bury him the same day, for a hanged man is accursed by God" (Deut 21:22-23).

Though contrary notes were sounded in Psalms 44 and 77, the general portrait of God in the Old Testament was that of a mighty and transcendent victor. He is frequently depicted as a warrior who conquers Israel's enemies and their gods, and brings Israel and the just to safe passage. The faithful Jews who followed Jesus were thus unprepared for the way he fulfilled God's will — through painful submission to evil out of obedience to the Father.

THE ANOINTING AT BETHANY

The PRN begins (and ends: the first person to encounter the risen Jesus is Mary Magdalene) consistent with Jesus' public ministry: his outreach to outcasts. Matthew and Mark describe an

---

PEAK PASSAGES

The Psalms are the most quoted Old Testament book in the PRN. Particularly prominent are Psalms 22, 31, and 69. The most influential passages from the prophets, the third through fifth "*Servant (of Yahweh) Songs*" in Isaiah (cf. Is 50:4-9; 52:13-15; 53), are never directly quoted, but are dramatized vividly:

"The prophet (Isaiah), who has rightly been called "the Fifth Evangelist," presents in this Song (Isaiah 53) an image of the sufferings of the Servant with a realism as acute as if he were seeing them with his own eyes: the eyes of the body and of the spirit. In the light of the verses of Isaiah, the passion of Christ becomes almost more expressive and touching than in the descriptions of the evangelists themselves" (Pope John Paul II, *Salvifici Doloris*, On The Christian Meaning of Human Suffering, 17).

---

unnamed woman (whom John identifies as Mary of Bethany) interrupting a meal to pour expensive ointment over Jesus' head. Jesus interpreted the act as anticipatory of his burial (cf. Mt 26:12; Mk 14:8) and predicts that it, like his Last Supper, will be remembered (cf. Mt 26:13; Mk 14:9). Luke places this or a similar incident earlier in his Gospel (cf. Lk 7:36-50).

THE PLOT TO KILL JESUS

The PRN begins with the plot by the chief priests and scribes to kill Jesus. Ironically, the religious groups charged with preserving Israel's most sacred treasures, God's word and temple, become the ones to crucify Jesus, who is God's word (cf. Jn 1:1-18) and temple/dwelling place (cf. Jn 2:19). A desire on the part of the religious leaders to do away with Jesus is noted earlier in each Gospel, but for fear of the people they do not act until Judas presents the opportunity.

THE LAST SUPPER

One of the interesting dimensions of the PRN are the nuances in and differences among the Gospels. This is particularly apparent in the accounts of the Last Supper. The various Eucharistic Prayers used at Mass echo this diversity.

Because Paul's letters predate the Gospels, the earliest account of the Last Supper is 1 Cor 11:23-26. The expression "the Lord's Supper" comes from 1 Cor 11:20. Since Luke was a companion of Paul, it is not surprising that his account of Jesus' words and gestures is closest to Paul's.

Only Luke and Paul (twice) include the words "Do this in remembrance of me" (Lk 22:19; 1 Cor 11:24, 25) and "This cup (Luke inserts "which is poured out for you") is the new covenant in my blood" (Lk 22:20; 1 Cor 11:25).

Whereas Luke and Paul emphasize the new covenant promised in Jer 31:31-34, Mark and Matthew use the phrase "my blood of the covenant" (Mt 26:28; Mk 14:24), which recalls

Moses' sprinkling of sacrificed animals' blood on the people during their acceptance of the Mosaic covenant in Ex 24:7-8. Jesus' action indicates that he will fulfill the people's (and our) broken promise of obedience.

As discussed in Chapter Eleven, Matthew is particularly concerned with presenting Jesus as the new Moses. Mark alone notes that the apostles drank of the cup, while Luke has Jesus take two cups.

JESUS' BETRAYAL

Jesus' revelation of his betrayer at the Last Supper was heartbreaking. Intimate betrayal is one of life's greatest pains. Jesus was susceptible to all human limitations, including the dissolution of intimate relationships and well-intentioned choices gone awry.

Jesus was not a merry martyr. He was openly irritated with Judas, and spoke ominously of his fate. However, he didn't retaliate or dwell on the betrayal. He moved on with life and his mission, focusing on his apostles: ". . . those who have continued with me in my trials" (cf. Lk 22:28).

John is the evangelist most critical of Judas. Only John tells us explicitly that Satan entered into Judas after he ate the morsel (cf. Jn 13:27) — the opposite of the divine presence in the Eucharist. Luke (cf. Lk 22:3) views this satanic influence as occurring prior to the meal (another example of the subtle parallels between Luke and John, as discussed in Chapter Nine).

Only John reports that Judas helped himself to the shared purse (cf. Jn 12:6). Only John does not report a direct exchange between Judas and Jesus at the moment of his arrest. To drive home the horrible nature of the crime, nine times John references Judas' betrayal of Jesus (cf. Jn 6:64, 71; 12:4; 13:2, 11, 21; 18:2, 5; 21:20). Only Matthew matches this total.

WRESTLING WITH THE WORD

How do I respond when I am in the position of Jesus or Judas? Do I despair or move on with life? What can I do to take steps in the right direction and move beyond my pain?

THE AGONY IN THE GARDEN

The event traditionally referred to as the agony (from the Greek word *agonia* in Lk 22:44, which described the struggle between wrestlers) in the garden can be found in Mt 26:36-46; Mk 14:32-42; Lk 22:39-46. Along with his cry of abandonment on the cross (cf. Mt 27:46; Mk 15:34), Jesus' crisis reveals the depths of his humanity.

The evangelists describe its location differently: Mark and Matthew identify it as "a place called Gethsemane" (which means oil press), Luke refers to "the place" at the Mount of Olives (the general area), and John speaks of a garden reached via the Kidron

---

WRESTLING WITH THE WORD

Because Judaism goes by a lunar calendar, Passover always occurs during a full moon. Archaeologists tell us that en route to Gethsemane, Jesus and his disciples walked by a graveyard. Imagine a sacred meal shared with loved ones followed by a moonlit walk by a cemetery en route to torture and death instigated by a friend.

Where do I go to take refuge and meditate in moments of crisis? What parallels can I draw between Jesus' agony and mine?

---

valley. Given John's previous references to Genesis, beginning with Jn 1:1, he may be drawing a parallel between the testing done in the garden of Eden and that in the garden of Gethsemane.

Jn 18:2 reports that Jesus met with his disciples often in the garden, while Lk 22:39 tells us it was his custom to go to the Mount of Olives. Lk 21:37 relates that Jesus would often teach in the temple by day and go to the Mount of Olives at night. It was natural for Jesus to go to a familiar, special place at such a stressful time.

PEAK PASSAGES

 The letter to the Hebrews offers a brief allusion to the Agony in the Garden, mentioning Jesus' tears (cf. Heb 5:7), which are not recorded in the Gospels. A major theme of Hebrews is that Jesus' sufferings enable him to act as our high priest and intercede for us (cf. Heb 2:18; 4:15-16). Of what significance to me is a vulnerable and interceding Jesus?

JESUS' AGONY IN MATTHEW AND MARK

I discuss Matthew and Mark together because their passion stories are so similar, with Matthew drawing heavily upon Mark. Most of the differences involve Matthew's injection of Old Testament themes (cf. Mt 27:39-44, 52; Wis 2:12-20).

Among the evangelists, Mark uses the strongest language to describe Jesus' grief and fear over his impending death. He shows Jesus throwing himself on the ground in a state of distress, while Matthew portrays Jesus assuming a prayer posture common in the Old Testament.

In Mark's Gospel, the last thing Jesus says to the apostles before the arrival of his captors is an ambiguous Greek phrase (cf. Mk 14:41), which is usually translated as "Enough." It literally means "the money is paid," and was used in business transactions to confirm the receipt of payment. Could this be a double entendre?

Jesus paid the price of human sinfulness while the Jewish rulers paid Judas his thirty pieces of silver.

JESUS' AGONY IN LUKE

Luke's version of Jesus' agony shows him fulfilling the Lord's Prayer. The fifth petition of the Lord's Prayer, "Lead us not into temptation," begins and ends the passage, thus bracketing the passage as a distinct unit (known by scholars as a *pericope*, pronounced pe-rik'-a-pee, from the Greek word for paragraph). This literary technique, akin to our paragraph breaks, is known as an inclusion or an envelope structure.

As you become more familiar with the Bible, you'll notice when passages begin and end with similar expressions. Literal translations particularly bring this out.

Jesus also prays the second petition of the Lord's Prayer, "Your will be done." Prayer is a favorite theme of Luke's. He portrays Jesus in prayer more often than the other Gospels.

Unlike the apostles, Jesus weathers the temptation and is comforted by an angel (cf. Mk 1:13; Acts 12:6-11). Jesus' angelic assistance and intense sweating are not reported in the other Gospels.

Angels are a frequent theme in Luke. He mentions them in the first two chapters of his Gospel and throughout Acts of the

---

WHAT DOES IT MEAN?

The fifth petition of the Lord's Prayer: "Lead us not into temptation" is alternatively translated as "subject us not to the test/trial. The traditional rendering of the Greek word *peirasmos* as "temptation" is often mistakenly understood as implying that God would somehow tempt us, a misconception addressed by Jas 1:13-15. Temptation ultimately comes from ourselves (the flesh), the devil, and the world. Jas 1:12 contains a beatitude congratulating those who endure temptation.

Apostles. Some ancient manuscripts omit Luke's reference to Jesus' angelic assistance, perhaps out of concern that Jesus' vulnerability would be misunderstood.

JOHN'S PARALLEL TO THE AGONY IN THE GARDEN

In John, Jesus' preparation for his passion is subtle and dignified. Jn 12:24-36 is John's closest parallel to the Agony in the Garden: Jesus expresses his sorrow, appeals to God, receives support from heaven, and accepts his imminent death. Further insight into Jesus' mind-set comes in his farewell meal, discourse, and prayer (cf. Jn 13-17), which can be subdivided as follows:

- The foot washing at the Last Supper (13:1-20).
- Jesus' betrayal: The hour of darkness (13:21-30).
- Jesus' abandonment (13:31-38).
- Jesus is the way to God (14:1-14).
- Jesus' sending of the Holy Spirit (14:15-31).
- The vine and the branches (15:1-17).
- The animosity of the world (15:18-16:4a).
- Jesus' departure and return (16:4b-33).
- Jesus' intercessory prayer (17:1-26).

In Jn 18, Jesus and his disciples travel across the Kidron valley to a garden where they immediately encounter Judas and the arresting party. There is no mention of any struggle on Jesus' part. Even more so than Matthew, John shows Jesus in control of the events surrounding his passion. At the Lord's Supper, he tells Judas to go about his business, and in the garden takes charge of the encounter with the arresting forces.

John's passion and resurrection narrative, Jn 13-20, is known as the *Book of Glory* because it presents Jesus as enthroned on the cross in anticipation of being glorified in heaven. Like a king, Jesus directs the events of his passion, remaining in firm control. Jesus came to give his life for the world and for his friends (cf. Jn 10:18). Fittingly, he says "It is finished" before giving up his spirit (cf. Jn 19:30).

SHARING THE PAIN

The Agony scene is one of the few recorded occasions in which Jesus shared important moments exclusively with his closest disciples, Peter, James, and John. Other instances include the Transfiguration (cf. Mk 9:2-9:9), where Jesus' glory is revealed in anticipation of his resurrection, and the healing of the synagogue official's daughter (cf. Mk 5:37-43).

Only Matthew and Mark note Jesus' request for intimate support. He asks them to keep awake (in line with his image of Jesus as "God with us," Matthew inserts "with him") and pray not to be put to the test. As described in the parables in Mt 25, "keep awake" also carries connotations of being vigilant. Matthew and Mark do not excuse the apostles' sleeping in Gethsemane as Luke does by attributing it to their grief.

Matthew, Mark, and Luke reveal Jesus praying to be spared "the cup." The cup signified God's punishment of unrepentant sinners (cf. Rev 14:10; 16:19; Is 51:17, 22), whose place Jesus was taking (cf. 2 Cor 5:21).

John uses the term "hour" instead of cup to describe Jesus' mission: "Now is my soul troubled. And what shall I say — Father, save me from this hour'? No, for this purpose I have come to this hour" (Jn 12:27). In John, "the hour" refers to Jesus' mission. Jesus first uses the term in rebuffing his mother's attempt to have him intervene at the wedding in Cana (cf. Jn 2:1-11).

The hour motif is also present in the other Gospels, though less frequently (cf. Mt 26:45; Mk 14:35, 41; Lk 22:14). The Greek language distinguishes between chronological time (*chronos*) and the time of decision or opportunity (*kairos*). In the Gospels, *kairos* signifies a pivotal or crisis moment, usually related to the end-times, the ultimate moment of decision and activity (cf. Mt 24:44; Mk 13:32; Lk 22:53).

What "hour" (time of decision/opportunity) are you currently facing? How might Jesus' approach to his "hour" inspire you to respond with integrity, courage, and wisdom?

Each of the Gospels and the letter to the Hebrews offer a unique perspective on Jesus' agony/struggle that can be adapted to your viewpoint and experiences. We would expect these perspectives to differ, as everyone's experience of suffering is unique. Each book offers powerful images and themes for responding to trials and suffering:

- Luke's agony account exhorts you to pray, particularly the Lord's Prayer, and look on others (e.g., the grief-stricken apostles) with eyes of mercy and compassion. If the angels come to Jesus' aid, they will also come to yours.

- Matthew reminds you to recognize the frailties of human nature in an unbroken chain from the Old Testament until today (cf. Mt 26:41) and to persevere "with Jesus," who knows from experience the toll such testing takes.

- Mark shows you that even Jesus can crack under such difficult testing, and that it is okay for you to lament and mourn before God. The most important and challenging spiritual value throughout such an ordeal/test is obedience to God's will, which remains the focus of Jesus' prayer.

- John opens your eyes to the dignity of suffering when undergone out of love for God and neighbor. Like a grain of wheat, we must die (to selfishness) to gain new life (cf. Jn 12:24).

- Hebrews reminds us that we need not feign invulnerability, and that we can entrust God with our prayers, tears, and fears.

THE TRIAL OF JESUS

Matthew, Mark, and Luke portray Jesus arrested and brought to trial before the Sanhedrin (a council of chief priests, scribes, and elders led by the high priest). Significant themes of the trial are the flaunting of Jewish juridical procedures, the false and contrasting witnesses, the predetermined verdict of blasphemy, and the mocking and beating of Jesus. The entire sequence of events from arrest to condemnation is characterized by injustice, an aspect particularly emphasized by Luke, to whom Jesus' innocence is a central theme.

Jesus is evasive in his response to questions about his identity, except for Mk 14:61-62, where he acknowledges that he is the messiah. This is a turnabout from the first part of Mark in which Jesus tried to keep his identity secret. Since his messiahship was now manifested in suffering, he could fully reveal his identity before Israel.

JESUS' INTERROGATION BY ANNAS

Only John (cf. Jn 18:12-27) records this non-juridical (unofficial) interrogation of Jesus by Annas, former Jewish high priest and father-in-law of Caiaphas, the current high priest. John does not mention the trial before the Sanhedrin that is reported by the other Gospels.

In response to both Annas' questions about his teachings and the guard's slap of Jesus' face, Jesus thrice repeats the word "spoken," which has special significance in John's Gospel. It represents the word of God that Jesus proclaims. The rejection of Jesus' words by Annas and the guard symbolizes the rejection of the people: "He came to his own home, and his own people received him not" (Jn 1:11).

THE DENIALS OF PETER

Peter's denials are one of the most significant and profound events in the New Testament. Proper interpretation identifies with rather than criticizes Peter condescendingly. Neither Jesus nor the evangelists looked down on Peter. As discussed in Chapters Twelve and Thirteen, he represents all of us.

JUDAS' DEATH

Only Matthew reports Judas' remorse, despair, and suicide, which is contrasted with Peter's humble repentance. It recalls the

suicide of Ahithophel (ah-hith´-oh-fel), David's counselor who
betrayed him (cf. 2 Sam 17:23). Old Testament texts brought to
mind by Judas's betrayal are Ps 41:9; 55:12-14.

Acts of the Apostles reports that Judas fell headlong in a field
and spilled his entrails (cf. Acts 1:18). This recalls the fate of a
wicked man in the Old Testament (cf. Ps 69:26; 109:8; Zech
11:12-13).

A fundamentalist might harmonize the accounts and infer
that Judas tried to hang himself, but the rope broke and his
innards spilled out in the fall. A Catholic approach would be to
look at the history of interpretation of the passage, along with the
theology and audience of Matthew and Luke and the context of
the passages, and focus on the religious meaning of the accounts,
rather than their historical dimensions. It is understandable why
Judas' death would be shrouded in mystery: he was likely alone
when he died, and not a focus for either Jesus or the apostles.

PONTIUS PILATE

Let us now move from one tragic individual to another. One
of the more prominent figures in the passion narrative is Pontius
Pilate. Pilate was governor of Judea for 10 years, A.D. 26-36. Judea
was a small, troublesome outpost of little consequence in the
Roman Empire. Pilate needlessly antagonized the Jews on
numerous occasions (cf. Lk 13:1). This explains his tense
interactions with the religious leaders and the people during Jesus'

trial. This callous man's desire to spare Jesus' life testifies to the impression Jesus made.

JESUS' INTERACTIONS WITH PILATE

Significant differences exist among the Gospels' accounts of Pilate. Only Matthew reports the dream of Pilate's wife, his washing his hands of Jesus' death, and the people's corresponding assumption of responsibility. Luke alone reports Pilate's transfer of Jesus to Herod Antipas, (whose father, Herod the Great, tried to kill the infant Jesus) and his subsequent reconciliation with Pilate (cf. Lk 23:12). John develops Jesus' interactions with Pilate more than the other Gospels do, reporting words and actions with timeless symbolic meaning. They are worthy of brief commentary even in this introductory book because they convey central themes of Jesus' message and ministry in succinct and profound fashion.

"My Kingdom Is Not of This World" (Jn 18:36)

Pilate begins his interrogation of Jesus by questioning him about being a king. Jesus sets the tone for the conversation by pointing out that this world is not his domain. Earlier in the Gospel he referred to it as the domain of Satan, the prince of this world (cf. Jn 12:31: 14:30; 16:11). As discussed in Chapter

Thirteen, John uses the term "world" both as an object of God's love (cf. Jn 3:16) and as an entity opposed to him.

Do I expect Jesus' kingship to be primarily exercised in this world or the next?

"What Is Truth?" (Jn 18:38)

Symbolizing worldly persons, Pilate shows that the truth is not in him, like some of those who opposed Jesus earlier in the Gospel (cf. Jn 8:44-47). For Pilate, truth is an abstract, impractical concept. Like Pilate, the more I compromise the truth, the more hardened I become.

"Behold the Man" (Jn 19:5)

Hoping to avert a death sentence, Pilate brings the whipped and mocked Jesus before the people to reveal him as a pitiful fool and harmless threat. Pilate, like Judas and the religious leaders before him, *handed him over* (a key expression in the PRN; cf. Mt 20:18; 27:2; 27:26) for crucifixion. Jesus experienced multiple betrayals, as have most of us. Jesus didn't condone such treachery, but he didn't let it embitter him.

Pilate's famous words "Behold the Man," referenced traditionally in their Latin form, *Ecce Homo*, have a meaning for John quite unintended by Pilate: This is the Word made flesh, the image of God whom we are to emulate, and what we have done to him. Though he looks the part of the ultimate loser, he triumphs through love, a power greater than status (the Jewish leaders), ignorance (the people), fear (Jesus' apostles), and military might (Pilate).

What is my response to Jesus "the man" in the person of my neighbor and myself?

The Judgment at Gabbatha (Jn 19:13)

One of the most subtle scenes in John's PRN occurs when Pilate brings Jesus out before the crowd for the final time. Most translations portray Pilate sitting on the judge's bench at the place called Gabbatha (stone pavement). However, translations such as the New Jerusalem Bible and many scholars interpret the Greek text as depicting Pilate seating Jesus on the judgment bench. This may be John's ironic way of revealing who the real judge was.

Who are the real judges today, those mocked, falsely accused, and rejected by society? In what situations am I mocked and misjudged? In what ways do I mock and misjudge others?

"Behold Your King" (Jn 19:14)

In John, Pilate and Jesus begin and end their discussion on the topic of kingship. This dramatizes John's image of the crucifixion as Jesus' enthronement, not in the sense of glorifying suffering, but of affirming gratuitous love, God's essential characteristic (cf. 1 Jn 4:8). Their interaction comes to a dramatic and ironic close as Pilate (and John) presents Jesus, fitted with a crown of thorns and royal robes, to the crowd as their king.

While all four Gospels describe the crowds as shouting for Jesus' crucifixion, only in John do the crowds exclaim "Away with him. Away with him" (cf. Jn 19:15). In Acts 21:36, a mob shouts the same about Paul. This epitomizes the rejection that has marked Jesus' public ministry and passion.

"What I Have Written I Have Written" (Jn 19:22)

The other Gospels report that an inscription reading "(This is) the King of the Jews" was placed above Jesus' cross. John affirms the universal nature of Jesus' mission by reporting that it was recorded in Hebrew and the universal languages of the time, Greek and Latin. Pilate ironically testifies to the authenticity of the title through his refusal to preface it with "This man said, I am . . ." at the request of the Jewish leaders.

THE GEOGRAPHY OF THE PASSION

We have a general idea where the events of the passion occurred. For example, we know where the Kidron Valley, Gethsemane, and the Mount of Olives are. However, we are not certain of the exact location of the Upper Room, the path on which Jesus carried the cross, Golgotha (where he was crucified), or the governor's palace.

Moving beyond geography, let us accompany Jesus on his way of the cross, discovering personalities, circumstances, and choices that reappear in our lives.

JESUS BARABBAS

Mk 15:7 and Lk 23:19 report that Barabbas was a murderer and rebel. There is no historical record outside of the Gospels of the custom of releasing a prisoner during a Jewish feast. While this does not preclude the historical dimension of the account, it does hint that its theological meaning is paramount.

The name Barabbas, composed of the roots *bar abba*, means son of the father. In Mt 27:15-16, he is called Jesus Barabbas. The people preferred the false to the authentic son.

SIMON OF CYRENE

"As they were marching out, they came upon a man of Cyrene, Simon by name; this man they compelled to carry his cross" (Mt 27:32). By stating the involuntary nature of his assistance, and not commenting on his state of mind, the Gospels invite you to reflect on Jesus' absolute abandonment and the

---

WRESTLING WITH THE WORD

Am I open to helping even those I do not know or who cannot repay me? As in Simon's situation, I never know who might need my help. Sometimes it is not friends or family who come through in times of trouble, but strangers.

---

subjective figure of Simon. John does not mention Simon because such assistance would be inconsistent with John's portrayal of Jesus as having complete control over his destiny.

THE ABUSE OF JESUS

In accordance with his image of the crucifixion as the enthronement of Jesus, John does not follow the other Gospels in presenting the soldiers spitting on Jesus, kneeling down before him, and striking him on the head with a reed.

Resembling John (as he often does) in emphasizing Jesus' dignity during the passion, Luke omits the crown of thorns, the royal robe, and the mockery of the soldiers prior to Jesus being placed on the cross. Though Jesus predicted his flogging (cf. Lk 18:33), and Pilate mentions it twice (cf. Lk 23:16, 22), Luke does not record that it actually occurred, stating only ". . . Jesus he delivered up to their will" (Lk 23:25).

FEMALE FOLLOWERS OF JESUS

Given his emphasis of the role of women in Jesus' ministry, it is not surprising that only Luke presents Jesus consoling and warning the grieving women who followed him as he carried the cross (cf. Lk 23:27-31). All four evangelists record the presence of women at the cross (cf. Jn 19:25-27) or looking on. These passages show that not all present were overtaken by the mob mentality.

THE STRIPPING OF JESUS

Prior to being crucified, Jesus is stripped of his garments (cf. Mt 27:35; Mk 15:24; Lk 23:34; Jn 19:24). The evangelists have in mind Ps 22:18: "they divide my garments among them, and for my raiment they cast lots," though only John references it.

In the ancient Near East, public nakedness was an abomination. In the Bible, three categories of people, other than children, are presented as naked: prisoners of war, condemned men, and slaves. When the high priest entered the most sacred part of the temple during religious ceremonies, he was appropriately covered, with no bare skin unnecessarily exposed. From Adam and Eve to Noah to Jesus, nakedness was the ultimate indignity.

Imagine how the followers of Jesus felt about this humiliation. It recalled the humiliation of the Jewish people throughout their history. They and Jesus were stripped to the bone.

In being stripped of his last earthly possessions, Jesus descends into the pits of human ignominy. While the soldier cast lots for Jesus' clothing, Jesus cast his lot with sufferers from all periods, taking upon himself the experience of abject poverty and humiliation.

SIGNS OF THE TIMES: THE BIBLE TODAY

The stripping of Jesus yields a multitude of applications. So many people are stripped of physical, economic, emotional, or social security. As with Jesus, it may be all they possess.

How do I strip others of their dignity? How might I clothe them and myself?

THE SEAMLESS GARMENT

While the other Gospels relate that the soldiers cast lots for Jesus' garments, John cites Ps 22:18 and records the detail of the seamless garment. The traditional explanation was that this represented the robes of the high priest and thereby Jesus' priestly ministry. Today scholars view it as a symbol of the Church — continuous and whole. Eisegetically and analogously, it can also represent the consistency and integrity that believers strive for in their moral and spiritual life.

In what ways do I respond to life and the Bible in disjointed and compartmentalized fashion? What steps can I take to become more whole and consistent?

THE FINAL TEMPTATION

Jesus' final temptation was the cruel taunting by the soldiers, passers-by, his fellow condemned men, and the religious leaders: "If you are the Son of God, come down from the cross" (Mt 27:40; cf. Mk 15:29-32; Lk 23:35-37; Wis 2:12-20). This resembles the temptation experienced by Jesus in the desert immediately preceding his public ministry (cf. Mt 4; Mk 1; Lk 4). The devil invited him to spurn the suffering messiahship called for by the Scriptures and to transcend the constraints of humanity, thereby using his divinity for his own purposes.

THE SEVEN WORDS FROM THE CROSS

Innumerable books and essays have been written on Jesus' final utterances (traditionally referred to as "the seven words") from the cross. Now it is your turn. You'll discover where to find these words in the Gospels, their literal meaning, and how they are relevant to you.

Jesus' Cry of Abandonment (Mk 15:34; Mt 27:46)

"At three o'clock Jesus cried out with a loud voice, 'Eloi, Eloi, lema sabachthani?' which means, 'My God, my God, why have you forsaken me?'" (Mk 15:34, New Revised Standard Version).

Mark gives the Aramaic address "*Eloi*" of Ps 22:1, while Mt 27:46 uses the Hebrew address, "*Eli,*" probably to explain why bystanders thought Jesus was calling Elijah (in Hebrew, *Eliyahu*, which means Yahweh is God). These are Jesus' only words from the cross. According to Matthew and Mark, he then dies with a loud cry, like a desperate animal.

Biblical commentators traditionally have softened the impact of Jesus' cry by pointing out that Psalm 22 ends on a note of faith, and that by referencing one verse of a psalm, the entire psalm is evoked. As with the Agony in the Garden, believers can become uncomfortable with the human vulnerability of Jesus. While some are troubled by Jesus' words, others are comforted. What is your response to his words?

Ps 22:1 is the only lament psalm in which a verse repeats the same version of God's name, i.e., "My God, My God", in its address. In the Bible, when a person speaks someone's name twice in succession, a special message is indicated. The psalmist and Jesus are posing a special, universal question to God, which we affirm: why? Only God knows.

A Final Mockery (Mt 27:48-49; Mk 15:36)

Misunderstanding Jesus' cry as an appeal for Elijah to save him, a bystander gets a sponge full of vinegar for Jesus to drink. Mark and Matthew view this final encounter with Jesus differently, one of the few instances in their passion accounts where they disagree. Mk 15:22 portrays Jesus rejecting wine filled with myrrh (to dull the pain). Mt 27:34 recalls Ps 69:21 in reporting that the wine was filled with gall/poison. In Mark, the person is taunting Jesus. In Matthew, his attentions seem compassionate, but other bystanders intervene with one final taunt. Even in tragic situations, it is possible to reach out. What is your reaction to your neighbor's appeal for help?

Jesus Forgives His Tormentors (Lk 23:34)

Only in Luke does Jesus forgive his tormentors. Jesus' attribution of their behavior to ignorance is paralleled by similar excuses in Acts 3:17; 13:27; 17:30. This reminds us to be merciful on ourselves and others. Many sins are committed out of ignorance.

Jesus Welcomes a Repentant Thief (Lk 23:43)

Luke presents Jesus as a reconciling force to the end. Only Luke reports that the arrested Jesus healed the ear of the slave struck by Peter's sword (cf. Lk 22:51). Only Luke reports the reconciliation of Pilate and Herod (cf. Lk 23:12). Matthew and Mark report that the criminals crucified alongside Jesus reviled him. Only Luke reports that one of them asked to be remembered by Jesus when he enters his kingdom. He became Jesus' first companion in paradise.

Jesus Hands Over His Spirit (Lk 23:46)

Luke is more interested in the reconciling and redeeming aspects of the passion than the gory details. Jesus' final words are a prayer of submission (cf. Ps 31:6). The gentle manner of Jesus' death is consistent with the gentle manner of his ministry. Stephen's final words amid his stoning recall Jesus' (cf. Acts 7:59-60).

SIGNS OF THE TIMES: THE BIBLE TODAY

When Pope John Paul II prayed about the Holocaust during his visit to the Holy Land in 2000, he quoted Ps 31:13 in memory of the victims: "I hear the whispering of many — terror on every side! —as they scheme together against me, as they plot to take my life."

The expression "terror on every side" was associated with Jeremiah (cf. Jer 20:3, 10), whose suffering and rejection was recalled by the early Church in reference to Jesus' passion.

Jesus Addresses His Mother and the Beloved Disciple (Jn 19:25-27)

The straightforward sense of Jesus' dying words involves the physical care of his mother, presumably a widow. However, John's words often have a symbolic meaning that we can discern through careful study. Both traditionally and currently, Catholic interpreters intuit such in this case, based on the ambiguous Greek phrase used here and in Jn 1:11.

According to this interpretation, Jesus was calling the beloved disciple, who is a representative figure (of the believer) in John, into spiritual intimacy with the mother of Jesus. He is to take Mary, the model disciple in Luke and John, into "his own" (his heart). A close relationship with someone's mother naturally brings you to a greater understanding of the person himself.

The significance of Jesus' interaction with his mother and disciple is underscored by the preface to Jesus' subsequent expression of thirst: "After this Jesus, knowing that all was now finished. . . ." (Jn 19:28)

Jesus Thirsts (Jn 19:28)

Just as Jesus' words to his mother and disciple are often interpreted symbolically, commentators have likewise interpreted Jesus' cry of thirst as expressing his desire to confer the Spirit upon believers, as he foretold in his farewell speech (cf. Jn 14-17). This is confirmed by John's portrayal of Jesus' death as an act of literally handing over his spirit (cf. Jn 19:30), and his description of the blood (representing life) and water (representing the Spirit, as in baptism; cf. Jn 3) that flow from Jesus' side when it is pierced after his death (cf. Jn 19:34), an event related only by John.

"It Is Finished" (Jn 19:30)

In accordance with his portrayal of Jesus as in complete control of the events surrounding his passion and death (cf. Jn 10:17-18), John reports Jesus' final words as an acknowledgment of the completion of his mission. Jesus had given permission for everything else to happen (e.g., he tells Judas to leave at the Last Supper, he lets Peter stumble though he sees it coming, and he informs Pilate that he [Pilate] was given his power from above), and now he permits himself to die. John's departure from the other Gospels' precedent of presenting a psalm verse as Jesus' dying words illustrates the importance he ascribes to Jesus' control and fidelity to his mission.

THE BURIAL OF JESUS

Each gospel identifies Joseph of Arimathea as the disciple who requested Jesus' body from Pilate. John adds that Nicodemus

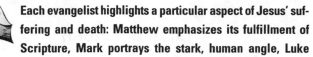
assisted in the Jewish burial process. Both fear the Jewish leaders, thereby anticipating the fear of the apostles on the evening after the resurrection before encountering Jesus (cf. Jn 20:19).

John alone notes that in the crucifixion area there was a garden (as in Gethsemane, recalling the garden of Eden) that contained the unused tomb where Jesus was laid.

Just as they accompanied Jesus in his ministry (in contrast to the exclusively male discipleship typical of rabbis at that time) and on the way of the cross, so the women followed Joseph and observed the tomb and how Jesus' body was laid.

Matthew alone relates a story (cf. Mt 27:62-66) of how the religious leaders had requested a tomb guard from Pilate, only to be told to take care of the matter themselves.

The stage is set for events that no one could have anticipated, despite forewarnings.

Chapter Fifteen

How to Contemplate the Resurrection Narratives

Contents of this Chapter

- Learn the geography of the resurrection appearances.
- Encounter the multiple endings in Mark, and his "Longer Ending's" synthesis of the other Gospels' accounts.
- Discover the differences in the evangelists' resurrection accounts.
- Consider the significance of the various "Marys."

The analyses and reflections of the last chapter were a bit rigorous because of the intense nature of the events and the material. Our analysis and comparisons of the resurrection accounts will be less taxing due to their shorter length, more distinct nature, and fewer Old Testament references. It is only fitting that the passionate nature of our activity in the last chapter should yield to the peaceful contemplation of the resurrection.

JESUS' RESURRECTION: MYSTERY OF FAITH

The resurrection of Jesus is a mystery of faith and of history. It is the culmination of Jesus' incarnation, ministry, passion, and death. By considering all four Gospel accounts, we will encounter the fullness of the ancient Christian witness, beginning with Mark. But first, let's situate ourselves by considering the locations discussed within the resurrection narratives.

THE GEOGRAPHY OF THE RESURRECTION APPEARANCES

In Matthew and Mark, Jesus appears to the disciples in Galilee, as he had predicted (cf. Mt 26:32; Mk 14:28). Jn 21 also contains a resurrection appearance in Galilee. In Luke 24 and Jn 20, Jesus' appearances occur in and around Jerusalem, which is where Jesus heads at a critical point in Luke's Gospel (cf. Lk 9:51), and is the location of much of Jesus' ministry in John.

— THE BIBLE SAYS WHAT? —

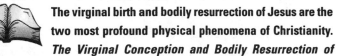 **The virginal birth and bodily resurrection of Jesus are the two most profound physical phenomena of Christianity.** *The Virginal Conception and Bodily Resurrection of Jesus* **by Raymond E. Brown, S.S., is accessible in length and presentation, and is a classic on the subject.**

MARK'S INITIAL ENDING (MK 16:1-8)

The most striking aspect of Mark's resurrection narrative is that there are several endings. Most likely, Mark's Gospel originally ended at Mk 16:8.

Mk 16:1-8 relates the visit of Mary Magdalene (the constant among the Gospel resurrection accounts) and companions to anoint Jesus' body. While wondering who will roll back the tombstone, they encounter a young man in a white robe who announces that Jesus has risen, and advises them to tell Peter and the disciples to meet Jesus in Galilee. They were afraid. End of story. Understandably, Mark's community wanted more; enter Mk 16:9-20.

MARK'S LONGER ENDING (MK 16:9-20)

Mk 16:9-20 received the title of the "Longer Ending" in comparison to the shorter endings (discussed below) found in less important manuscripts. It probably dates from the late first century, and its style differs from the rest of Mark. Because of its antiquity and acceptance by the early Church, it is considered to be inspired and therefore is included in the canon.

A credible explanation of the Longer Ending's composition is that to correct for the sparse and abrupt original ending of Mark, the early Church constructed a composite account from passages in the existing Gospel accounts:

- Mk 16:9-11 seems influenced by Lk 24:10-11 and Jn 20:11-18.
- Mk 16:12-14 seems influenced by Lk 24:13-49 and Jn 20:19-23.
- Mk 16:15-16 parallels Mt 28:18-20.
- Mk 16:17-18 may have been influenced by Jesus' words in Lk 10:19 and Paul's encounter with a snake in Acts 28:3-6.
- Mk 16:19-20 seems influenced by Lk 24:50-53 and Acts 1:3-9.

MARK'S SHORTER ENDING

"And all that had been commanded them they told briefly to those around Peter. And afterward Jesus himself sent out through them, from east to west, the sacred and imperishable proclamation of eternal salvation."

This concludes Mk 16:8 in an old Latin manuscript and comes between Mk 16:8 and Mk 16:9-20 in four late (seventh to ninth century) manuscripts. It is usually contained in Bible footnotes, and is not considered canonical.

THE FREER LOGION

This ending, two paragraphs in length, was found after Mk 16:14 in a fourth- or fifth-century manuscript now preserved in the Freer Gallery of Art in Washington, D.C. Though not canonical, it is nonetheless inspiring, and can be found in the footnotes of most study Bibles.

In my judgment, one of the Bible's most sublime testimonies to the role of women in the ministry of Jesus and the Church is the Gospel of John's portrayal of the women at the cross, two named Mary (Miriam) and two identified only as his mother (i.e., Mary) and his mother's sister.

Though the Greek is unclear as to whether three or four women are present, it is unlikely that Jesus' mother and her sister would have the same first name, thus making the Mary, the wife of Clopas and Jesus' mother's sister two separate persons. The female disciples at the cross outnumbered the males three or four to one, perhaps foreshadowing the more prevalent presence of women in the Church at a pastoral level.

In all four Gospels, Mary Magdalene is among the first to encounter the empty tomb. In John, she is the first to encounter Jesus. People often presume Mary to be a woman of ill repute, perhaps based on Lk 7:36-50, though that woman is unnamed. We know only that she had seven demons cast out of her (cf. Lk 8:2), and that she was a disciple.

Though he obviously knew all the women present, it was only to his mother and the beloved disciple that Jesus spoke. Acts 1:14 mentions Mary, but not Mary Magdalene, present with the disciples in the room where they were staying.

All four women are worthy of contemplation and emulation. Two represent the anonymous dimension of discipleship, those persons (particularly women) whose service escapes the notice of most, but not God. Another represents maternal love and the fourth deep friendship.

How feminine and frequently re-enacted is this passage! A mother's sister, friend, and her son's closest female friend accompany her to the most dreaded event imaginable: the premature and tragic death of her son. How worthy of admiration are the Marys, and indeed all of the women disciples in the Gospels!

MATTHEW'S RESURRECTION NARRATIVE (MT 28)

Matthew alone records both a cosmic earthquake at the death of Jesus and a peculiar event that links Jesus' death to his resurrection. Tombs are opened and the bodies of holy persons are raised. After the resurrection, they leave their tombs and appear to some in Jerusalem (cf. Mt 27:51-54).

The Fathers of the Church interpreted this in light of Rev 21:2, 10; 22:19, in which Jerusalem is a metaphor for heaven. The more literal sense is that of Ez 37, Dan 12:2, and Is 26:19, which prophesied the raising of the dead, the first fruits of which occur at Jesus' death. Matthew also relates a story that circulated among the Jews as an explanation of Jesus' empty tomb (cf. Mt 28:11-15).

Matthew concludes with the great commission to make disciples, baptize them in the name of the Father, Son, and Holy Spirit (the first complete articulation of the Trinity in the Bible), and remember Jesus' presence within the Church (Matthew's fundamental theme).

PEAK PASSAGES

1 Cor 15:3-9 is the earliest account of Jesus' resurrection appearances. It contains the only New Testament reference to Jesus' appearances to five hundred believers, and to James.

LUKE'S RESURRECTION NARRATIVE (LK 24)

Women play a significant role in all of the resurrection narratives, but particularly in Luke and John. In Luke, they report the empty tomb and Jesus' resurrection to the apostles, who deem it nonsense. Peter runs to the tomb (a detail also recorded by John), his guilt over his denials no doubt contributing to his anxiety.

Lk 24:13-35, often referred to as "the road to Emmaus," brings together several of Luke's key themes. An incognito Jesus listens to two disciples summarize the events of recent days, then interprets the events in light of the Old Testament. Only in the breaking of the bread did they recognize Jesus, at which point he disappeared. Luke shows the unity of the breaking open of the Scriptures and of the bread (the Eucharist), thus providing a model for Christian spirituality and worship.

Why does Jesus disappear here, and in Jn 20:17 tell Mary Magdalene not to touch him? Based on his response to Thomas and the lack of a recorded post-resurrection appearance to his mother, I believe Jesus wants believers to walk by faith rather than by sight (cf. 2 Cor 5:7; Jn 20:29), and to avoid clinging to physical realities.

JESUS' ASCENSION

Matthew does not record the Ascension, though Mark does (cf. Mk 16:19) and Luke does twice (cf. Lk 24:51; Acts 1:9-11). Jesus' ascension into heaven rekindled memories of Elijah's ascension (cf. 2 Kings 2:11).

Jesus' final address to his disciples in Lk 24:44-49 resembles his dialogue with the two men on the way to Emmaus. He opens their minds to the Scriptures and recalls his public ministry in which he showed himself to be the fulfillment of the law, the prophets, and the Psalms (a term used within the Bible to signify the Writings, the least-defined part of the Hebrew Bible at the time of Jesus).

Jesus' command that the apostles stay in Jerusalem and await the gift promised by the Father (the Holy Spirit; cf. Lk 24:49) serves as a transition to Acts of the Apostles. Jerusalem is the site of Acts' early chapters, and the Holy Spirit is the central character.

Luke's Gospel ends with Jesus blessing the apostles and their companions prior to his ascension. They respond by worshiping Jesus joyfully and praising God in the Jerusalem temple.

JOHN'S RESURRECTION NARRATIVE

There are five scenes in John's resurrection narrative, sandwiched around two summations:

- The empty tomb and appearance to Mary Magdalene (20:1-18).
- Appearance to the disciples (20:19-23).
- Appearance to the disciples and Thomas (20:24-29).
- First summation: the meaning of these signs (20:30-31).
- Jesus with the disciples by the sea (21:1-14).
- Jesus with Peter and the beloved disciple (21:15-23).
- Appendix summation: authentication of the Gospel's testimony (21:24-25).

Unique aspects of John's narrative include Mary Magdalene's brief encounter with the empty tomb prior to summoning Peter and the beloved disciple, and the latter's entry into the tomb and immediate belief.

Jesus' exclamation ("Mary!") and Mary's reply ("Teacher!") in Jn 20:16 symbolizes his personal relationship with believers. Jesus almost seems to be teasing Mary by not revealing himself immediately.

A main theme of Jesus' farewell discourse in Jn 14-17 was the peace that he would give. This continues in Jn 20:24-29, Jesus' *shalom* being mentioned thrice. The other Gospels record some doubt among the apostles (cf. Mt 28:17; Mk 16:14; Lk 24:11), while John identifies it with Thomas.

Jn 20:30-31 sums up the purpose of the Gospel: to convince the listener that Jesus is the Christ, God's son, so that they may have life in his name. These verses and Jn 21:25 affirm that Jesus did many more things than reported, the only place in the Gospels this is noted.

JOHN'S APPENDIX

Jn 21 is centered around Peter's and the beloved disciple's relationship to Jesus. The tension between Peter and the beloved disciple with which the Gospels conclude is a fitting segue to a chapter on St. Paul, an adventurous theologian like the beloved disciple who also experienced tension with Peter (cf. Gal 2:11-14).

Chapter Sixteen

—— How to Read and Experience —— the Letters of St. Paul

Contents of this Chapter

- Recognize the profound, influential, and provocative nature of Paul's personality and letters.
- Learn about Paul the person.
- Recognize the many hardships, obstacles, and disappointments endured by Paul.
- Recognize that Pauline authorship of six of his letters is disputed.
- Survey the context, main themes, highlights, and contemporary applications of Paul's letters.

ST. PAUL'S CHALLENGING LETTERS

St. Paul is perhaps the most influential and controversial theologian in history. His writings have altered the course of religious and secular history. His teachings have been at the center of two of history's most painful schisms: that between Jews and Christians in the first century, and the Protestant Reformation. More denominational disputes occur over St. Paul's letters than all other biblical books combined.

Such controversy extends back to New Testament times. Speaking in reference to Paul's letters, 2 Pet 3:16 observes: "There are some things in them hard to understand, which the ignorant and unstable twist to their own destruction, as they do the other scriptures."

Like most geniuses, Paul was a complex person who recognized the paradoxes and inconsistencies of life. Consequently, his writings and actions were not always straightforward, and could even seem inconsistent. His thought evolved over time and in accordance with the community he addressed.

Neither his letters nor the commentaries on his letters by the Church Fathers contain a systematic presentation of his thought. Biblical scholars who summarize Paul's thought do so with numerous qualifications and nuances, as Paul's letters are filled with his own clarifications. Since he did not present his thought in a systematic fashion, it is difficult to present a synthesis of his theology.

Both theologically and exegetically (from the standpoint of biblical criticism/interpretation), Paul is a challenge to scholars as well as beginners. His letters must be taken as a whole and interpreted within the context of the other New Testament books.

If you would like to sample Paul's letters, some of the most influential passages are Rom 5-8; 1 Cor 1:10-2:16; 7; 9; 11-13; 15; 2 Cor 5; Gal 1:11-3:14; 5; Eph 1:3-14; 5:1-6:18; Phil 2:1-11; 3:1-4:1, 11-13; Col 1:15-29; 3:1-4:5; 1 Thess 4:13-5:11; 1 Tim 2:1-4:5; 2 Tim 2:8-13.

THE POIGNANCY OF PAUL

St. Paul's writings are filled with pithy expressions that capture the essence of profound Christian truths. My favorite is: "If for this life only we have hoped in Christ, we are of all men most to be pitied" (1 Cor 15:19). This poignantly expresses the sober yet hopeful testimony of the New Testament and Christian experience.

I particularly find St. Paul helpful during pivotal points in my life. I suspect this is partly due to his volatile personality and well-documented character flaws. Like Peter and the rest of the apostles, he is everyman, and can relate to common human difficulties.

St. Paul's writings are like an assortment of chocolates or wines. Everyone has their own favorite selections, which at particular times really hit the spot.

The Gospels are the core of my Bible-reading diet, supplemented by the Psalms, and I make sure I get a steady diet of the other New Testament letters and classic passages in the Old Testament, but on special occasions, for example, when I need spiritual encouragement or a gentle kick in the pants, I know just the man to turn to.

Like a close friend or loved one, there are times St. Paul frustrates or confuses you to no end, and there are other times that you feel so close and grateful to him that you want to give him a cheer or a hug.

THE BIBLE SAYS WHAT?

 From an exegetical/analytical standpoint, reading St. Paul's letters is simpler than reading the Gospels in that we don't have to consider the various sources underlying his letters. While some of his letters may be a composite of several letters (e.g., Philippians and 2 Corinthians), they do not contain the multiple layers of tradition that are part of the Gospels and many of the Old Testament books.

ABOUT ST. PAUL

We'll begin our exploration by learning about St. Paul's life and world. We'll then consider the style and purpose of his letters, and the communities and individuals to whom he wrote. This will provide a foundation for experiencing Paul's letters as addressed to us.

Paul was born in Tarsus, a major city in Cilicia, on the southeastern coast of Asia Minor (present-day Turkey), and was educated as a Pharisee by a prominent rabbi named Gamaliel I (cf. Acts 22:3; 23:6; 26:4-5; Phil 3:5). Paul thus received extensive exposure to the Old Testament, Jewish tradition, and Greek culture.

Paul started out as a zealous persecutor of Christians. He first appears in the Bible in Acts 7:58-8:1, where he approves of the stoning of St. Stephen (the first Christian martyr, and a leader of the Christian community in Jerusalem).

Paul's initial encounter with the risen Jesus occurred on the road to Damascus, sometime around A.D. 34-36 (cf. Acts 9:1-9). Though the popular image associated with this event is of Paul being thrown off his horse, the Bible says only that a light from the sky flashed around Paul and he fell to the ground. Cardinal Carlo Martini, S.J.'s *The Testimony of St. Paul* is an insightful and accessible discussion of this event and Paul's life and teachings.

Paul received much of his information about Jesus from his advocate Barnabas (cf. Acts 9:27), the larger and older communities (Jerusalem, Damascus, Antioch) he visited, and from his fifteen-day visit with Peter in Jerusalem (cf. Gal 1:18). Oh, to eavesdrop on that conversation . . . a good subject for imaginative reflection.

In the chronology below, there is a large gap between Paul's conversion and his assimilation as a missionary. He was not accepted by the Christian communities overnight. He had plenty of time to process information about Jesus and formulate his unique way of understanding and presenting it. Likewise, most of us have a considerable gestation period before we give birth/expression to our faith in a mature manner.

Scholars consider Paul's undisputed letters (see below) as the most reliable source for information on his life, followed by Acts of the Apostles, and then his disputed letters. The timing and details of Paul's missionary journeys as reported in Acts and Paul's

PAUL'S CHRONOLOGY	
Event	*Year (A.D.)*
Birth	ca. 5-10
Conversion to Christianity	ca. 34-36
First Post-Conversion Visit to Jerusalem	ca. 37-39
In Tarsus and other areas of Cilicia	40-44
In Antioch	44-45
First missionary journey (from Antioch to Cyprus, Southern Asia Minor, and back)	46-49
Council of Jerusalem	ca. 49-50
Second missionary journey (from Antioch through Southern Asia Minor, to Northern Galatia, Macedonia, and Corinth, then back to Jerusalem and Antioch)	50-52
Third missionary journey (from Antioch through N. Galatia to Ephesus, possible imprisonment)	54-58
Return from Prison (through Macedonia toward Corinth and back to Jerusalem)	57-58
Arrested in Jerusalem and imprisoned in Caesarea	58-60
Shipped to Rome	60-61
Imprisoned in Rome	61-63
Martyred in Rome under Nero	64-66

letters do not always agree, presumably because Luke is more concerned with the message about Jesus and the needs of his community than he was about historical precision. This is not to deny the historical basis of the events told in Acts, but to view them in their theological and pastoral context.

PAUL'S PROFESSION

Paul worked as a tentmaker (cf. Acts 18:3). Given his travels, he probably had difficulty maintaining his clientele. He worked day and night (cf. 1 Thess 2:9; 1 Cor 15:10; 2 Cor 11:27) so as not to be a burden to his communities (cf. 1 Cor 9:14-15; 2 Cor 11:9). His letters acknowledge his acceptance of money for his individual needs only from one of his favorite communities, the Philippians (cf. Phil 4:10-20).

Paul should be viewed not only as a Christian leader and brilliant theologian, but also as a homespun preacher. Because of his profession, it is likely that he did much of his evangelizing in small numbers, perhaps while he was working. It is inconceivable that he would keep his faith distinct from his work. As a maker of tents and related leather goods, he dialogued with common folks who gave him a sense of grassroots faith and issues. We can continue this dialogue with Paul.

PAUL'S BAGGAGE

Paul went through life with heavy baggage. He never completely shook off his reputation as a former persecutor of Christianity and as a participant in the stoning of Stephen (cf. Acts 7:58; 8:1). He discussed his trials and pains frequently, and suffered an undisclosed "thorn in the flesh" (cf. 2 Cor 12:7-10). Like Peter (cf. Jn 21:18; 1 Pet 1:6-7; 2:19-21), Paul recognized the redemptive value of innocent suffering (cf. Rom 5:3-5; Phil 3:10-11; Col 1:24).

APPRECIATING THE APOSTLE TO THE GENTILES

Following Peter's lead (cf. Acts 10-11), Paul was largely responsible for opening up the Church to the Gentiles. Because of this and his pre-conversion persecution of the Church, he ran afoul of conservative Jewish Christians from Jerusalem. Paul fashioned himself "the Apostle to the Gentiles" (cf. Rom 11:13; 1 Tim 2:7), and referred to Peter as the one entrusted with presenting the Gospel to the circumcised (cf. Gal 2:8).

In 2 Cor 11-12, Paul contrasts himself with the "super-apostles" who favored style over substance and who criticized him for his unimpressive physical and public speaking presence (cf. 2 Cor 10:10; 11:6). This passage sheds light on Paul's many trials and reveals that he was not above sticking up for himself. Paul was not a motivational speaker with slick phrases, compelling gestures, and glittering promises, but neither was he a mumbling milquetoast. Among the biblical authors, only Jeremiah matches Paul in autobiographical details and emotional expression.

HUMANIZING ST. PAUL

Like many gifted persons, Paul could be difficult to get along with. He had a very painful breakup (cf. Acts 15:36-39) with Barnabas over the role of John Mark in what would be Paul's second missionary journey (cf. Acts 15:40-18:22). Paul's later comments hint of remorse over his inability to reach a compromise with these two key figures of the early Church (cf. 1 Cor 9:6; Col 4:10). Perhaps this is why he was understanding of marital difficulties and allowed separation in extreme circumstances (cf. 1 Cor 7:10-16). Who is Barnabas in my life? Someone who has been an advocate for me but with whom I have had a falling out due to difficult circumstances?

Whether Paul was a widower or never married, there was undoubtedly an area of loneliness in his life. Passionate people who have to live without sexual intimacy and companionship often come to a great appreciation of it, thus Paul's profound sentiments and counsel on love and marriage (cf. 1 Cor 7; 13; Eph 5:21-33).

WRESTLING WITH THE WORD

Who are the Pauls (authentic prophets) and the super-apostles (false prophets) in today's world? Whom do I listen to and imitate?

THE WRITING OF PAUL'S LETTERS

Not being a scribe himself, Paul wrote his letters with the help of a secretary. One of his secretaries, Tertius, extends his greetings in the first person in Rom 16:22. 1 Cor 16:21, Gal 6:11, 2 Thess 3:17, Phlm 19, and Col 4:18 contain Paul's comments that he himself is writing.

Since Paul made tents and preached during the day — and because of the physical demands of transcription a scribe could only write for two or three hours at a spell — Paul's letters were probably composed and transcribed in the evening. His Greek is fluent and eloquent, though occasionally grammatically incorrect. His prodigious writings and ministry are a testimony to what you can achieve with limited resources when your purpose is aligned with God's will.

LETTERS THAT PAUL MAY NOT HAVE WRITTEN

Differences in vocabulary, style, and theology among Paul's letters lead scholars to propose that some of the letters may have been written by his disciples up to thirty years after his death. 1 Thessalonians, Galatians, Philippians, 1 and 2 Corinthians, Romans, and Philemon are undisputed Pauline letters. Paul's authorship of 1 and 2 Timothy and Titus is most disputed, followed by Ephesians, then Colossians and 2 Thessalonians. The disputed letters are also referred to as *deuteroPauline*, meaning the second grouping of Paul's writings.

Excluding Rome, the undisputed Pauline letters were addressed to communities founded by Paul. He didn't found the community at Colossae or Ephesus, but was very active preaching and writing in Ephesus.

Epistles 1 and 2 Timothy and Titus contain more sayings and teachings passed down within the Christian tradition than the undisputed letters do. Also, the disputed letters are more traditional and patriarchal in their attitude toward women and their role in the family and society.

Because a dynamic prophet like Paul would change over time as well as receive input from others, it is possible, although unlikely, that Paul wrote all the letters attributed to him. For this and literary purposes, I will often refer to the author of the disputed letters as Paul. Few laypersons reading the disputed letters would detect traces of non-Pauline authorship unless informed of such.

THE PURPOSE AND CONTEXT OF PAUL'S LETTERS

As indicated in 1 Thess 5:27 and Col 4:16, Paul's letters were designed for oral proclamation in a public-worship context. The practice of reading Paul's letters in public worship alongside the Old Testament books undoubtedly contributed to their becoming inspired Scripture. Try reading Paul's letters aloud and listening as if you were at church in ancient Asia Minor.

Paul's letters were written to address specific theological and pastoral issues and to keep in touch with the Christian communities. They contain both universal and community-specific teachings. They reflect his and his communities' evolving faith, identity, and circumstances. For example, his earliest letter, 1 Thessalonians, lacks the breadth and depth of later letters.

THE STRUCTURE OF PAUL'S LETTERS

Paul's letters follow the structure of ancient religious letters. They begin with a greeting and follow with a thanksgiving/blessing (Galatians has no thanksgiving because Paul was upset with them). Then comes the body of the letter, followed by an exhortation (a brief moral pep talk) and conclusion/farewell. Paul's letters integrate various types of information:

- Personal perspectives and received revelations on the message and person of Jesus.
- Theological and moral doctrines.
- Explanations and applications of the links between the Old Testament and Jesus.
- Hymns (cf. Phil 2:6-11) and teachings handed down within the Christian community.
- Pastoral counsel.
- Autobiographical details and disclosures of his self-understanding as an apostle.

PAUL AND THE HISTORICAL JESUS

Paul's focus is the crucified and risen Jesus. His stock phrase was "we proclaim Christ crucified" (cf. 1 Cor 1:23). Paul was insistent about his personal knowledge of the risen Jesus (cf. 1 Cor 9:1; Gal 1:11-16), but he probably never met Jesus in the flesh. Accordingly, of the few references he makes to the life of Jesus, most concern his death and resurrection:

- Jesus was born of a woman under the law (Gal 4:4).
- Jesus was betrayed (1 Cor 11:23).
- Jesus commanded that his followers partake of his body and blood under the form of bread and wine through a commemorative meal, which has become known as the Eucharist (1 Cor 11:23).
- Jesus was crucified (Gal 2:20; 3:1; Phil 2:5; 1 Cor 2:2, 8), died (1 Cor 15:3), was buried (1 Cor 15:4), was raised from the dead (1 Cor 15:5), and ascended to heaven (Eph 4:9).
- Jesus acquitted himself well in his testimony before Pontius Pilate (1 Tim 6:13).

WHAT DOES IT MEAN?

Paul's favorite expression for Jesus is "Lord," a title meaning God. With the exception of Acts 24:24, only Paul among the New Testament writers refers to Jesus as Christ Jesus.

Paul's unique expression for the Church is "the body of Christ" (cf. 1 Cor 12:27; Col 1:24; Eph 4:12). Absent from his early letters (1 Thessalonians, Galatians, Philippians), it appears first and most prominently in 1 Cor 10-12, in which he addresses the divisiveness within the Corinthian community.

PAUL'S AFFIRMATION OF JESUS' TEACHINGS

Paul's letters indicate familiarity with Jesus' teachings:

- **Rom 12:44/Mt 5:44:** Prayerful, loving disposition toward enemies.
- **Rom 13:8-10/Mt 22:39-40:** Love of neighbor fulfills the law.
- **Rom 14:14/Mk 7:15:** Nothing external to people can defile them.
- **Rom 16:9/Mt 10:16:** Be wise as serpents and innocent as doves.

- **1 Cor 7:10-11/Mt 19:6.** Divorce and remarriage is not part of God's original plan and direct will.
- **1 Cor 10:27/Lk 10:8:** Eat what is put before you when you are a guest in another's home. Paul included in this admonition meat offered to idols, unless it offended the conscience of others.
- **1 Thess 5:2/Mt 24:42-43:** The Lord will return like a thief in the night.

"It is more blessed to give than to receive" (Acts 20:35) is a saying of Jesus that was recalled by Paul, but does not appear in the Gospels.

CATEGORIZING PAUL'S LETTERS

Paul's letters can be divided into four groups, dated approximately as follows:

- **Early Letters:** 1 and 2 Thessalonians (A.D. 51-52: presuming Pauline authorship of 2 Thessalonians);
- **The Great Letters:** Galatians, Philippians, 1 and 2 Corinthians, Romans (A.D. 54-58);
- **Captivity Letters:** Philemon, Colossians, Ephesians (A.D. 61-63); Philemon and Colossians may have been written from Ephesus in the mid fifties. If Ephesians was written by Paul, it probably occurred during his imprisonment in Rome.
- **The Pastoral Letters:** 1 and 2 Timothy, Titus (A.D. 64-67) if by Paul or his secretary/close disciple(s).

READING PAUL'S LETTERS

Paul's letters are arranged first according to whether the audience is a community or an individual, and within that, by length. Thus Paul's longest letter to a community, Romans, appears first, and his shortest letter to an individual, Philemon, appears last. A simple and acceptable approach is to read them in the order they appear in the Bible.

If Paul is new or confusing to you, consider reading his letters in the order they were written, beginning with his undisputed letters. With the exception of 2 Thessalonians, I discuss the undisputed letters first, beginning with the oldest letters.

1 AND 2 THESSALONIANS

1 and 2 Thessalonians are a good place to start because of their brevity and simplicity. They give you a sense that Paul's writings are letters first, and sources of doctrine and counsel second. They substituted for his physical presence. Because he was a gifted writer as well as a theologian, his letters could be read in the assembly and manifest his presence.

1 Thessalonians is the oldest New Testament document. It was written around 50-51, probably from Corinth and a few months after Paul's visit to Thessalonica. Thessalonica was a commercial city in Macedonia, Greece, whose Christian community was composed of both Gentiles and Jews. 1 Thessalonians addresses the community's expectation that Jesus would be returning to earth soon (cf. 4:13-5:11). Paul's oldest ethical instructions are found in 1 Thess 4:1-12.

2 Thessalonians was written around A.D. 51-52 if by Paul, and by the late first century if written by a disciple. Like 1 Thessalonians, it addresses Jesus' return (cf. 2 Thess 2:1-12) and provides ethical instructions (cf. 2 Thess 3:6-15), including such cautions against idleness as "If any one will not work, let him not eat" (cf. 2 Thess 3:10).

GALATIANS

The letter to the Galatians was probably written from Ephesus around A.D. 54-55 to churches in the province of Galatia in Asia Minor. Paul bluntly expresses his disappointment in the Galatians, who despite Paul's teachings let themselves be influenced by Jewish Christians who wanted to impose the Mosaic law on Gentile converts to Christianity.

Galatians' primary themes are Christian liberty, life in the Spirit, and justification by faith rather than by works (observance) of the law. Paul expands and refines this discussion in Romans. Galatians contains a classic passage that contrasts the works of the flesh with the fruits of the Spirit (cf. Gal 5:19-23).

PHILIPPIANS

Philippi was a thriving Roman colony (cf. Acts 16:12) in northeastern Greece. Paul helped form its Christian community during his second missionary journey around A.D. 50. Philippians was written circa A.D. 56 if from Ephesus, or A.D. 61-63 if from prison in Rome.

As Paul indicates in Phil 4, the Philippians were very supportive of him; thus, his letter is warm and personal. Read this letter and Philemon (below) as if it were from a dear spiritual friend.

In Phil 1:12-26, Paul reflects on his imprisonment and attitude toward death. In Phil 2:1-11, Paul encourages his community to imitate Christ's *kenosis* (emptying/giving of himself) as portrayed in an early Christian hymn.

PHILEMON

Philemon was written around A.D. 55 if from Ephesus, or A.D. 61-63 if from prison in Rome. It is addressed to a prominent Christian, Philemon, and two other persons, perhaps his wife and son, along with local Christians who gathered at Philemon's house.

This shortest and most informal of Paul's letters contains Paul's plea on behalf of Onesimus, a slave owned by Philemon. Details are sketchy, indicating that they may have previously corresponded.

After having been evangelized by Paul, the runaway slave Onesimus is seeking to return to Philemon. Paul offers to reimburse Philemon for any losses incurred, and exhorts him not only to forgive Onesimus' offense, but to free and receive him as he would Paul. Such intermingling of religious values and social mores, and Paul's relationship to both master and slave, makes for an awkward situation, thus necessitating Paul's diplomatic approach.

This letter testifies that biblical principles can be applied sensitively to awkward social and economic circumstances. Applications of the Bible should not be suspended because of social norms or personal or communal inconvenience.

1 AND 2 CORINTHIANS

1 Corinthians was written between A.D. 56 and 57 from Ephesus; 2 Corinthians was written in mid to late A.D. 57 from Macedonia. Corinth was a Greek cosmopolitan seaport known for its revelry and polytheistic shrines and practices. Because of the temptations faced by the Christian community there, Paul corresponded with them frequently. Given its variations in tone and topics, 2 Corinthians may be a composite of up to five letters.

Because he founded and related frequently to the community at Corinth, Paul's letters to them are personal and pastoral. Conversely, because Paul did not found the community at Rome, his letter to them has a more formal and theological tone.

In 1 Corinthians, Paul's pastoral concerns are conveyed cohesively and in refined theological teachings, while 2 Corinthians is more personal and raw/reactive, in part owing to Paul's unpleasant visit to Corinth (cf. 2 Cor 2:1-11), which precipitated the letter.

Because they address timeless issues (e.g., sex, money, family relationships, diversity sensitivity, competition) with compelling theological, pastoral, and personal perspectives, the Corinthian letters are probably the most relevant of Paul's writings. Following are highlights of 1 Corinthians:

- Paul's passionate statement of the folly of the cross (1 Cor 1:17b-31).
- Practical advice on factions within the community (1 Cor 1:10-17a; 3-4), disputes (1 Cor 6:1-11), sexual matters (1 Cor 5; 6:12-7:40), and the appropriateness of eating food sacrificed to idols (1 Cor 8; 10).
- The earliest biblical account of the commemoration of the Last Supper (1 Cor 11:23-26).
- Reflections on the Christian community as the body of Christ (1 Cor 12; 14).
- Paul's beloved hymn of love (1 Cor 13).
- Paul's most extensive disclosures on the resurrection and the afterlife (1 Cor 15).

2 Corinthians is the most frank, revealing, and personal of Paul's letters. It speaks graphically of his sufferings, revelations he has experienced personally and secondhand (cf. 2 Cor 12:1-7a), and his understanding of his apostolic vocation (cf. 2 Cor 3:1-7:16; 10-11).

2 Cor 8-9 presents a practical model for charitable giving, highlighted by the memorable saying "for God loves a cheerful giver" (2 Cor 9:7).

ROMANS

The most inspiring, studied, and influential of Paul's letters, Romans is a theological treatise packaged in a letter. While in Corinth in the winter of A.D. 57-58, Paul wrote to the Romans, a community he had not previously visited, though he had friends there. He intended to bring money from other Christian communities to the Jerusalem community, and to visit Rome on his way to Spain (cf. Rom 15:24-28).

Because Paul could anticipate resistance in Jerusalem and, in fact, was arrested there, it may be that he viewed a letter to the large and influential community at Rome as his last opportunity to offer extended reflections on the Gospel. Alternatively, he may have been refining his thoughts in preparation for his encounter with the Jerusalem church.

Following are major themes of Romans:

- Both Jews and Gentiles have sinned and need redemption (1:16-3:26).
- Believers are justified by faith in Jesus rather than through the works of the law (3:27-4:25).
- The mystery of redemption (Ch. 5).
- Moral responsibilities in response to God's grace (Ch. 6).
- The nature and dominion of the law (Ch. 7).
- Life in the Spirit (Ch. 8).
- The Jewish people in God's plan (Ch. 9-11).
- Counsel on Christian living (Ch. 12-13).
- Being sensitive and respectful toward persons immature in their faith (Ch. 14:1-15:13).
- Paul's long good-bye. (15:14-16:27).

Read Romans slowly and meditatively, consulting a commentary or a study Bible when necessary. Don't attempt to get through the whole letter at once. Because of its progression of thought, reading it in order provides context and flow.

COLOSSIANS

Colossae was a small, once prominent city located in Asia Minor. Several possibilities for its dating exist. If written by Paul from Rome, it could date from the early to mid sixties. If written by Paul while he was in Ephesus, it would have been composed between A.D. 54 and 56. If written by a disciple of Paul, it would date from the eighties. A slight majority of scholars deny its Pauline authorship.

Col 1:15-20 contains a beautiful hymn to Christ, followed by a personal exhortation to the Colossians (cf. Col 1:21-23), and Paul's oft-quoted linkage of personal suffering to Jesus' suffering and the Church's redemption (cf. Col 1:24). Col 3:1-4:6 is a beautiful exhortation to personal and familial holiness that is expanded upon in Eph 5:21-6:4.

Colossians bears considerable resemblance to Ephesians and the undisputed Pauline letters in theology, vocabulary, and style. Though not as profound theologically as Ephesians, it is very readable, eloquent, and inspirational, and of considerable pastoral and personal value.

EPHESIANS

Ephesus was a thriving Christian community located in western Asia Minor about 110 miles west of Colossae. Its dating is uncertain. If by Paul, it would be in the early to mid sixties. If by a disciple, it could be as late as the nineties. This late dating is a reflection of its profound and innovative linkage of such central topics as the risen Jesus, the Church, and marriage.

Ephesians lacks the intricate argumentation of Romans, yet is almost as profound. Because it is much easier to read than Romans and only slightly more difficult than Colossians, it has become a grassroots favorite. It is less susceptible to misinterpretation and polemics than Romans and Galatians.

Ephesians' long sentences and thought patterns, and its integration of Paul's thought, are two reasons its Pauline authorship is questioned. Paul tended to write in shorter bursts and phrases, and he was not prone to synthesize his thought.

The unknown author of Ephesians has rightly been called the disciple of Paul par excellence. In some respects (e.g., Eph 5:21-33), Ephesians may be a case of the student surpassing the teacher. Following are the key themes and passages in Ephesians:

- 1:3-14 is a lofty hymn announcing the blessings bestowed by Jesus.
- 1:15-23; 3:13-21 are beautiful prayers.
- 2:1-3:12 is a summation of Pauline themes and personal revelations.

- 4:1-24 is a moral pep talk that integrates numerous Pauline themes. It is more theologically oriented than pastoral/practical.
- 4:25-5:20 shows how 4:1-24 can be put into practice.
- 5:21-6:4 is Christianity's most succinct and ideal presentation of domestic life.
- 6:10-20 offers eloquent and comprehensive spiritual counsel on how to battle evil.

If you want a practical, concise, and articulate portrayal of Paul's thought in a pastoral setting, you can't do better than Ephesians.

THE PASTORAL LETTERS

Timothy lived in Lystra in Asia Minor, and was presumably a convert during Paul's mission there around A.D. 46. He joined Paul on his next trip, around A.D. 50, and also accompanied him on Paul's second missionary journey in A.D. 50-52. He is mentioned frequently and endearingly in Paul's letters; 1 and 2 Timothy and Titus received their designation as "pastoral" in the eighteenth century. This recognized their focus on established communities whose founders or leaders had left or died. Paul's other letters focused on new or growing communities. 1 Timothy and Titus discuss the proper functioning of the local Church, whose leaders have come to be known as pastors.

The Pastoral Letters are similar in style and focus. If written by Paul, they would have been composed in the mid sixties, shortly before his death. If not written by Paul, they probably date

---

PEAK PASSAGES

The following are influential and representative Pastoral Letters selections that can get you started: 1 Tim 2; 3:16; 4:4-9; 2 Tim 2:11-13; 4:6-8.

to the late first or (less likely) early second century; 1 Timothy is first in the canon not because it was written before 2 Timothy, but because it is longer. Neither letter indicates knowledge of the other.

When you read the pastoral letters, look for these highlights:

- Cautions against false teachers and corrections of false teachings (1 Tim 1:3-11; 4:1-5; 6:3-10; 2 Tim 2:14-3:9; Titus 1:10-16).
- Instructions on Church order, leadership, and worship (1 Tim 2:1-3:16; Titus 1:5-9).
- Instructions on social justice and relations (1 Tim 5:1-6:2; Titus 2:1-3:11).
- Instructions to and encouragement of Timothy (1 Tim 1:12-20; 4:6-5:2; 6:11-21a; 2 Tim 1:6-18; 3:10-4:18).

The pastoral letters are of greatest relevance to persons in leadership roles in the Christian community. Because they seek to preserve the purity of their communities and leaders, they are written from a conservative standpoint. Their practical and communal focus is representative of Paul and constitutes a fitting way to end our survey of his letters.

Chapter Seventeen

—————— How to Read and Persevere ——————
With the Letter to the Hebrews

— Contents of this Chapter —

- Appreciate the unique and elegant motivational classic, the Letter to the Hebrews.
- Survey the style, main themes, and highlights of the Letter to the Hebrews.
- Discover similarities between Hebrews, Matthew, and John.
- Consider applications of Hebrews' message to our lives.

You have made your way through several long chapters, so it's time for a short one. Conveniently, conciseness fits the intense and intricate letter that we are about to explore. Better to let the Letter to the Hebrews speak for itself, once we have gotten our contextual and thematic bearings.

The Letter to the Hebrews is an inspiring letter that is one of the finest literary works in the Bible. It is organized carefully and makes persuasive use of logic and emotion. I speak of persevering with the letter both because it is challenging and it exhorts us to persevere in following Jesus (cf. Heb 10:36-39; 12:1-13).

The authorship of Hebrews has always been a mystery. The Church's first great biblical scholar, Origen (ca. 185-254), observed that only God knows who wrote Hebrews. It has traditionally been attributed to St. Paul because it refers to "our brother Timothy" in Heb 13:23, but its style, vocabulary, and perspectives are sufficiently unlike Paul's letters that scholars almost universally believe that he did not write it.

Hebrews was most likely written in the eighties, though a dating in the sixties is possible. The book is attributed "to the Hebrews" because it addresses the relationship of Jesus and the new covenant he established at the Eucharist and on the cross to the Hebrew covenant.

HIGHLIGHTS OF HEBREWS

- 1:4-2:18 uses the Psalms to demonstrate Jesus' superiority to the angels.
- 3:1-4:13 uses the Psalms and Pentateuch to show how Jesus surpasses Moses like a son exceeds a servant, and invites us to learn from the disobedience of the Israelites.
- 4:14-7:28 reveals that Jesus' intercessory role makes the Old Testament priesthood obsolete.
- 8:1-10:18 demonstrates the superiority of Jesus' sacrifice and ministry to that exercised in the Old Testament.
- 10:19-39 is an exhortation to take refuge in Jesus' high priesthood and to persevere amid the suffering that accompanies discipleship.
- 11:1-40 portrays Old Testament men of faith as inspirational models and forerunners of Jesus. In accommodating this passage to modern sensibilities, we could rightly add names of women of faith.
- 12:1-13 exhorts us to keep focused on Jesus and his sufferings as we experience God's paternal discipline.
- 12:14-29 exhorts us to recognize Jesus' superceding of Old Testament revelations and respond appropriately to the call and grace of God.
- 13:1-19 exhorts us to observe the moral essentials of Christian life (love, hospitality, compassion, chastity, obedience, perseverance, and avoidance of greed and strange

teachings) in light of the themes of this letter (e.g., the high priesthood of Jesus and the inspirational example of holy persons, beginning with the Old Testament heroes and heroines).

PEAK PASSAGES

Following are texts that I have found accessible and enlightening: Heb 1:1-4; 2:1-3a, 10-18; 4:12-16; 5:7-10; 6:4-6, 10; 7:23-25; 8:8-12 (the New Testament's longest citation of an Old Testament passage, Jer 31:31-34); 10:16-17 (another citation of Jer 31:33-34); 10:32-39; 11:1-3, 6, 39-40; 12:1-3, 7-14; 13:1-8.

HEBREWS' SIMILARITIES TO MATTHEW AND JOHN

Hebrews is a motivational classic and a wonderful companion to the Gospel of Matthew. Both show how the Old Testament priesthood, sacrifices for the atonement of sins, and ritual and moral prescriptions are fulfilled and surpassed by Jesus. Both quote the Old Testament extensively and use rabbinical reasoning and rhetorical techniques to exhort believers to live moral lives inspired by a personal relationship with Jesus, the new Moses.

Hebrews also brings to mind the Gospel of John. Both feature a cosmic prologue, inspirational sayings, subtle references to the Old Testament, extended allocutions, and an emphasis on the majesty of Jesus.

Reading Hebrews with Matthew and John in mind will keep you busy awhile. Hebrews also forms a natural bridge between the letters of Paul and the other New Testament letters. We'll encounter the latter in the next chapter.

Chapter Eighteen

How to Read and Apply the Catholic Epistles

Contents of this Chapter

- Consider the composition, context, and focus of the Catholic Epistles.
- Recognize the diversity among the Catholic Epistles.
- Explore key themes and highlights of the individual books.
- Discover that these overlooked books are rich in practical directives, grassroots spirituality, and motivational exhortations.

The Catholic (i.e., universal) Epistles is the traditional name for the New Testament letters not attributed to St. Paul and not addressed to a specific community or an otherwise known individual (2 and 3 John are addressed respectively to an "elect lady and her children" and an individual named Gaius). These include James, 1 and 2 Peter, 1, 2, and 3 John, and Jude. The letter to the Hebrews was not included among these because traditionally it was associated, however tenuously, with St. Paul. Protestants often refer to these as the General Letters. Because of their similarities to John's Gospel, we discussed 1, 2, and 3 John in the same chapter (thirteen).

We know much less about the background of the letters discussed in this chapter than we do of the Gospels and the letters of Paul. Though they are tucked away in the back of the New Testament, the Catholic epistles fulfill an important niche in the New Testament and life. They provide inspiring and practical insights into Christian morality and spirituality. In this chapter, you'll discover the main themes and highlights of these books, and how they relate to contemporary challenges.

THE LETTER OF JAMES

The best place to begin our exploration of the Catholic epistles is with the practical and straightforward letter of James. James is the Dutch uncle and grassroots sage (wisdom teacher) of the New Testament. He integrates common sense, morality, and Gospel values.

Illustrating the synchronicity of faith and works, James corrects those who would use St. Paul's doctrine of justification by faith (as elaborated in his letters to the Galatians and Romans) to justify moral laxness (cf. Jas 2:14-26). James and the Sermon on the Mount (with which it shares numerous teachings) are the closest New Testament parallels to Old Testament wisdom literature and modern self-help literature.

The letter does not give more than the name of its author. Several persons named James are mentioned in the New Testament. The letter was written too late (sometime in the eighties or nineties) to be composed by either the Apostle James "the Greater" (son of Zebedee, brother of John) who was beheaded under Herod Agrippa (cf. Acts 12:2) in the early forties, or the Apostle James, son of Alphaeus, who is known (and depicted in religious art) as "the Lesser" because of that description in Mk 15:40, though most translations render it as "the younger."

The most likely candidate for authorship is James the (step/half) brother or cousin of the Lord (cf. Mk 6:3; Mt 13:55), to whom Jesus appeared (cf. 1 Cor 15:7), and who met with and is identified as an apostle by Paul (cf. Gal 1:19).

Though he is not mentioned as following Jesus during his public ministry, James the "brother" of the Lord became a prominent figure in the Jerusalem Church (cf. Acts 12:17; 15:13-21; 21:18). For credibility purposes, the author of Jude refers to him in identifying himself.

According to the Jewish historian Josephus, James the brother of the Lord was stoned as a martyr in the early sixties under the high priest Ananus II (son of Annas, who interrogated Jesus in Jn 18:19-24). While if true this would predate the writing of the epistle by two decades, it is possible the work could be pseudonymous, like Paul's disputed letters. As with works of art attributed to the great masters but completed by their pupils, so the early Church felt no compunction about attributing works to their inspiration or source, who may not have been the actual composer or supervising editor.

HIGHLIGHTS OF JAMES

James can be read in one sitting or contemplated deeply in several. Each section outlined below contains inspiring pointers:

- How to view trials (1:2-4).
- Petitioning confidently for wisdom (1:5-8).
- Perspectives on poverty and riches (1:9-11).
- The origins and purpose of temptations/tests (1:12-16).
- All good originates in God (1:17-18).
- Avoid rashness, anger, and all forms of excessive, sordid behavior (1:19-21).
- Hearers of the word must practice it (1:22-25; cf. Mt 7:21).
- Sins of the tongue are incompatible with true religion (1:26).
- True religion is purity and reaching out to those who are vulnerable and suffering (1:27).
- Avoid favoritism toward the rich (2:1-7).
- Sounding like Paul's letter to the Romans, James reminds us that failure in one aspect of the law is enough to render us incapable of judging others (2:8-13).

- Faith without works is dead (2:14-26).
- Harnessing the tongue (3:1-12).
- Contrasts between earthly and spiritual wisdom (3:13-18).
- The origins of sinfulness are the flesh, the world, and the devil. The remedy is humility, purity, and taking refuge in God (4:1-10).
- Prohibition of gossip, slander, calumny (name-calling), and judgment of others (4:11-12).
- Take life day by day with the attitude "if the Lord wills" (4:13-16).
- The classic definition of sin: "Whoever knows what is right to do and fails to do it, for him it is sin" (Jas 4:17).
- Warning to the rich who cheat and oppress the poor (5:1-6).
- In anticipation of Jesus' return, we should exercise Job-like perseverance (5:7-11).
- Avoid oaths (5:12; cf. Mt 5:33-37).
- Recommends appropriate attitudes and responses for when you are suffering, cheerful, or sick. The source of the sacrament of the anointing of the sick (5:13-15).
- Exhortation to mutual confession and prayer (5:16-18).
- Positive consequences of bringing back those who wander from the faith (5:19-20).

James' practical instructions and frequent denunciation of verbal violence (sins of the tongue) echoes the Hebrew wisdom tradition (see Job, Proverbs, Sirach, and the wisdom Psalms).

1 PETER

The best way to read 1 Peter is with the apostle in mind. The main theme in 1 Peter is suffering. Some form of the word suffer or suffering(s) appears in Greek sixteen times (2:19, 20, 21, 23; 3:14, 17, 18; 4:1 [twice], 4:13, 15, 16, 19; 5:1, 9, 10), and is implied at least three other times (3:17 [twice]; 4:16).

As pointed out in our discussion of Peter's denials in Chapters Twelve and Thirteen, suffering and caring for the brethren was a major aspect of the apostle's ministry. If you wish to reflect on the role of suffering in discipleship and your life, 1 Peter is a great source, and the texts referenced above are highlights.

DID PETER WRITE 1 PETER?

Whether Peter wrote 1 Peter is a matter of scholarly debate, but its emphasis on perseverance amid suffering seems to reflect his influence. If Peter wrote it, he did so between A.D. 60 and 63; if not, it was probably written between A.D. 70 and 90. If Peter didn't write it, it must have been either by a disciple or someone very familiar with both Peter's and Jesus' life and teachings.

Peter's authorship of 1 Peter is questioned because of the letter's superb Greek, eloquent style and vocabulary, and its frequent quotation of the Septuagint (the Greek Old Testament). Such literary and biblical competence would normally not have been the province of a Galilean fisherman, but such are not normally tutored by the Word of God (cf. Jn 1:1) either. Further, 1 Pet 5:12 alludes to a secretary, Silvanus, so the author had help.

2 PETER

2 Peter is probably the last New Testament book to be written. Its concern with false prophets and the second coming of Christ indicate a composition date in the early second century. Because the letter of Jude addresses these issues (cf. 2 Pet 3:3/Jude 18) and likewise contains language about the judgment of angels (cf. 2 Pet 2:4/Jude 6), it is possible that 2 Peter may have drawn from Jude. 2 Pet 2 may be influenced by Heb 2:1-3; 6:4-8; 10:26-30 as well.

2 Peter is considerably shorter than 1 Peter, and lacks its breadth of pastoral counsel and skillful interweaving of a primary theme (suffering). Like 1 Peter (cf. 1 Pet 2:13-17/Rom 13:1-8;

1 Pet 3:1-2, 7/Eph 5:22-33), it exhibits similarities with Paul's letters (cf. 2 Pet 3:8-10/1 Thess 5:2; 1 Tim 2:4; cf. 2 Pet 3:15-16).

2 Pet 1:17-18 offers a link to Peter through a recollection of Jesus' transfiguration, which only Peter, James, and John witnessed. The letter also contains an earthy and blunt Old Testament-influenced characterization of wavering false prophets that sounds as if it could come from the impetuous fisherman (Peter): "The dog turns back to his own vomit, and the sow is washed only to wallow in the mire" (2 Pet 2:22; cf. Prov 26:11).

HIGHLIGHTS OF 1 AND 2 PETER

Along with the passages referenced above, 1 Pet 1:3-9, 13-25; 2:9-10, 13-17; 3:1-12; and 2 Pet 1:3-8, 20-21; 2:20-22 are accessible and prominent passages in 1 and 2 Peter.

THE LETTER OF JUDE

Jude is the most obscure book in the New Testament. Its place and date of composition are ambiguous. It claims to be written by Jude, the brother of James. If this is a reference to Mk 6:3 or Mt 13:55, it would make him Jesus' relative. Such kinship would have provided the credibility necessary to address Church issues in an authoritative way.

Like the other late letters, Jude is concerned with false teachers, sexual promiscuity, and the community's disappointment over Jesus' delay in returning. The earliest New Testament letter, 1 Thessalonians, dealt with problems related to the second coming of Jesus, but mentioned little about false teachings. The latter became a sore spot with Paul, as evidenced by his diatribe in 2 Cor 10-12 and 2 Thess 2. Paul warns that the devil may appear as an angel of light (cf. 2 Cor 11:14). The Sermon on the Mount ends with a similar warning against false prophets (cf. Mt 7:15-23).

Jude makes reference to Old Testament persons and images in the context of Last Judgment themes, as well as an apocryphal (excluded from the Bible) work, the Assumption of Moses (cf. Jude 9). The latter contains a warning against slander, the practice of which has been rationalized and absorbed into the moral and legal fabric of modern western societies.

Jude is not a book for children, nor for persons starting out with the Bible. Its imagery is harsh and it presumes familiarity with the Old Testament and apocryphal works. However, it also includes standard New Testament counsel: Watch out for false teachers and Judgment Day, cling to your faith and the merciful love of God, pray in the Holy Spirit, and be responsive to the weak in faith (cf. Jude 20-21).

Jude is valuable for its depiction of late first-century Christianity and its jarring imagery connected with the Last Judgment. If Jude spoke gently and politely to chronically sinning, hard-hearted persons (like us), how likely would they/we pay attention?

2 Peter's and Jude's obscurity and foreboding tone is a fitting segue into the last and most cryptic book of the New Testament, Revelation. Since these deal with the end of the world, we will also discuss basic precepts of biblical teaching on the topic.

Chapter Nineteen

How to Read and Understand ─── the Book of Revelation: Where Do We Go From Here?

┌─ **Contents of this Chapter** ──────────────────

- Learn the context and purpose of the book of Revelation.
- Recognize the purpose of apocalyptic literature.
- Survey the symbolism, main themes, and highlights of Revelation.
- Discover the true relevance of Revelation to today.
- Consider the development, nuances, and practical import of the Bible's teachings about the end of the world.

└───

In this chapter, we will survey the book of Revelation and point out its most accessible passages and how to interpret them both contextually and personally (how they apply to us, today). We'll encounter the Bible's teachings on the end of the world and the criteria for entrance into the next world.

Biblical passages on the end-times and the Last Judgment have both straightforward (the moral dimension, the criteria of judgment) and mysterious (the descriptive aspect, how and when these events will occur) dimensions. We will touch on both of these, with an emphasis on the former, on which the Bible is much clearer.

REVELATIONS ON REVELATION

The book of Revelation received its name from the book's title in the Latin Vulgate. The Latin word "*revelare*" means to reveal or uncover what had been hidden. The other name by which the book is identified, "Apocalypse," comes from the first word of the Greek text, "*apokalypsis,*" in Rev 1:1, and has a similar meaning. The revelation/unveiling concerns "what must take place soon."

There are good reasons why Revelation is placed last in the New Testament. It uses vivid, cosmic imagery and numerical symbolism to describe the future in light of the past and present. This is not something that a beginner to Christianity or the Bible would immediately understand.

Contrast this to the first book of the New Testament, the Gospel of Matthew, which is written in an orderly sequence of seven sections and contains mostly straightforward moral instructions, miracle stories, and parables.

Revelation was only accepted into the Bible after much debate. The book deals with the accountability of individuals and churches and presumes familiarity with Christian morality. Revelation addresses the struggle between good and evil, the persecution of the Church, and the reward of the just, and makes frequent reference to the book of Genesis, particularly the serpent and the tree of life. As such, it functions as a consummation of the Old and New Testament.

In light of the above, it makes sense to read Revelation after you have become familiar with the rest of the New Testament and the most important parts of the Old Testament (e.g., Genesis, Exodus, the Psalms, and the major prophets), Catholic hermeneutics (i.e., principles and methods for interpreting the Bible, as introduced in this book), and Revelation's historical context.

According to an Early Church Father, Irenaeus (ear-in-ay'-us), Revelation was written to Christians who were suffering persecution under the emperor Domitian, who ruled from A.D. 81-96. Most scholars believe the book was written around A.D. 95.

REVELATION'S SYMBOLISM

The symbols used in Revelation are cryptic references to the early Church's perilous situation. For example, Babylon refers to Rome, and "the beast" (which is associated with the number "666"; cf. Rev 13:18) refers to Neron Caesar (Nero), the first emperor to persecute the Christians. "666" equals the numeric value of the Aramaic letters which form Nero's name.

To avoid further recriminations, the author disguises his language so that the message is comprehensible only to Christians. Paradoxically, when the symbolism is deciphered with respect to historical rather than future contexts, the message applies to Christians of any era, as fidelity to the Gospel inevitably brings opposition and even persecution. Focus on its meaning for the biblical audience, yourself, and the Church, rather than on how it applies to others or the world at large.

A study Bible or commentary by a Catholic scholar can help you decipher Revelation's symbols and their historical context. Avoid a fundamentalist commentary that neglects the latter and suggests fanciful correlations to modern persons and events that do not correspond to the book's original purpose. An excellent resource for beginners is George T. Montague, S.M.'s *The Apocalypse and the Third Millennium: Today's Guide to the Book of Revelation*.

Examples of apocalyptic literature in the Bible besides Revelation include Daniel, parts of Zechariah and Ezekiel, and the sections of Matthew, Mark, and Luke immediately preceding the Last Supper. There are numerous apocryphal (outside the Bible) apocalyptic books, but these are mainly of interest to biblical scholars, historians, or curious readers.

HIGHLIGHTS OF REVELATION FOR BEGINNERS

The best way to approach Revelation as a beginner is to concentrate on the least cryptic and most accessible passages:

- **Rev 2-3:** Messages to seven churches in Asia Minor.
- **Rev 7:9-17:** A vision of the reward reserved for martyrs and those who endure persecution.
- **Rev 12-13:** The magnificent and timeless image of the individual believer and the Church under siege in a sinful society.

This passage dramatizes the daily conflict between the forces of good and evil. In the Bible and in other ancient Near Eastern religious literature, issues on earth, in Revelation's case, religious persecution, are interpreted in light of heavenly parallels, such as the battle between the angels and the devils described in Rev 12-13.

For example, the chaotic, promiscuous, and violent nature of the Canaanite and Mesopotamian gods were a reflection of their disordered societies. Conversely, the more serene Egyptian gods reflected the well-ordered Egyptian society, a civilization that lasted longer than any other in history. You must also factor in the more predictable weather patterns in Egypt, particularly the annual flooding of the Nile, in contrast with the turbulent climate in Mesopotamia and to a lesser extent, Canaan.

- **Rev 17:** A condemnation of Rome, and by analogy, immoral cultures of all times.
- **Rev 20-22:** A dramatic image of the end-times and the fulfillment of God's plan.

INTERPRETING REVELATION IN A COMMUNAL SETTING

As apocalyptic literature, Revelation naturally evokes allegorical and mystical meanings such as discussed in Chapter Eight. Because these levels of meaning are more subject to misinterpretation than the literal/historical or applied/homiletic levels, I suggest that you conduct your exploration of Revelation in the context of a Bible study or with the aid of a spiritual guide or commentary.

A community context is particularly appropriate for interpreting Revelation. Images of the community of believers under siege and eventually rewarded in heaven abound in the book, and seven Christian communities/churches are affirmed and reproved in Rev 2-3.

Revelation's cryptic symbolism was comprehensible to members of the Christian community, but gibberish to outsiders. The common believer got their Bible knowledge and clues (decoding information) primarily through clergy preaching, family and catechetical teachings, and discussions at community gatherings.

Not only Catholics, but most Orthodox and mainline Protestants accept the approach to Revelation discussed above, and do not interpret the book primarily in a futuristic sense. They focus on the rich moral and spiritual meaning of the book, and do not indulge in subjective associations of the symbolism with contemporary entities. They do not speculate on the timing or location (Armageddon; cf. Rev 16:16) of the end of the world or the current identity of the beast (cf. Rev 13:11-18).

THE LEGACY OF REVELATION

Probably the most poignant application of Revelation is for people who are undergoing acute suffering. The whole book is concerned with two primary issues:

First, Christians will not be abandoned by God, despite present persecutions. This recalls similar messages addressed to the Jews in the books of Esther, Judith, and Maccabees. Second, amid suffering, Christians must not abandon their faith. Revelation is a heavenly pep talk that reassures us that our suffering is not beyond God's providence and our ability to endure it (cf. 1 Cor 10:13), and that God will richly reward us in heaven for persevering.

Revelation reminds us that the war between good and evil continues throughout history, and at times seems to reach a terrifying level. Jesus and the martyrs who have followed in his footsteps are a source of inspiration and hope.

We may not be to the point of shedding blood (cf. Heb 12:4), but we are, nonetheless, suffering for our faith (cf. Jn 16:33), and can take comfort in the consolations offered in Scripture, of which the most mysterious and dynamic are found in Revelation.

It is significant that the New Testament book that is concerned with suffering from beginning to end (of both the book and human history) would be selected by the early Church to conclude the Bible, the book of suffering.

Having peered through Revelation's window into the end-times, we will now define and distinguish the latter's key concepts and doctrines.

THE RESURRECTION OF THE BODY

The Jewish understanding of death and the afterlife evolves in the Bible. Initially, the dead lived only through the memories of their descendants. Later, the dead were understood to inhabit the shadowy netherworld known as *Sheol*. Eventually, belief in the resurrection of the body developed.

One of the earliest biblical references to the resurrection of the dead can be found in Is 26:19: "Your dead shall live, their corpses shall rise. O dwellers in the dust, awake and sing for joy! For your dew is a radiant dew, and the earth will give birth to those long dead" (New Revised Standard Version).

By Jesus' time, the concept of the resurrection of the body was accepted by most observant Jews. The main exception was the Sadducees, the elitist temple priests, whose acceptance of only the first five books of the Old Testament (the Torah/Pentateuch) as Scripture, which do not refer to the afterlife, naturally led them to reject this concept. The Gospels narrate their conflict with Jesus over this teaching (cf. Mt 22:23-33; Mk 12:18-27; Lk 20:27-40).

Although Jesus often conflicted with the Pharisees, his spirituality had many parallels with theirs, including belief in the resurrection of the body. Paul's most specific discussion of the afterlife, and in particular the resurrection of the body, is 1 Cor 15:35-54.

THE IMMORTALITY OF THE SOUL

The concept of the immortality of the soul reflects the Greek philosophical distinction between body and soul. The Bible makes no such distinction: the immortality of the soul is linked to the resurrection of the body. The Bible views humans as whole persons.

Several references to immortality are made in the Wisdom of Solomon. This reflects the more biblical notion of eternal life in God's presence rather than the philosophical notion of the Greeks. The most common New Testament expression to denote the afterlife is eternal life. It is particularly prevalent in the Gospel and letters of John.

PERSONAL ACCOUNTABILITY

Personal accountability is a consistent teaching in both the Old and New Testament. God rewards us according to our actions: "For we must all appear before the judgment seat of Christ, so that each one may receive good or evil, according to what he has done in the body" (2 Cor 5:10).

Initially, the Hebrews viewed divine justice solely in terms of this world. God rewarded or punished both the individual and community in this life. However, as shown in later books such as Daniel and the Wisdom of Solomon, they gradually incorporated a more defined concept of the afterlife, including belief in the resurrection of the body. This paralleled their evolving belief in the concept of a spiritual adversary known as Satan.

One reason for the transition into a more defined concept of the afterlife was the growing recognition of individual responsibility highlighted by the prophets (cf. Ezek 18). In the earliest books and societies of the Bible, the individual's destiny was directly linked to his community's and ancestors' (cf. Ex 20:5-6; 34:7).

We encounter this tension between community accountability and individual destiny in Abraham's questioning of God about the fate of the righteous in Sodom in Gen 18:22-33. The Bible gradually recognizes that each person stands on his own before God. When belief in the afterlife grows to where questions of eternal destiny are evoked, the New Testament is clear that people and deeds are judged on an individual basis (cf. Mt 25:31-46).

PARTICULARITY AND SUBSIDIARITY

In his emphasis on "just one" person or good deed (cf. Mt 25:40), Jesus consummates this evolution. He proclaimed that the repentant rejects of society would enter heaven before the hard-hearted religious and social elite who took great pride in their community standing and illustrious ancestry (cf. Mt 21:31).

With Jesus, things are particularized. This contrasts with Moses, the man of big numbers, who hasn't the time or energy to immerse himself effectively in particularities. His father-in-law, Jethro, recognizes this, and invites him to invoke the principle of subsidiarity, whereby responsibility is delegated to those in closest proximity to the activity or situation (cf. Ex 18:13-27).

THE EVOLVING ESCHATOLOGY OF THE BIBLE

In summary, in the Old Testament there was a gradual evolution and clarification of beliefs in an afterlife, but still not to the point of a universally accepted doctrine. This continues in modern Judaism, which includes a diversity of perspectives.

Because of explicit New Testament teachings on the subject, Christian belief in the afterlife is more standardized and universal. However, as far back as the first Christian biblical scholar, Origen (A.D. 185-254), individual Christians (and today, persons of other faiths and belief systems) have questioned the existence of hell. This belief in universal salvation, designated by the Greek term *apokatastasis*, was deemed unorthodox by the Church at the synod of Constantinople in A.D. 543.

PEAK PASSAGES

A good place to sample the New Testament's teaching on individual responsibility is Mt 25. It presents three accountability parables, concluding with the famous Last Judgment parable found only in Matthew.

The latter brings together New Testament teaching on daily morality, Jesus' identification with vulnerable persons, the relationship between creation and salvation (cf. Mt 25:34), God's judgment of individuals, and the second coming of Jesus. It shows how the teaching and person of Jesus bears on all persons, even those who may not have heard of him.

DISTINGUISHING PERSONAL JUDGMENT FROM THE SECOND COMING

The Bible also distinguishes between each individual's judgment by God that occurs after death and the *parousia* (Jesus' return to earth and his universal judgment of the world). You can usually determine by the context and language whether Jesus is speaking of personal or universal judgment. A study Bible or commentary will offer guidance as well.

New Testament teaching on Jesus' return focuses on daily vigilance and moral preparedness. It highlights the relationship of morality to immortality, and the surprise nature of Jesus' return: he will come like a thief in the night (cf. Mt 24:43-44; Lk 12:39-40). Only the Father knows the day and the hour (cf. Mt 24:36; Acts 1:7). Christians who venture predictions of the end-times with startling precision apparently have information to which Jesus was not privy.

PEAK PASSAGES

"Moreover it is required of stewards that they be found trustworthy. But with me it is a very small thing that I should be judged by you or by any human court. I do not even judge myself. I am not aware of anything against myself, but I am not thereby acquitted. It is the Lord who judges me. Therefore do not pronounce judgment before the time, before the Lord comes, who will bring to light the things now hidden in darkness and will disclose the purposes of the heart. Then every man will receive his commendation from God" (1 Cor 4:2-5).

Like the New Testament, the Catholic Church focuses on preparation rather than speculation in regards to Jesus' return: live right and let God worry about the details. The just in the Last Judgment parable were so busy reaching out to the vulnerable that they failed to notice it was Jesus they were serving (cf. Mt 25:37-39).

THE EUCHARIST AND THE AFTERLIFE

The Eucharist is the context for the Gospels' most extensive and definitive discussions of the afterlife. The Eucharist is a foreshadowing of the Messianic banquet that will celebrate the kingdom of God inaugurated by Jesus' return. In regards to the Eucharist and the afterlife, the Gospels' focus is on what Jesus has done for us and how we should respond, rather than vice-versa.

Matthew, Mark, and Luke discuss personal judgment and the second coming immediately prior to preparations for the Last Supper. In Jn 14-17, Jesus' farewell speech that follows the Last Supper, Jesus begins with an allusion to the afterlife (cf. Jn 14:1-3), and then focuses on the trials his followers will experience. They will be able to endure these through his presence with them in the person of the Advocate (the Holy Spirit; cf. Mt 10:19-20; Jn 14:16, 26; 16:14).

Without describing the exact nature of heaven, the Bible offers a promise of the next life with ample guidance and models (the communion of saints; cf. Heb 11-12; 13:7-8; Rev 7:9-17) for getting there. What better way to end our exploration of the New Testament than with Jesus' greatest gifts to us: himself (as offered in the Eucharist), the promise of eternal life, the Church and the communion of saints, and the Holy Spirit? Let us now explore their roots in the Old Testament.

Section Three

—— How to Read the Old Testament ——

Chapter Twenty

—— The Context of the Old Testament ——

MAKING THE OLD TESTAMENT MANAGEABLE

The objective of this section of the book is to help you become comfortable with the Old Testament by becoming an informed and discerning reader. The Old Testament is too vast, ancient, and complex a body of literature to assimilate as a whole. The events span from the nineteenth to the second century B.C., and the formal writing process occurred from the tenth through the second century B.C.

Thus, we will take a selective approach that focuses on essentials, highlights, and accessible parts, especially those that illuminate the New Testament, modern life, and our personal experiences. This serves as a foundation for tackling the more difficult and obscure parts later.

When you break the Old Testament into manageable chunks, you discover that much of it is comprehensible and stimulating even to persons new to the Bible. The Old Testament is God's word, the context for the New Testament and the Bible for Jesus and his followers, and a deposit of great spiritual and human wisdom. The big picture it provides is necessary for a mature understanding of salvation history (God's redemptive initiative in human affairs) as revealed in the Bible.

From a literary and functional standpoint, much of the Old Testament has no parallel in the New Testament. For example, the New Testament does not contain a book of hymns/prayers such as the Psalms, nor does it contain books of practical wisdom such as Proverbs and Sirach (the letter of James comes the closest) or an account of creation.

This chapter introduces you to the geography, peoples, and politics of the Old Testament. The chapters that follow introduce you to the divisions and books of the Old Testament.

RECOGNIZING OUR HEBREW HERITAGE

As you read through the Old Testament, you will be struck by its pervasive influence in western civilization, beginning with the foundation of western morality, the Ten Commandments. Human equality and ecology are founded on principles of human dignity and stewardship narrated in the first two chapters of Genesis. The spirituality that helped fuel the abolition of slavery and the civil rights movement was greatly influenced by the book of Exodus. Our fundamental notions of sexuality and marriage are based largely on the creation accounts in Gen 1-2, and the derivative accounts in the New Testament (cf. Mk 10:2-12; Mt 19:3-9; Eph 5:21-33). Many well-known characters, stories, and expressions are found in the Old Testament: Adam and Eve, Cain and Abel, Noah's ark and the flood, the collapse of the walls of Jericho, Samson and Delilah, Hallelujah, holy Moses, the wisdom of Solomon, and the patience of Job.

NEAR EASTERN GEOGRAPHY

The ancient Near East is roughly equivalent to what is referred to today as the Middle East. It has the remarkable feature of balancing amazing change and a timeless quality. Shepherds, camel drivers, and Bedouins ply their trade alongside computer specialists and global traders. Seas, deserts, mountains, farmland, and cities form a diverse terrain.

Jews, Christians, and Muslims each view the land, particularly Jerusalem, as sacred. This fascinating cultural, topographical, and geographical mix is the epitome of the challenge of diversity. Both literally and figuratively, the Middle East has always been a hot spot.

"Fertile Crescent" is a modern term for the half moon area of fertile land extending from the Tigris and Euphrates rivers westward over Syria to the Mediterranean, and southward through Canaan and the northern part of Egypt beginning with the Nile Valley. It forms a land bridge between Africa, Asia, and Europe that has been utilized for religious, military, and commercial reasons since the beginning of civilization. For travel purposes, all other routes eventually lead to sand or sea.

Not only in the Bible, but throughout history, the Jewish people have been at the crossroads of civilization. Their outstanding ethical, cultural, and spiritual contributions are in a part a consequence of their being where the action is.

The name Mesopotamia comes from the Greek expression for "between the rivers," i.e., the Tigris and Euphrates (the Great River). It is a region rather than a country. For example, Assyria occupied northern Mesopotamia, and Babylonia the southern area.

The Transjordan is the area east of the Jordan river, currently in the Kingdom of Jordan. It is sometimes referred to in the Bible as "the other side of the Jordan" (cf. Deut 3:20; Josh 7:7).

The promised land is the biblical name for Canaan. It was later known as Palestine, the name given by the Roman Emperor

Hadrian, after suppressing the Bar Kochba (named after its leader, Simon) revolt in A.D. 135. It is derived from the name *Philistia*, the Mediterranean coast area first inhabited by the Philistines around the 12th century B.C.

THE POLITICS OF BIBLICAL GEOGRAPHY

The three main areas in the Old Testament are Mesopotamia, Canaan, and Egypt. In the New Testament, Asia Minor, the collection of states bordering the Mediterranean and Aegean Seas to the northwest of Canaan, come into play as the site of Paul's missionary journeys.

The dominant ancient Near Eastern powers during the biblical era were, chronologically, Egypt, Assyria, Babylon, Persia, Greece, and Rome. The reigning power had much to do with the development and layout of the territories. Israel wielded significant power only during the reigns of Kings David, Solomon, and Josiah, when the traditional powers were dormant, and even this was concentrated in Canaan and its borders.

The splitting of the monarchy after the death of King Solomon resulted in the tribes of Judah and Benjamin forming the southern kingdom and the remaining ten tribes composing the northern kingdom. The kingdoms were known by their largest and most influential tribes, Judah and Israel.

Political intrigues (infighting [including several assassinations] and international conflicts and uneasy alliances) and religious infidelity characterized both kingdoms while they lasted. The northern kingdom was more spread out and internally unstable, and was closer to the greatest military threat, Assyria.

The climate and agriculture of Egypt was relatively stable, largely due to the predictable spring flooding of the Nile. Accordingly, Egypt had a well-ordered society and economy, as well as a diverse pantheon of comparatively optimistic and serene gods.

In contrast, the peoples of Canaan and Mesopotamia were subject to violent and unpredictable weather swings. Their geographical terrain was remarkably diverse. Accordingly, their economies were subject to numerous variables, and given the diversity of peoples occupying the land, the political situation was generally unstable.

WHO'S WHO IN MESOPOTAMIA

The first known inhabitants of Mesopotamia were the Sumerians, a non-Semitic people who inhabited the southern section of Mesopotamia. The only reference to Sumer in the Bible is a disputed one, *Shinar*, which occurs four times in Gen 10-14. By the time of Abraham (ca. nineteenth century B.C.), the Sumerians had disappeared from the scene.

One of the most fascinating ancient Near Eastern topics is Sumer, the world's first civilization. Buried for centuries, it was rediscovered in the late nineteenth century. The seeds of many moral, cultural, and historical patterns in the Bible and western civilization are found in Sumerian documents and artifacts.

Following the Sumerians into prominence were a Semitic people, the Akkadians, who lived to the north of Sumer. Both Sumer and Akkad were located in what became Babylonia and is now Southern Iraq.

Following the Akkadians were the Babylonians in southern Mesopotamia and Assyria in northern Mesopotamia. Both became world powers during biblical times, and destroyed the southern (ca. 587-586 B.C.) and northern (ca. 722-721 B.C.) kingdoms respectively. Both biblical and secular history attests that the Assyrians were the cruelest conquerors in the ancient Near East. With this in mind, Jonah's dismay over his prophetic assignment to Nineveh (Assyria's capital) and over the latter's subsequent repentance is more understandable.

EMBRACING THE BIG PICTURE

Much of this book is devoted to helping you identify important nuances in the Bible and life. This chapter focused on the larger horizon, the historical context of the Old Testament, which helps put the minutiae in perspective.

It is helpful to periodically take a step back and reflect on the flow of both biblical and personal salvation history. Contemplate and perhaps journal on the key events, places, and circumstances in the Bible and your life, and note how God is active.

Gradually, biblical names, stories, and events will become familiar and evoke parallels in your life. The Bible then becomes not only history, but your story, and the promised land, your turf. Next stop, the beginning of the Bible, the Pentateuch.

Chapter Twenty-One

How to Read and Receive — the Pentateuch

Like the Jews (cf. Ex 19:1-9), we receive the Pentateuch as a divine gift. We are in familiar territory, but the vocabulary may be foreign. Let's begin by acquainting ourselves with relevant terms and groupings.

The first section of the Old Testament in Christian Bibles is known as the historical books. Within them, there is a sub-category known to Christians as the *Pentateuch* (Greek for "five scrolls.") With the exception of Gen 1-11, they cover the period in Hebrew history from Abraham to Moses.

Jews classify these books by themselves and refer to them in several ways: as the *Torah* (teaching/instruction, though usually translated as law), *Chumash* ("a fifth"), or the traditional biblical term "the book ("of the law" is sometimes added) of Moses." The

Torah is the most important part of the Hebrew Bible, and the Torah scroll is stored in a separate place within the synagogue.

The term Torah is also used in reference to Jewish law in general. Rabbinical tradition identifies 613 commandments in the first five books of the Bible. A frequent source of Jesus' conflicts with the Pharisees was their legalism in regards to these, at the expense of common sense and compassion.

THE DOCUMENTARY HYPOTHESIS

Until modern times, the traditional belief among Jews and Christians was that Moses wrote the Pentateuch. The first Jewish scholar to propose a credible alternative theory was Baruch Spinoza (1632-1677). He attributed the authorship of the Pentateuch to the scribe Ezra.

The first Roman Catholic scholar to scrutinize the Mosaic authorship of the Pentateuch was Father Richard Simon (1638-1712). The French Catholic physician Jean Astruc published a literary analysis of Genesis in 1753 that built upon the work of his predecessors and is regarded as formally initiating the scientific study of the Pentateuch.

German Protestant scholars of the nineteenth century developed the foundations of what Julius Wellhausen (1844-1918) would synthesize and promote as the "documentary hypothesis."

The documentary hypothesis proposes that there are four main literary sources woven together in the Pentateuch. These are commonly identified by their first letter: J (Yahwist, German spelling begins with "J"), E (Elohist), D (Deuteronomist), and P (Priestly).

Most likely, J (10th century) and E (9th-8th century) came from the southern (Judah) and northern (Israel) kingdoms respectively (the monarchy split in 930 B.C.).

D (8th-7th century) came from the southern kingdom, while P arose during the Babylonian exile (6th century).

It is postulated that survivors of the fall of the northern kingdom to Assyria in 722-721 B.C. handed down the E tradition until it became united with J around 700 B.C. This synthesis is referred to as JE.

Sometime after the exile (587-538 B.C.), D and P were integrated with JE. The priests and scribes responsible for P edited the various traditions until it reached its final form after 500 B.C. This final redaction (edited version) may be similar to what Ezra the priest-scribe read aloud in Neh 8:13-18 in the mid-fifth century B.C.

Scholarship on this subject continues to evolve. On the conservative side, respected scholars such as Umberto Cassuto have disputed the hypothesis and argued for a more ancient dating of the books. Others question the existence or prevalence of pre-exilic sources J and E, and instead focus on P and D. Recent scholarship ascribes a later, post-exilic date to much of the Pentateuch, thereby giving the P source a larger role in its composition and compilation.

The following chart summarizes the general characteristics of each source:

Source	Dating (B.C.)	Probable Location	Characteristics and Themes
Yahwist (J) from the German word Jahweh; story-teller with keen psychological insights.	10th cent.	Solomon's court or a scribe(s) in Judah, probably Jerusalem.	Uses the Tetragrammaton (YaHWeH); refers to God in human/anthropomorphic terms; refers to God's holy mountain as Sinai. Compelling characters and images include Adam and Eve, Cain and Abel, the sons of Noah, and the Tower of Babel. Emphasizes David's link to Abraham; Prominent in

Continued on page 264 ...

... continued from page 263

Source	Dating (B.C.)	Probable Location	Characteristics and Themes
			Gen 1-11. Promotes Jerusalem as center for Jewish worship; favors the southern kingdom.
Elohist (E) (Uses the name Elohim for God).	9th-8th cent.	Northern kingdom.	Substitutes Horeb for Sinai. Emphasizes Jacob and northern locations such as Bethel and Shechem and issues such as charismatic leadership, worship rituals, and idolatry. More difficult to identify separately than the other sources. Probable compositions include Gen 22:1-19; 40:1-23; Exod 20:1-26. Begins at Gen 15.
Deuteronomist (D) (historian and theologian).	8th-7th cent.	Southern kingdom.	Source for Deuteronomy through 2 Kings. Reassesses J & E in light of polytheistic influences and corruption in the divided monarchy. Identified with the "book of the law" that was found and promulgated under the reformer King Josiah ca. 622 B.C. (cf. 2 Kings 22:8). D explains to an exilic audience the source of Israel's suffering: their infidelity.
Priestly (P) (theologian).	During the Babylon exile (587-538).	Babylonian (priests who survived Jerusalem's destruction).	Injects hope based on God's irrevocable blessing and covenant. Stresses fidelity to the law, the cult of worship, and personal faith.

THE UTILITY OF THE DOCUMENTARY HYPOTHESIS

We have just started the Old Testament, and I'm already exposing you to a scholarly hypothesis that doesn't appear relevant to a simple reading of the text. The alternative is to ignore the complex historical and literary context of the Pentateuch, and be vulnerable to fundamentalist notions of its composition. The primacy of the literal sense of Scripture mandates that we expose ourselves to relevant contextual issues.

You are going to encounter the documentary hypothesis in even the most basic study Bible and commentary, so you might as well be exposed to it now.

— WHAT DOES IT MEAN? —

 The word tradition comes from the Latin noun, *traditio*, meaning a giving up or handing on. Catholics read the Bible with an eye to traditional interpretations that have gained acceptance in the Church. Within mainstream Protestantism, there has also been a rediscovery of the importance of patristic (the Church Fathers) sources.

The Pentateuch itself (and much of the Bible) is a collection of normative material handed down within the community of believers. In the Pentateuch, we distinguish these according to their hypothesized source.

As defined in the Second Vatican Council document *Dei Verbum*, there is no dichotomy between the Bible, Tradition, and the living Church. The Bible is the word of God handed on and interpreted within the context of Tradition and the guidance of the magisterium for the edification of the living Church.

GENESIS

In the Pentateuch, you can learn much about the book from its Hebrew name, which is also the first Hebrew word of the book. Genesis is known to Jews by its first word, *bereshith*, beginning. This aptly describes Genesis' objectives in narrating the origins of both human and Hebrew history.

UNIVERSAL ORIGINS

As Mass begins with music, so the Bible opens with a hymn (cf. Gen 1-2:4a). We immediately encounter the work of P, the Priestly author discussed above. P narrates the origins of creation from the divine viewpoint, with the recurring theme being God said/ordered, saw/observed, and sanctified/approved.

The storyteller, J (the Yahwist), then follows with the story of Adam and Eve (cf. Gen 2:4b-3:24). J offers a human perspective on the proceedings, narrating the simultaneously joyful and painful ethos of life while portraying God as a potter, matchmaker, father of the Bride, and disapproving but loving parent.

The best way to understand this story is to recognize the historical connotations of the symbols in the passage (e.g., the garden, the snake, the trees, the act of eating, nakedness) and then translate this into applications indicative of how the drama is continually re-enacted.

ACCOMMODATION

Many scholars and spiritual writers have pointed out the many applications to life and psychological insights contained in the Adam and Eve story. "Accommodation" is the technical term for moving from the primary, literal sense of Scripture to its applied, or adapted, sense, that is, to accommodate it to our situation.

As pointed out in the Pontifical Biblical Commission's 1993 document *The Interpretation of the Bible in the Church*, this was frequently practiced by the Church Fathers, but in a non-fundamentalist way. When done in a prayerful and humble manner, and with its basis in the literal sense, accommodation is a natural and efficacious way of interacting with the Bible.

Later books of the Bible accommodate parts of the previous books. The biblical writers did not feel that their quotations of previous books had to correspond in a rigidly literal manner. As discussed in Chapter Three and in a much debated and critical passage in *Dei Verbum*, Part II, section 8, divine revelation and human understanding (guided by the Holy Spirit) continue to evolve:

"For there is a growth in the understanding of the realities and the words which have been handed down. This happens through the contemplation and study made by believers, who treasure these things in their hearts (cf. Lk 2:19, 51) through a penetrating understanding of the spiritual realities which they experience, and through the preaching of those who have received through episcopal succession the sure gift of truth. For as the centuries succeed one another, the Church constantly moves forward toward the fullness of divine truth until the words of God reach their complete fulfillment in her.

"The words of the holy fathers witness to the presence of this living tradition, whose wealth is poured into the practice and life of the believing and praying Church."

GENESIS 1-11

Gen 1-11 is referred to as the primordial, or primeval, history. (Here's a memory aid: Prime means first and most of those folks were evil). The most universal section of the Bible, it exposes in dramatic fashion the roots of the tensions between the human condition and divine providence that give rise to so many of our "Why?" questions. It explains origins or causes from a theological and anthropological perspective. It is not intended to be literal history.

Gen 1-11 is framed in the language of mythology. This does not imply that the material is untrue or of a lesser degree of inspiration or value. Myths were an oral society's way of grappling with mystery and shedding light on the otherwise unexplainable.

Both Cardinal Ratzinger (in his book *In the Beginning: A Catholic Understanding of the Story of Creation and the Fall*) and Pope John Paul II have pointed out the importance of distinguishing the sources and literary forms in the Pentateuch. Speaking with reference to Gen 1-11, Pope John Paul observes "... In fact, the term "myth" does not designate a fabulous content, but merely an archaic way of expressing a deeper content" (Pope John Paul II, November 7, 1979).

WHY ARE THERE TWO CREATION STORIES?

Seeing things from multiple perspectives can be a sign of sophistication. Because people perceive things differently, there are multiple sides to most stories. The presence in the Bible of two versions of a single event is an indication that the story was popular and viewed as important.

Significant events (e.g., creation, the paschal mystery) are so mysterious, contextual, and multi-faceted that to convey the whole truth it is necessary to engage multiple viewpoints and explanations. As another example, the Pentateuch gives two explanations for Moses' inability to enter into the promised land (cf. Num 20; Deut 1).

WHAT'S IN A NAME?

In the Bible and antiquity, names were of great importance. Names gave identity to a person. Naming a person signified exerting power over them. Note how God maneuvers Moses' request for his name at the burning bush (cf. Ex 3:13-14).

A name change symbolized a change of destiny. Sarai and Abram have their names changed to Sarah and Abraham (cf. Gen 17:5, 15). Jacob becomes Israel, which means "El (God) fights." Israel the person and the nation wrestles with God.

Barbara K. Shuman, a lay leader in the reform movement of American Judaism, describes the spiritual dimensions of this dynamic from the perspective of Judaism in an article titled, "Agenda: Jewish Education," for JESNA (Jewish Education Source of North America):

Were you aware that, according to the Bible, the first male identity crisis occurred during creation, long before adolescence or mid-life?

The Hebrew word translated as "the man" or "the human person" in Gen 1-3 is *ha'adam*. "*Ha*" is the definite article ("the"). When *adam* is preceded by the definite article, it is a collective noun, that is, it speaks not only of an individual, but of the species.

Without the definite article preceding it, *adam* is a proper name. This usage does not occur until Gen 4:25, although the Hebrew text is ambiguous in verses such as Gen 2:20; 3:17; 21, where some translators feel the proper name "Adam" is indicated.

Adam is a play on the word *adamah*, which appears in the same verse and means "ground/soil/earth." Thus, man's name is derived from his origins.

The root of *adam* also forms the words for red and blood. A man working in the fields gets red from the sun, and to the Hebrews, blood represented life. In the Bible, a name reveals much about a person or place.

"In the story of Jacob wrestling with the angel, according to Rashi (Judaism's most authoritative commentator on the Bible), the Hebrew word for 'wrestle' (*avek*) may imply that Jacob was 'tied.' Rashi refers to the talmudic passage where the same word is used to describe fringes that are twined with loops, or knotted. His commentary continues, 'for thus is the manner of two (people) who struggle to overthrow each other, that one embraces (the other) and knots him with his arms.'

"To wrestle with God is to be tied to God; it suggests an intimacy. Through our struggle we are brought closer together. When we grapple with God we embrace the Holy One. We commit ourselves to a relationship in which we are eternally bound up together. We struggle — not to win — not to beat our opponent, and not to escape. We struggle to discover meaning, to

WHAT DOES IT MEAN?

 In the Old Testament, you will frequently see the word "LORD" in capital letters. This translates the *Tetragrammaton*, the four Hebrew letters "YHWH" that are more precisely rendered "Yahweh" than the inaccurate medieval form "Jehovah."

In instances such as Ps 86:3-5, when "Lord" is used in reference to God but is not presented in capital letters, it translates the Hebrew word *Adonai*, which means "(My) Lord." Ps 16:2 is a rare example of the two terms being used in the same verse:

> "I say to the LORD, 'Thou art my Lord; I have no good apart from thee.'"

Psalm 8:1 is a similar example of community praise:

> "O LORD, our Lord, how majestic is thy name in all the earth!"

The name of the chief Canaanite God, *Baal*, meant lord, master, or husband, and was also infrequently used in early Old Testament texts to refer to God. Such usage was avoided in later Old Testament books because of its pagan connotations:

> "And in that day, says the LORD, you will call me, 'My husband,' and no longer will you call me, 'My Baal'" (Hos 2:16). (To clarify this distinction, Hosea uses a different Hebrew word than Baal for "husband.")

Such use of marital imagery to indicate Israel's (and in Eph 5:21-33, the Church's) relationship with God reminds us that we should use God's name in a personal and endearing, as well as reverential, sense. Jesus exemplifies this in referring to his father as "Abba," an affectionate term akin to "Daddy." If we remember that our primary lover and father is God, we will be better able to endure the disappointments that we experience in corresponding human relationships.

Scholars are uncertain as to the *Tetragrammaton's* original pronunciation. Vowels were added to the Hebrew text in the eighth century A.D.

by the Masoretes (Jewish scribes) to aid pronunciation. In their honor, the Hebrew text is referred to as the Masoretic Text (MT).

The *Tetragrammaton* is God's name revealed particularly to the Hebrews, beginning with Moses at Mt. Sinai (cf. Ex 3:15). Other names for God, such as *El* or *Elohim*, were also used by Israel's polytheistic neighbors.

To this day, pious Jews do not write or speak the *Tetragrammaton*. Instead, they refer to God as *Adonai* ("[My] Lord") or *Hashem* ("the Name"). Muslims likewise display a reverential attitude toward God's name. Christians can surely learn from their Near Eastern siblings.

understand God's will, to fulfill the expectations of our Creator. We are tied to the One that challenges us to grow and who assists us in that struggle. In our wrestling we are not adversaries but partners; we wrestle not against God but with him.

"The spiritual journey into meaning is a journey we undertake with God. When we study, we continue the struggle. When we engage with the text we wrestle with God's words. Perhaps this is why learning is a lifelong obligation, for it fulfills our identity as *Israel* (one who struggles with God). When we wrestle with Torah, with teaching, we remain tied to God; as long as we continue to learn, we are blessed."

In the New Testament, Jesus renames Simon "Peter," which means rock. This reflects his new identity and destiny, and signifies Jesus' benevolent authority over him. Saul, an enemy of the early Church, is henceforth referred to as Paul after encountering Jesus on the road to Damascus.

The Joseph Cycle

Gen 37-50 is often referred to as the Joseph cycle. Though not matching the stories of Abraham and Jacob in biblical significance, it nonetheless captivates and adapts well to modern drama, as demonstrated by the various plays associated with Joseph, the most famous involving his "amazing Technicolor dream coat," and the tetralogy of Thomas Mann (four historical novels considered to be among the finest literary works of the twentieth century).

An interesting caveat of Jewish tradition is that Joseph is not referred to as a patriarch. Jewish tradition gives various explanations for this. He did not have a Hebrew wife, he was buried outside of the promised land, and most of his exploits were in Egypt.

Perhaps the simplest reason is that he is the ancestor of only one of the twelve tribes, whereas the three patriarchs (Abraham, Isaac, and Jacob) are the ancestors of all the tribes. Joseph cannot be defined because he is a transitional figure. He is a bridge between the patriarchal sagas in Mesopotamia and Canaan and the Mosaic saga in Egypt and the desert.

TWO JOSEPHS

Joseph and his New Testament namesake, the foster father of Jesus, are regarded as guardians in Jewish and Christian tradition. Joseph took care of his brothers and father, who symbolize Israel (the twelve tribes originate with Joseph and his brothers (cf. Gen 49:1-27), and Jacob was renamed Israel). The New Testament Joseph looked after Mary and Jesus.

Many Jewish boys have been named after the favorite son of Jacob. Pope John Paul II's apostolic exhortation on Joseph is entitled *Guardian of the Redeemer*. Both Josephs were men of integrity who exhibited sensitivity, trust in divine providence, and mercy.

HEBREW FAMILY NARRATIVES

Gen 12-50 is known as the patriarchal narratives, though the word patriarch is never used in the Old Testament. It is found in Acts 2:29 and Heb 7:4. The matriarchs also played a significant role in these narratives. For example, Rebekah is portrayed as much more influential and proactive than Isaac.

The most prominent Jewish families in the Bible experience difficulties and challenges we can relate to. Their stories contain insights into the way we interact within our family system. Though they didn't use our terms, the biblical writers recognized the patterns and indicated so through similar words and events.

Following are the biblical verses pertaining to Judaism's first families:

Family	Primary Themes	Biblical References
Abraham and Sarah	Faithfulness and mutual support	Gen 12-22
Isaac and Rebecca	Deception and favoritism	Gen 25-27
Jacob, Rachel, and Leah	Wrestling with God and self	Gen 28-36
Joseph and his brothers	Betrayal, providence, and reconciliation	Gen 37-50
David and sons	Incest, murder, favoritism	2 Sam 11-24; 1 Chr 11-29
Solomon and sons	Wisdom, sensuality, idolatry	1 Kings 1-11; 2 Chr 1-9:31

David and Solomon are included due to their significant role in Hebrew history.

LESSONS FROM THE FIRST FAMILIES

Like Abraham, take a risk and follow God into the unknown (cf. Gen 12).

Don't give up because you act in ways of which you are ashamed. Abraham and Isaac passed their wives off as their sisters to save their skins (cf. Gen 12; 20; 26). "Like father, like son" is a frequent theme in the Bible.

You can't fool God. Abraham and Sarah laughed at the prophesy that she would give birth even though her periods ceased (cf. Gen 17:17; 18:12). Isaac means "he laughs." When

God confronted Abraham about Sarah's laughter, she nervously denied it. God's terse response, "No, but you did laugh" sounds like a father's benevolent correction of his child.

Like Abraham, dare to dialogue vigorously and persistently with God (cf. Gen 18:16-33). Like Jacob, dare to wrestle with God (cf. Gen 32:22-32). He is transcendent but approachable (cf. Heb 4:16).

Dare to dream and achieve — Jacob and Joseph did, and accomplished great things, despite their character flaws and sibling rivalries. Jacob was a scoundrel and Joseph a spoiled brat, but God called them and they cooperated, fulfilling an important role in salvation history while growing as individuals.

God can likewise help us cope with the fiercest of opponents. He can work with us no matter how glaring our weaknesses and hurts. Neither Moses (cf. Ex 4:10-16) nor Paul (cf. 2 Cor 10:10; 11:6) were impressive speakers, but with God's help they got their audience's attention.

THE BIBLE TODAY: SIGNS OF THE TIMES

The ancient peoples surpass us in the art of storytelling. They had great memories and were highly sensitive to nature, their experiences, and God's presence and actions.

Ancient peoples marveled at the world. We analyze it incessantly or try to shut it out with distractions of all kinds. We view life from a technological, scientific perspective, and exercise our memory muscles little. Often our concept of God is static and intellectual rather than dynamic and personal. Reading the Bible can help us recover a sense of wonder and appreciation.

EXODUS

Exodus is the most important book in the Bible for Jews, and is also accorded special emphasis within Christianity. The defining event of the Old Testament is the Exodus.

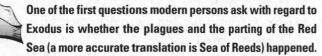
The Hebrew name for Exodus is *shemot*, which means names. Exodus begins by listing the twelve tribes of Israel that migrated to Egypt. This bridges the almost five-century gap between Joseph and Moses.

Despite the order of the Bible, the ancient Hebrews knew God as deliverer/liberator (i.e., the Exodus) before they knew him as creator (i.e., Genesis). Only after experiencing his personal and saving initiative did the Hebrews perceive him as Creator. This personal to universal process is how individuals typically come to know God.

EXODUS HIGHLIGHTS

- The Hebrews are threatened by a new Pharaoh (1:1-22).
- Moses in Egypt (2:1-22).
- Moses in the desert (2:23-4:31).
- Moses and Pharaoh (5:1-12:32).

- The story of the Passover and Exodus (12:33-15:21).
- Trials in the wilderness (15:22-18:27).
- Moses receives the Ten Commandments (i.e., the Decalogue, meaning "ten words") from God at Mt. Sinai (referred to as Mt. Horeb by the "E" and "D" sources of the Pentateuch) (20:1-17).
- God's covenant with Israel (20:22-24:11).
- Moses and God (24:12-18).
- Sabbath regulations (31:12-17; 35:1-3).
- The golden calf (32-34).

PEAK PASSAGES

 When Moses found the Israelites dancing around the golden calf, he melted and ground it down, sprinkled it on the water, and made the revelers drink it. Talk about getting a taste of your own medicine!

Statues of bulls and other animals were frequently worshiped in the ancient Near East. Moses' spokesperson and brother, Aaron, had let the wavering Israelites return to the idolatrous milieu they had left. The text adds that Israel's revelry disgraced them before their enemies — losing "face" or dignity has always been an abomination in the Eastern cultures. Read Ex 32:21-24, and note Aaron's all-too-human evasion of responsibility.

LEVITICUS

Though Leviticus contains mostly legal code, chapters 19-20 of its holiness code (cf. Lev 17-26) are excellent reading for persons at all levels of familiarity with the Bible.

The Hebrew title for Leviticus is *vayikrah*, meaning "and he called." Much of Leviticus is Moses conveying God's regulations for life and worship. When we read Leviticus, we need to modify its moral prescriptions according to New Testament principles, and recognize that God is also calling us to listen and respond.

NUMBERS

Numbers gets its name from the census that opens the book (Num 1:2; cf. Num 3:14-39; 26). The Hebrew title for Numbers is *bamidbar*, which means "in the wilderness," the context of the book.

NUMBERS' STRUCTURE

Numbers is composed of three main sections:

- Preparations in the wilderness for the journey to the promised land (1-10:10).
- The journey itself (10:11-21:9).
- Various battles and final preparations for entry into the promised land (21:10-36:13).

PEAK PASSAGES

Num 20:1-21:9 relates the deaths of Miriam and Aaron, the crisis at Meribah, the Edomites' lack of hospitality, and the serpent attack and antidote.

Num 33 gives an account of Israel's journey.

ISRAEL IN THE DESERT

The New Testament commentary on the Israelites' desert experience is Jesus' temptation in the desert (cf. Mt 4:1-11; Mk 1:12-13; Lk 4:1-13) and the "Bread of Life" discourse in Jn 6. In the former, the tempter quotes Psalm 91, while Jesus counters with texts from Deuteronomy (cf. Deut 8:3, 6:6, 13). Their interaction has a rabbinical quality: both make and refute a point using Scripture.

The New Testament presents Jesus as being faithful where Israel (and we) has failed. Jesus sets an example by his decision(s) to live by the word of God, refuse to test God, and seek no glory for himself.

I once told a priest that I would have grumbled along with the Israelites in the desert. He remarked that they probably would have eaten grass if they could find it. Trusting in the word of God brings a banquet in heaven rather than a picnic on earth.

— WRESTLING WITH THE WORD —

Why did Israel wander in the desert for forty years? Divine retribution? Bad directions? Misguided leaders or followers? Clan clashes?

Why do I resist God so stubbornly, failing to trust him even after I have discovered his initiative in my life?

Why do I continually make the same mistakes, and fall into the same traps? Why do I often feel like I am going around in circles, taking one step forward and two backward?

Why do I have to undergo a challenging, usually painful period of adjustment when I embark on new endeavors? Why are transitions so difficult and often protracted?

In what deserts (testing or transition periods) do I find myself? How might I learn from Israel and Jesus?

DEUTERONOMY

The name Deuteronomy comes from the Greek *deutero* (second) and *nomos* (law). The Hebrew title, *devarim*, means words or things. These complementary expressions summarize the book's content and purpose: it affirms Moses' and God's words, the law.

Read Deuteronomy as an extended homily and reminiscence by an aging leader who reminds his people of significant events and teachings, sometimes presenting them in a new way. At the end, Israel and Moses bid each other good-bye.

After the book of Joshua, Moses is not mentioned as frequently in the Old Testament as we would expect: Ps 106, Sir 45, and 2

Mac 2 are prominent exceptions. Israel moves on, and Moses' role as lawgiver takes precedence over his personality. Moses died peacefully in full possession of his powers and in obedience to the word of the Lord (cf. Deut 34:5-7). Jewish tradition refers to this as "the divine kiss," since the text mentions God's mouth.

Jesus and Stephen are the only other biblical characters who are reported as dying with the word of God on their lips. Moses died as he lived, and is remembered as Israel's greatest prophet, the "servant of the Lord" who interacted intimately with God.

DEUTERONOMY'S BRIDGE TO THE FUTURE

Deuteronomy synthesizes the message and ministry of Moses, integrating its legal and prophetic aspects.

Just as Joseph serves as a transition between the patriarchs and the birth of Israel as a nation (more like a rag-tag collection of clans/tribes), so Deuteronomy offers a moral compass for Israel's transition from slavery to freedom. The legal tone of Leviticus and the disorientating experiences of Numbers give way to Deuteronomy's spirituality of the heart as well as of the law.

Deuteronomy's influence extends beyond the Pentateuch. The next six books in the canon (Joshua-2 Kings) are known as the deuteronomic history. They flow into each other and reflect the influence of the book of Deuteronomy and the "D" source. The deuteronomic principle (based on Deut 30:15-19) reflexively linked suffering with sin and prosperity with holiness, and was challenged in the books of Job, Jeremiah, Koheleth, and the lament Psalms.

HIGHLIGHTS OF DEUTERONOMY

- Review of past events (Ch. 1-3).
- Moses' exhortations (Ch. 4).
- Ten Commandments and commentary (Ch. 5-11).
- Review of the law (Ch. 12-26).
- Blessings and curses (Ch. 27-30).

- Moses' farewell address (Ch. 31).
- Moses' farewell song (Ch. 32).
- Moses' farewell blessing (Ch. 33).
- Moses' death and epitaph (Ch. 34).
- Deut 31-34 serve as a bridge between the Pentateuch and the Deuteronomic history, summarizing the former and anticipating the latter.

PEAK PASSAGES

Deut 6:4-9: The *Shema* (meaning "listen, hear this") is Judaism's most sacred prayer. Jesus quotes the *Shema* in the New Testament (cf. Mt 22:37; Mk 12:30; Lk 10:27).

READING GUIDELINES

Keep these pointers in mind:
- Avoid getting bogged down in genealogies, legal code, and antiquated historical descriptions by referencing the book highlights presented above.
- The book of Genesis is intriguing, mostly accessible literature. The first eleven chapters use symbols and popular stories to explain the roots of the human condition, and the remaining chapters are classic accounts of the patriarchs and matriarchs and their families.
- The first twenty chapters of Exodus are action packed. After an interlude in the middle for legal code, things heat up again at Ex 31:12.
- Read Lev 19-20 in the context of New Testament spirituality and contemporary moral and spiritual challenges.
- Numbers documents the wandering in the wilderness (the desert). Sequential reading works fine as long as you judiciously skip passages that confuse you.

- Deuteronomy is great if you like speeches, exhortations, and dramatic endings, but it does not have the fast pace, colorful characters, and intrigue of Genesis and Exodus.

THE PENTATEUCH: ISRAEL'S IDENTITY

The Pentateuch is an account of Israel's identity, manifested in two primary ways: through genealogies and their covenant with God.

Genealogies are particularly prominent in Genesis. The patriarchal traditions describe Israel's origins and the "blood dimension" of an Israelite's identity. You are an Israelite if you are a descendant of Abraham, Isaac, and Jacob, and if you are a member of one of the twelve tribes of Israel.

The remaining books of the Pentateuch define Israel differently. They view an Israelite as someone who entered into a covenant with God whereby they promised to live according to God's rules, or "the law." Unlike the birthright dimension of Israelite identity, the covenantal dimension is one of choice, and can be lost. If an Israelite transgressed the law in a major way, he could be excluded from the community. Idolatry is an example of a transgression that is incompatible with being an Israelite.

WRESTLING WITH THE WORD

It is natural and appropriate for the Pentateuch to inspire us to emulate the Israelites and consider our spiritual identity. How do we know that we are true to ourselves and God?

For Christians, the answer is love of self and neighbor (cf. Jn 13:35; Mt 25:31-46; Lk 10:25-37; 1 Jn 4:20-21), which is based upon love of God (cf. Mk 12:28-34; Lk 10:38-40), and reaches it heights in the rejection of revenge, a central theme in the New Testament (cf. Mt 5:43-48; Rom 12:14-21; 1 Pet 3:9).

POSTPONING THE PROMISED LAND

In the next chapter, we will temporarily leave the historical books and move to the Psalms, the most accessible book of the Old Testament for beginners, and a staple of the Catholic liturgy and of the Bible reading plans articulated in Chapter Five. Like the Pentateuch, the Psalms are a microcosm of the Bible. We will then discuss the remainder of the historical books in the chapter of that name.

Chapter Twenty-Two

—— How to Pray and Live the Psalms ——

The Hebrew name for the book of Psalms is *sefer tehillim*, which means book of praises. Psalms comes from the Greek *psalmos*, which means songs. The Psalms were sung at worship services.

Along with Genesis and Exodus, the Psalms are a good place to begin reading the Old Testament. Most Psalms are straightforward and of manageable length. With the exceptions of Proverbs and Sirach, no other book of the Bible is broken down into such compact, self-contained units.

The Psalms echo the other sections of the Old Testament, and are the most frequently quoted book in the New Testament.

┌── **SAINTS AND SAGES ON THE BIBLE** ─────────────────┐

 "The Psalms: a mirror in which each man sees the motions of his own soul" (Rowland E. Prothero).

└──┘

They are used in the New Testament as a representative term for the Writings, the final grouping of the Hebrew Bible (cf. Lk 22:44). They are particularly prominent in the Gospels' accounts of Jesus' suffering and death.

Though thoroughly Hebrew in mentality and expression, the Psalms have a universal dimension that transcends culture, circumstance, and creed. You can always find something in the Psalms to speak to you.

The writers of the Psalms typically don't specify details of their circumstances or what God has done to deliver them. By keeping the language general, they invite you to fill in the rest.

WHO WROTE THE PSALMS, AND WHEN?

The authorship and dating of the Psalms is ambiguous. Only a very few, such as Psalms 51 and 137, seem to refer directly to identifiable events in the Bible. The traditional belief was that King David wrote most of them, but scholars reject this. However, just as the influence of Moses is felt throughout the Pentateuch, David's influence is pervasive in the Psalms.

THE PSALMS' POETIC STRUCTURE

A characteristic feature of Hebrew poetry is its balanced rhythm. Parallelism is a poetic way of relating consecutive expressions to each other in order to communicate a coherent meaning. Either a verse or half a verse affirms, contrasts with, or completes the preceding verse or half a verse. Identifying these parallelisms slows your reading down and alerts you to the values the psalmist (psalm author) is emphasizing. After you read this section, you will literally be well-versed in the Psalms:

- **Synonymous parallelism (corresponding expressions):** The second clause of the verse affirms or rephrases the first: "Therefore the wicked will not stand in the judgment, nor sinners in the congregation of the righteous" (Ps 1:5).

- **Antithetic parallelism (contrasting expressions):** The second clause presents a contrast to the first: "for the LORD knows the way of the righteous, but the way of the wicked will perish" (Ps 1:6).
- **Synthetic parallelism (complementary expressions):** The second clause completes the first: "My flesh and my heart may fail, but God is the strength of my heart and my portion forever" (Ps 73:26).

THE STRUCTURE OF THE BOOK OF PSALMS

For symbolic (to correspond with the Pentateuch) and unclear liturgical reasons, the Psalms were divided into five books, each ending with a blessing:

- **Book 1:** Psalms 1-41
- **Book 2:** Psalms 42-72
- **Book 3:** Psalms 73-89
- **Book 4:** Psalms 90-106
- **Book 5:** Psalms 107-150

The numbering of the Psalms in the Hebrew Psalter differs slightly from that in the Greek and Latin versions. Usually the numbers in the latter are one less than in the Hebrew version.

In the Greek and Latin Psalters, Psalms 9 and 10, and 114 and 115, are combined, and both Psalms 116 and 147 are divided into two. Most Bibles follow the Hebrew numbering system.

Catholic Bibles have traditionally followed the Latin Psalter. In the Mass missals, you will see the Hebrew version number in parentheses next to the Latin version number.

THE PSALMS' CLASSIFICATIONS

Scholars have grouped the Psalms into categories based on their content and intended usage. Terms and classifications vary among scholars. I prefer the categories and assignments used in *The Catholic Study Bible*, as follows:

- **Hymns:** Primarily used in a liturgical setting. Their function is to facilitate praise of God. You can find hymns in Psalms 8, 19, 29, 33, 100, 103, 104, 111, 113, 114, 117, 135, 136, and 145-150.
- **Laments:** Prayerful complaints and petitions for God's help, as distinguished from self-pity and bitter griping. In the Bible, there are two kinds of laments:
  - **Community laments:** The community as a whole is suffering, and seeks relief. Psalms 12, 14, 44, 53, 58, 60, 74, 79, 80, 83, 85, 89, 90, 94, 106, 123, 126, and 137.
  - **Individual laments:** The largest group in the Psalms. Psalms 3-7, 13, 17, 22, 25-28, 31, 35, 36, 38-40, 42, 43, 51, 52, 54-57, 59, 61, 63, 64, 69-71, 77, 86, 88, 102, 109, 120, 130, and 140-143.
- **Communal Psalms of confidence:** The community affirms that God will support and deliver it. Psalms 115, 125, and 129.
- **Individual Psalms of confidence:** An individual expresses trust in God. Psalms 11, 16, 23, 62, 91, 121, and 131.
- **Communal Psalms of thanksgiving:** The community offers general or specific thanks to God. Psalms 65-68, 75, 107, 118, and 124.
- **Individual Psalms of thanksgiving:** The individual offers general or specific thanks to God. Psalms 9, 10, 30, 32, 34, 41, 92, 116, and 138.
- **Royal (messianic) Psalms:** Messiah means "anointed one." Kingship was conferred in Israel by anointing the head with oil (cf. 1 Sam 10:1, 16:13). Historically, these Psalms refer to the rulers of Israel. However, the early Church saw in these Psalms a prophetic reference to Jesus. Psalms 2, 18, 20, 21, 45, 72, 101, 110, 132, and 144.
- **Wisdom Psalms:** These Psalms illustrate how to live morally and prudently. Psalms 1, 37, 49, 73, 119, 127, and 128.

- **Psalms of assent:** The people sang these as they processed into the temple. Psalms 15, 24, and 95.
- **Prophetic Psalms:** In biblical parlance, prophecy does not necessarily mean speaking of the future. It primarily means communicating a message from God or an angel (angel means messenger). Psalms 50 and 81.
- **Historical Psalms:** These Psalms praise God for his interventions in Israel's history. Psalms 78 and 105.
- **Composite Psalms:** These Psalms have attributes of several of the groupings. Psalms 108, 133, and 139.
- **Liturgical psalm:** Meant to be recited in public worship, this psalm contains a verse that was sung repeatedly. Psalm 134.
- **Penitential Psalms.** Penitential means evoking remorse and repentance. The penitential Psalms are a subgrouping. All but Psalm 32 (an individual psalm of thanksgiving) are classified as laments. These Psalms reflect intense consciousness of personal sinfulness and a corresponding desire for forgiveness. Psalms 6, 32, 38, 51, 102, 130, and 143.

PSALM HEADINGS

All but thirty-four of the Psalms contain a heading or title. The headings were inserted long after the Psalms were composed. They usually indicate musical instructions, and identify the person credited as the psalm's author.

SAMPLING THE PSALMS

You can read the Psalms in order, randomly, by the groupings discussed above, or as they are presented in the lectionary or the liturgy of the hours. The latter provide structure, a comprehensible and liturgical arrangement, and a nice mix of other biblical passages.

Some publishers offer the New Testament packaged with the Psalms. This is a non-intimidating way for newcomers to the Bible to get started.

The characters and contexts of the Psalms have changed, but the emotions and spiritual dispositions have not. Following is an example of a modern-day lament.

In 1978, Aldo Moro, the prime minister of Italy, was kidnapped by an Italian terrorist group, the Red Brigade. After a long hostage period, his bullet-ridden body was found in the trunk of a car. Pope Paul VI was a longtime friend of Aldo Moro. This excerpt from Paul's prayer at Moro's funeral Mass reads like the responsorial psalm at Mass, with "Lord, hear us" as the refrain:

"And now our lips, closed as if by an enormous obstacle, like the great stone rolled to the entrance of Christ's tomb, wish to open to express the *De profundis* [an expression from the Psalms meaning "out of the depths"; in our terminology, "the pits"], that is, the cry and the weeping of the unutterable grief with which this tragedy suffocates our voice.

"Lord, hear us!

"And who can listen to our lament, if not You, O God of life and death? You did not hearken to our supplication for the safety of Aldo Moro, this good, meek, wise, innocent and friendly man; but You, O Lord, have not abandoned his immortal spirit, sealed by Faith in Christ, who is the resurrection and the life. For him, for him.

"Lord, hear us!

"Grant, O God, Father of mercy, that there will not be interrupted communion which, even in the shadows of death, still exists between those who have departed from this temporal existence and ourselves still living in this day in which the sun inexorably sets. The program of our being as redeemed is not a vain one: our flesh will rise again, our life will be eternal! Oh! Let our faith match this promised reality right now. We will see them again, Aldo and all the living in Christ, blessed in the infinite God!

"Lord, hear us!"

Because the order of the book of Psalms is purposeful, beginning with Psalm 1 is a good idea if you have self-discipline. I tried this and found it beneficial. If you go this route, take your time and savor it. When you encounter Psalms you can't understand or relate to, just move to the next psalm. You can always come back later.

The advantage of sequential (beginning with Psalm 1) or liturgically based reading of the Psalms is that you'll get a balanced spiritual diet. You can always depart from the menu when necessary. By sampling all the Psalms, you expose and acclimate yourself to readings that may not suit your tastes. This may also help you adjust to life's distasteful situations.

READING INDIVIDUAL PSALMS

Don't feel compelled to read every verse of a psalm at a single sitting. An individual verse or two can strike a nerve and provide the nourishment and guidance that you need. Other times, reading the whole Psalm, particularly a short one, will provide a more complete picture and experience. In general, it is a good idea to break the longer Psalms into manageable portions and read them over several sittings.

Even a short, simple psalm contains nuances that are perceptible only through study and repeated readings. If you periodically read a psalm slowly and repetitively, these will gradually become apparent.

A BALANCED READING OF THE PSALMS

Balance time spent on the Psalms that are most appealing and relevant to your life with gradually getting to know the whole Psalter. Try to find personal parallels to elements (e.g., Psalms about the king) that seem remote or dated. Psalms (or other biblical passages) that we initially struggle with can help us grow in surprising ways.

If we stick exclusively to what ratifies our opinions and experiences, the Bible becomes stale and one-dimensional, and we stagnate. Instead of God's word forming us (cf. Heb 4:12), we fashion it into our own image.

An example of this was the Jewish practice of *korban*, which substituted a self-imposed dedication to God for the fifth commandment (cf. Mk 7:9-13). Obedience is better than sacrifice (cf. 1 Sam 15:22; Prov 21:3).

Because the Bible alone doesn't always give us sufficient guidance, we should also turn to other ways God reveals his truths, such as Tradition (the wisdom of the Church handed down through the ages) and the living Church (the teachings of the magisterium, the pastoral care provided by clergy, religious, and competent laypersons, and the wisdom of fellow Christians).

ADAPTING THE PSALMS TO THE RHYTHMS OF LIFE

When I have had an intense day, I may not have the energy for a formal, disciplined, and detailed reading of the Psalms. Sometimes I just open up to the Psalms and eyeball them, turning the pages until I come to a psalm that seems compatible with my mood. Other times, I'll pick one that is not compatible with how I feel, so that I stretch and open myself to new horizons. For example, if I feel like lamenting, I'll read a hymn of praise to remind me that God deserves praise even when I feel down.

Once you get to know the Psalms and become familiar with the classifications discussed above, you will be able to skim the Psalter quickly and recognize when you come upon a psalm that suits your mood and situation. You'll also have favorite Psalms to return to, such as listed below.

PROMINENT PSALMS

Every Psalm is worth reading, but some Psalms are so rooted in ancient Hebrew culture that you may initially have difficulty relating to them. The following are accessible Psalms that have been prominent in Jewish and Christian history, and in my own life:

- **Psalm 1:** A contrast of the two fundamental paths of life.
- **Psalms 6 and 13:** Short and bitter laments suitable for sad situations.
- **Psalm 8:** An uplifting creation Psalm that celebrates human potential.
- **Psalm 19:** A Psalm that praises God's law, a concise version of the longest Psalm, 119.
- **Psalm 22:** Chronicles the movement from feelings of abandonment to trust and deliverance. Jesus lived and prayed this on the cross (cf. Mt 27:46; Mk 15:34).
- **Psalm 23:** "The Lord is my shepherd. . . ." The most beloved Psalm for individuals.
- **Psalms 27 and 40:** Touching affirmations of trust in God amid difficult circumstances.
- **Psalm 31:** A literary symphony of the movements of the spiritual life. My second favorite, and another Psalm prayed by Jesus on the cross.
- **Psalm 44:** Great to pray as a family or community during troubled times. Quoted in St. Paul's most inspiring passage (cf. Rom 8:36).
- **Psalm 51:** The Bible's most beautiful expression of hope amid remorse. As befitting a community of redeemed sinners, the Church has always treasured this Psalm. See the quotation at this chapter's conclusion.

    Read and return to Psalm 51. Repentance and trust in God's compassion and forgiveness beats denial or wallowing in guilt. Better to project sins and hurts upward than inward or outward.
- **Psalm 55:** "O that I had wings like a dove! I would fly away and be at rest; yea, I would wander afar; I would lodge in the wilderness, I would haste to find me a shelter from the

raging wind and tempest" (Ps 55:6-8). Don't we all feel like this at times?

- **Psalm 69:** A desperate and passionate Psalm applied by the early Church to the passion of Jesus.
- **Psalm 77:** Chronicles the movement from doubt and disillusionment to trust empowered by recollection of God's fidelity: "I think of God, and I moan; I meditate, and my spirit faints" (Ps 77:3; cf. 77:7-12).
- **Psalm 88:** A reminder that prayer can occur amid despair, this is the only Psalm that ends on a down or incomplete note. We're supposed to finish it.
- **Psalm 91:** An expression of trust in dire circumstances.
- **Psalms 103 and 104:** Beautiful creation Psalms, the first focusing on human beings, the second on nature.
- **Psalm 118:** Part of the Easter liturgy, it exudes joy.
- **Psalms 109 and 137:** These "cursing Psalms" inspire us to pray rather than act out our anger.
- **Psalms 18 and 139:** Psalms of divine providence.

CONCLUDING WITH COMPASSION

We'll conclude this chapter with a beautiful tribute to Psalm 51, perhaps the most universal prayer in the Old Testament:

"Psalm 50 (51, according to Hebrew numbering) has inexhaustible riches. It is the daily prayer of the Church, beginning in Latin: *Miserere mei Deus* (Have mercy on me, Lord).

"It is found all through the history of the Church and Christian spirituality. It forms the underlying plan of the Confessions of St. Augustine. It was loved, meditated, and commented upon by Gregory the Great. It was the battle cry for Joan of Arc's soldiers. It was closely studied by Martin Luther, who wrote unforgettable pages on it. It is the hidden mirror of conscience for the characters of Dostoievsky and is the key to his novels.

"This, then, is the Psalm of great men and women of God. Musicians like Bach, Donizetti, and others nearer to our time have conveyed it in music. Famous painters have delineated it in wonderful engravings.

"It belongs to the history of humanity, not only to the Hebrew Near East or the Christian civilization of the West" (Carlo M. Martini, S.J, *What Am I That You Care For Me: Praying with the Psalms*, Collegeville, MN: The Liturgical Press, 1992, 82-83).

Many people read and develop a love for the Psalms without any formal preparation. The sooner you begin reading the Psalms, the better.

Our detour completed, let us now return to the historical books.

Chapter Twenty-Three

How to Read and Relate to the Historical Books

┌─ **Contents of this Chapter** ─────────────────────┐

- Survey the variety, style, and context of the historical writings.
- Identify key persons, kings, and passages in the historical books.
- Discover which books are suitable for beginners and which are not.
- Encounter Hebrew heroes and heroines.
- Discover overlooked books with great stories and characters.

└──┘

THE HISTORICAL BOOKS

Genesis	Exodus	Leviticus
Numbers	Deuteronomy	Joshua
Judges	Ruth	1 & 2 Samuel
1 & 2 Kings	1 & 2 Chronicles	Ezra
Nehemiah	Tobit	Judith
Esther	1 & 2 Maccabees	*(In order, left to right)*

The historical books are a diverse collection spanning more than a millennia of Hebrew history. If you enjoyed reading about the Exodus in the Pentateuch, and want to see how the Israelites settled in the promised land, Joshua and Judges pick up where Deuteronomy leaves off.

WHAT DOES IT MEAN? ──────────────

The term *Hexateuch* was coined to describe the first six books of the Old Testament. It recognizes the common authorship and themes of Deuteronomy and Joshua as epitomized in two speeches (cf. Deut 26:5-11; Jos 24:1-28).

These speeches recall God's actions on behalf of Israel, beginning with the promise to the patriarchs and continuing through the conquest of Canaan, and exhort the people to fidelity.

The term "judges" as used in the book of Judges means ruler and military leader as opposed to judge, although their duties often involved mediation. The Hebrew word for judges means one who dispenses justice.

Resolving disputes was a leadership function in Israel, as demonstrated by Moses (cf. Ex 18:13-27) and Solomon (cf. 1 Kings 3:16-28), though neither were referred to as judges.

Joshua and Judges are not literal history in the modern sense. They are orally transmitted historical accounts that reflect a theological and nationalistic perspective. Archaeological and extra-biblical historical data give us additional insights, but not certainty, into what happened.

IDOL WORSHIP

The Hebrews did not go out of their way to worship idols. They lived among and were surrounded by peoples who practiced idolatry. Baal was the chief god of the agrarian pantheon worshiped by the Canaanites, while Marduk headed the Babylonian pantheon.

Participating in idol worship offered a sense of security and belonging. It is more difficult to trust in a seemingly distant, morally demanding and mysterious God who won't be manipulated than to get caught up in superstitions and orgiastic rituals designed to bring fertility to women and crops.

Morally, cultural temptations are more ominous than military threats. Jesus said not to fear those who destroy the body but cannot harm the soul (cf. Mt 10:28). Cultural temptations are subtle and deceptive, eroding integrity and both internal and external harmony. Frequently using the word "abomination(s)," the prophets' strongest condemnations are against idolatry.

What are the abominations and idols in modern society?

SAMUEL: PROPHET AND KING-MAKER

Samuel was a transitional figure in Israelite history. Both judge and prophet, he reluctantly inaugurates the monarchy. His story is recounted in 1 Sam 1:1-25:1.

The birth (cf. 1 Sam 1) and call (cf. 1 Sam 3) of Samuel are among the most compelling stories in the Bible. He was born to the previously infertile Hannah, whose conception was predicted by the priest Eli, under whom Samuel would serve as a boy.

While sleeping, Samuel received the uncommon "double call," i.e., "Samuel, Samuel." This is a rare occurrence in the Bible and signifies an important encounter between God and an individual. Other examples are Abraham at the sacrifice of Isaac (cf. Gen 22:11), Moses at the Burning Bush (cf. Ex 3:4), Martha (cf. Lk

---

THE BIBLE SAYS WHAT?

In 1 Sam 10:1-13 and 19:18-24, we read about prophets and those who encounter them in a state of prophetic frenzy or ecstasy. Exactly what occurred is difficult to determine. Suffice to say that when God shares his message and spirit, a strong reaction can occur.

Prophetic ecstasy/frenzy is known not only in the Bible, but also among Israel's neighbors. The latter's experience could be either self-induced (the power of suggestion) or an occult experience. See Morton Kelsey's *Discernment: A Study in Ecstasy and Evil.* In the New Testament (cf. 1 Cor 12; 14), we encounter the movement of the Spirit in the form of the charismatic gifts.

10:41), Peter (cf. Lk 22:31), and Paul/Saul (cf. Acts 9:4; 22:7; 26:14).

Samuel served as an adviser to both Saul and David, though he and God soured on Saul (cf. 1 Sam 15:10-16:1). Like Moses and Joshua before him and Jesus (cf. Jn 14-17) after him, Samuel gives a farewell address (cf. 1 Sam 12).

God's respect for Samuel is conveyed by this tribute: "Then the LORD said to me: Though Moses and Samuel stood before me, yet my heart would not turn toward this people" (Jer 15:1).

KEY KINGS

You might crown me if I asked you to keep track of all the kings of Israel and their neighbors. Because of the political instability (including assassinations and coups), this information is on a need-to-know basis. These kings you need to know:

King	Kingdom	Reign (B.C.)	Comments
Saul	United Monarchy	1050/45-1011/10	Reign marred by jealousy of David. Samuel warned against a king, but the people insisted (cf. 1 Sam 8).
David	United Monarchy	1011/10-971/70	The king through whose line the Messiah was promised.
Solomon	United	971/70-931/30	Guru of the wisdom movement and the epitome of misdirected potential.
Rehoboam	United; Judah (S)	931/30-913	Solomon's son, last king of the united monarchy, and first southern king. Continued father's oppressive internal policies despite counsel by elders to ease up. Hence the revolt.

Continued on page 298 . . .

... continued from page 297

King	Kingdom	Reign (B.C.)	Comments
Jeroboam I	Israel (N)	931/30-910/09	Overseer of laborers under Solomon. Incited a revolt and became first northern king. Encouraged idolatry.
Omri	Israel (N)	876-869	Founder of the Omrid dynasty. Established Samaria as Israel's capital. This politically neutral site helped bring stability and prosperity.
Ahab	Israel (N)	869/850	Many encounters with Elijah. Abided Queen Jezebel's scheme to murder and despoil Naboth (cf. 1 Kings 21). Through Jezebel's influence, Baal worship spread.
Jehu	Israel (N)	843-816	General known for charioteering (cf. 2 Kings 9:20). Replaced Omrid dynasty with his own in a bloody purge condemned in Hos 1:4.
Jeroboam II	Israel (N)	782/81-753	Strong king who oversaw Israel's last and most prosperous period.
Tiglath-pileser III	Assyria	745-727	Expanded and revitalized Assyria and made Israel a vassal.
Ahaz	Judah (S)	732/31-716/15	Became Canaanite king at twenty. Followed practice by sacrificing his son and worshiping at the "high places" — pagan cult sites (cf. 2 Kings 16:1-4). A wicked king.
Hezekiah	Judah (S)	716/15-687/86	"He trusted in the Lord the God of Israel; so there was none like him among all the kings of Judah after him, nor among

King	Kingdom	Reign (B.C.)	Comments
[Hezekiah continued]			those who were before him" (2 Kings 18:5). Closed down high places and banned nature-related superstitious rituals.
Josiah	Judah (S)	640/39-609	"Before him there was no king like him, who turned to the Lord with all his heart and with all his soul and with all his might, according to all the law of Moses; nor did any like him arise after him" (2 Kings 23:25; cf. Sir 49:1-4). Great reformer who purged idol worship. Died in an avoidable battle (cf. 2 Kings 23:29; 2 Chron 35:23-24).
Zedekiah	Judah (S)	597-587	Installed as a puppet ruler by Nebuchadnezzar. Ignored Jeremiah's pleas to surrender (cf. Jer 38:17). Watched his sons murdered by the Babylonians, and was blinded and taken in fetters to Babylon. Last Jewish king.
Nebuchad-nezzar II	Babylonian	605-562	The most powerful Babylonian king. Famous encounters with Daniel, and Shadrach, Meschach, and Abednego (cf. Dan 3). His madness is described in Dan 4. Called "my servant" in Jer 25:9; 27:6 because God used him in his plan for Judah's purification.
Cyrus II	Persian	539-530	Conquered Babylon and permitted Jews to worship freely and return to Jerusalem. Identified as the messiah/anointed in Is 45:1-3. At this

Continued on page 300 ...

... continued from page 299

King	Kingdom	Reign (B.C.)	Comments
[Cyrus II continued]			point in history, "messiah" did not carry the connotations and expectations it would in Jesus' time.
Darius I	Persian	522-486	Great administrator and military leader. Affirmed Cyrus' plan to help Jews rebuild temple (cf. Ezra 4-6). Capable of extreme cruelty and kindness. Lost to Greeks at Marathon in 490 B.C.
Karleno the Great	His country requested anonymity.	Expunged from the annals and lost to history.	The only monarch identified as "the great" by his enemies. Mandated that his subjects read his books, thereby setting education back two centuries. Prophets didn't bother vilifying him, as neither he nor his subjects knew what he was doing or saying. Had coin minted with rival king's image on it by mistake.

HIGHLIGHTS OF JOSHUA AND JUDGES

- **Josh 1:1-18:** Joshua's commission and preparations.
- **Josh 2:** Reconnaissance of the promised land.
- **Josh 5:13-6:27:** Joshua's vision and the destruction of Jericho.
- **Josh 8:30-35:** Joshua reads the law.
- **Josh 23-24:** Joshua's farewell speech.
- **Judg 13:2-16:31:** The birth and saga of Samson: judge, warrior, and betrayed lover.

HIGHLIGHTS OF 1 AND 2 SAMUEL

- **1 Sam 1:1-2:10:** The prophesied birth of Samuel.

- **1 Sam 3:** The call of Samuel.
- **1 Sam 4:1-10:** The Philistines capture the ark of the covenant.
- **1 Sam 8:** Israel pleads for a king.
- **1 Sam 9-10:** Samuel anoints Saul as king.
- **1 Sam 12:** Samuel's farewell address.
- **1 Sam 15:** Saul disobeys the Lord (cf. 1 Sam 15:22: obedience is better than sacrifice).
- **1 Sam 16:** Samuel anoints David as king.
- **1 Sam 17:** David and Goliath.
- **1 Sam 18-31:** Saul pursues David and dies in battle with the Philistines.
- **2 Sam 1:** Israel mourns Saul.
- **2 Sam 7:** God's covenant with David.
- **2 Sam 11-12:** David and Bathsheba.
- **2 Sam 13:** Rape and murder in David's family.
- **2 Sam 15-19:** Absalom revolts against David.
- **2 Sam 22:** David's song of praise.
- **2 Sam 23:1-7:** David's last words.
- **2 Sam 24:** David sins by ordering a census.

HIGHLIGHTS OF 1 AND 2 KINGS

- **1 Kings 1-2:** The death of David and succession of Solomon.
- **1 Kings 3; 4:29-34:** The wisdom of Solomon.
- **1 Kings 8:** Solomon dedicates the temple he built as described in 1 Kings 6.
- **1 Kings 9:1-9:** God's second appearance to Solomon.
- **1 Kings 10:1-10:** Solomon amazes the Queen of Sheba.
- **1 Kings 11:1-13:** Solomon's foreign women influence him toward idolatry.
- **1 Kings 11:14-40:** Rebellion against Solomon.
- **1 Kings 11:41-43:** Death of Solomon.
- **1 Kings 12:1-19:** Rehoboam's heavy hand incites the northern tribes' succession.

- **1 Kings 12:20-14:20:** The evil reign of Jeroboam in the north.
- **1 Kings 17-19; 21:** The prophetic activities of Elijah.
- **2 Kings 4-8:6:** Elisha the miracle worker.
- **2 Kings 8:7-15:** Elisha participates in a coup.
- **2 Kings 9-10:** Jehu's bloody coup and the ending of the Omrid dynasty.
- **2 Kings 13:14-21:** Death of Elisha and a symbolic miracle.
- **2 Kings 18-20:** Good king Hezekiah's reign.
- **2 Kings 22:1-23:28:** Discovery of Deuteronomy triggers good king Josiah's reform.
- **2 Kings 23:29-30:** Josiah's death.
- **2 Kings 24:1-25:21:** The fall of Judah.

1 AND 2 CHRONICLES

Originally one book, 1 and 2 Chronicles were written in the mid-fifth century B.C. Scholars refer to the unknown author as the Chronicler.

Traditionally, Judaism credited Chronicles to Ezra, whose book follows Chronicles in the Christian canon and picks up where Chronicles leaves off. Chronicles follows the books of Samuel and Kings, which cover approximately the same period and present an earlier, more critical perspective. It is interesting to compare their treatments of the same events.

Chronicles received their name from the Hebrew title, which means annals. St. Jerome, the translator of the Vulgate, suggested that we might call it the "chronicle of the whole sacred history," hence the title "Chronicles." A main source of the books' information is the public records and genealogies (i.e., chronicles) handed down within Israel. If you like history, you'll probably like Chronicles.

The Septuagint and older Bibles entitle these *Paraleipomenon*, which means "things omitted," or "supplements," because they modify the accounts given in the books of Samuel and Kings.

STRUCTURE OF 1 AND 2 CHRONICLES

1 Chronicles can be divided into two sections: 1Chron 1-9 contains genealogies down to David, and 1Chron 10-29 chronicles David's reign from a more sympathetic standpoint than the books of Samuel.

2 Chronicles also has two main sections. 2 Chron 1-9 chronicles Solomon's reign, and 2 Chron 10-36 tells the story of the southern kingdom, Judah, through the liberation of the exiles by King Cyrus of Persia (538 B.C.).

GENEALOGIES

Though they are tedious to modern readers, genealogies had implications for inheritance and property-ownership issues, as well as individual identities. We have the same issues, though our tools are not as primitive. We don't identify with our family roots as much because we don't live in a clan culture.

The modern branch of psychology known as family-systems theory (see the writings of Murray Bowen) shows how family history and interactions affect our personal development and marital and parental functioning.

EZRA AND NEHEMIAH

Ezra and Nehemiah are pivotal figures in the post-exilic period. They helped Israel move from a temple-oriented religion to a Bible-based one. They collected, preserved, proclaimed, and handed on the Scriptures.

The key passage of these books, Neh 8-9, shows the priest and scribe Ezra reading the law, the people proclaiming obedience, and the Levites (the priestly tribe) and Ezra leading them in prayer and recollection of God's works.

Ezra and Nehemiah are best understood by persons familiar with Hebrew history, and in particular the Exodus and Deuteronomic history (i.e., Deuteronomy through 2 Kings). Read Neh 8-9, but hold off on the rest of these books until you have a

┌─── **PEAK PASSAGES** ───────────────────────────────

Neh 5:1-7 shows that the most painful manifestations of economic and social injustice often come not from conquerors and outsiders, but from our own.

clearer picture of why the reforms of Ezra and Nehemiah were necessary.

TOBIT

Tobit contains clearly non-historical details that mark it as fiction. The story is set in eighth century B.C. Nineveh, among the exiles from the fall of the northern kingdom to Assyria (of which Nineveh was the capital).

Tobit was written around the second century B.C. The author and his domicile are unknown. It was originally written in Aramaic, then translated into Greek.

Tobit integrates prayers, hymns, and wisdom teachings in a delightful story. It has enjoyed wide popularity in Judaism and Christianity. The moral is that God will watch over God-fearing and compassionate Jews both in and outside of the promised land.

The main characters are Tobit (the patriarch of the clan), his wife Anna, son Tobias (also spelled Tobiah), and his bride and kinswoman, Sarah, the demon Asmodeus, and the archangel Raphael, who appears in disguise as Tobit's relative Azarias (which means "God helps" in Hebrew).

Key elements of the story line are as follows: Tobit experiences financial reverses and is blinded, thereby forcing Anna to support the family. Sarah has seven husbands die during her wedding night, and Tobias is set to be the eighth. The bridal chamber demon-repellant is the heart and liver of a fish.

RUTH

Ruth was a childless Moabite (a traditional enemy of Israel) widow who left her country, religion, and security to accompany her mother-in-law Naomi to Bethlehem (cf. Ruth 1:16-18). Ruth ended up marrying Boaz, a relative of her late husband, and bearing David's grandfather. Boaz is a hero for the protection extended to the foreigner Ruth, and for his securing of land for Naomi.

Widows, widowers, abandoned spouses, and discontented singles can find in Ruth a source of hope. God can reverse situations and dignify even the most sorrowful circumstances.

Along with Job and Jonah, Ruth is an example of the Old Testament's growing universalism. A foreign woman becomes a hero of Israel, and with Tamar (cf. Gen 38), Rahab (cf. Jos 2; 6), and Bathsheba (cf. 2 Sam 11), a participant in the Davidic line into which Jesus was born (cf. Mt 1:1-17).

All of these women have sexual improprieties connected with them. Tamar impersonated a prostitute, Rahab was one, Bathsheba committed adultery, and Ruth's ploy to hook Boaz on the threshing floor (cf. Ruth 3) had sexual connotations. God accomplishes his plan amid human weakness.

ESTHER

Esther was a beautiful and shrewd Jewess who became a queen and averted the slaughter of the Jewish people. Esther and the books of Maccabees (where Antiochus Epiphanes IV tried to exterminate the Jews) prefigure attempts throughout history to persecute the Jews.

The Jewish feast of *Purim* (meaning "lots," because lots were used by the persecutor of the Jews, Haman, to fix the day of their extermination) commemorates their deliverance.

JUDITH

Written by an unknown author around 150 B.C., the book of Judith can be divided into three sections:

- The Assyrians lay siege against the Jews (Jud 1:1-7:32).
- Judith encourages the people to trust in divine deliverance and works her plan to overcome King Nebuchadnezzar's commander in chief, Holofernes (Jud 8:1-14:10). The John and Mable Ringling Museum of Art in Sarasota, Florida (www.ringling.org), has two stunning paintings entitled *Judith with the Head of Holofernes*, by Fede Galizia and Francesco Cairo.
- The Jews rout and scatter the Assyrian army (Jud 14:11-16:25).

The name Judith means Jewess. Her victory is a *haggadah* a biblically-based midrash/story with a moral teaching) on the continuing meaning of the Exodus and subsequent divine deliverances.

The story contains the familiar motif of a woman dressing up, utilizing mistaken identity, and duping a man (cf. Esther 5; 7; Gen 38:13-26). In Gen 38:26, the deceived father-in-law Judah says of the pseudo-harlot Tamar: "She is more righteous than I" (Gen 38:26). Let us now move from righteous women instrumental in the preservation of Judaism to a righteous man, Judas Maccabeus.

1 AND 2 MACCABEES

The name *Maccabee*, whose likely meaning is "hammer," is taken from the family name of its hero, Judas Maccabeus, who along with his brothers and supporters lead the Maccabean revolt against the Seleucid (Greek) king, Antiochus Epiphanes IV, who persecuted the Jews (cf. 1 Mac 2:4, 66; 2 Mac 8:5, 16; 10:1, 16) while trying to establish Hellenism (Greek culture and religion) in Judea. Judas and his successors were part of the Hasmoneans, Jewish rulers during the period of political independence from 142 to 63 B.C., when the Romans conquered the Near East.

1 and 2 Maccabees contain separate narratives of similar but historically distinct events surrounding the liberation of the Jews from foreign domination in the second century B.C. Whereas 1 Maccabees covers the period from the reign of Antiochus Epiphanes IV (175 B.C.) to the accession of John Hyrcanus I (134 B.C.), 2 Maccabees narrates events from the time of the high priest Onias III and King Seleucus IV (ca. 180 B.C.) to the defeat of Nicanor's army (161 B.C.).

The books were written around 125 B.C. in Hebrew, but survive in a Greek version that contains so many Hebrew idioms that we are confident that a Hebrew original existed.

The Jewish feast of Hanukkah is based on the Maccabean revolt. Its menorah symbol derives from a Jewish legend about the oil lamp burning continuously in the temple, which Judas Maccabeus reclaimed and rededicated in 164 B.C. The books of Maccabees' concern with the temple, Jewish nationalism, and the consoling authority of Scripture (cf. 1 Mac 12:9; Rom 15:4) are also New Testament themes.

The heavy historical and nationalistic dimension of 1 and 2 Maccabees makes it prohibitive for beginners who are not history buffs. It suffices to know that this chronicle of Jewish history and the inter-testamental period exists, and is edifying reading once you grow comfortable with the Bible.

PEAK PASSAGES

2 Mac 12:42-46 is Old Testament precedent for the New Testament belief in the resurrection of the dead and the Catholic practice of intercession for the dead.

THE EVOLUTION OF JEWISH IDENTITY AND VALUES

We began our exploration of the Old Testament by surveying its background, and then moved to its foundational books, the Pentateuch. These impart the earliest identity, beliefs, and values of the Jewish people. We then surveyed the Psalms, which present developed versions of these in liturgical and poetic form. In this chapter, we saw how these evolved through a millennia of Jewish history. In the next chapter, we will see how the wisdom books translate these into practical guidance.

Chapter Twenty-Four

—— How to Read the Wisdom Books —— and Wise Up

┌─ **Contents of this Chapter** ─────────────────────────────┐

- Recognize the historical context and purpose of the wisdom books.
- Identify key passages and themes in the wisdom books.
- Distinguish the wisdom books from ancient polytheistic and contemporary secular personal-growth resources.
- Discover the contemporary utility of the wisdom books.

└──┘

WISDOM LITERATURE

The wisdom books of the Bible are literally designed to help us "wise up," that is, live more prudently and morally, particularly in daily affairs. They were designed to help persons negotiate everyday life, familial, and business situations, and experience prosperity and wellness. Their religious bent distinguishes them from modern self-help literature.

Given the pragmatic, functional mentality prevalent today, and our interest in potential fulfillment, we may find these books easier to relate to than other parts of the Old Testament.

The wisdom books are the most universal section of the Bible. Just as the human sciences have aided modern interpretation of the Bible, so Israel's wisdom literature was preceded and influenced by its neighbors' (particularly Egypt and the various Mesopotamian peoples).

Wisdom Teachings Permeate the Bible

Not all of the Bible's wisdom teachings are located in the wisdom books. Because the wisdom movement was integrated within Judaism, it is reflected throughout the Old Testament and in parts of the New Testament.

For example, the story of Adam and Eve is understood by scholars to have a wisdom dimension. A very influential and readable article on this topic was written by Luis Alonso-Schockel and is entitled "Sapiential and Covenant Themes in Gen 2–3" (Theology Digest 13 (1965) 3–10). The books of Amos, Tobit, and Jonah also contain a wisdom dimension.

In the New Testament, the Beatitudes have their origins in the wisdom movement, and the Sermon on the Mount offers wisdom counsel. The Gospel of Matthew (cf. Mt 11:19; 12:42) and the letter of James particularly reflect wisdom influence. The Gospel of Luke has several additional references to wisdom (cf. Lk 1:17; 2:40, 52; 7:35; 11:49).

Wisdom Balances the Law and Prophets

The wisdom books promote observance of the law and mindfulness of the prophetic exhortations within the framework of daily life. Their human perspective complements the divine perspective that is pervasive in the Pentateuch and prophetic books. For example, Gen 1-2:4a literally presents God's perspective ("And God saw ..."), while the wisdom-influenced story, Gen 2-3, focuses on humanity's experience and perspective.

Literary Diversity in Biblical Wisdom Literature

The wisdom writings in the Bible include poetry (Psalms, Song of Songs, Job, parts of Proverbs and the Wisdom of Solomon), proverbs (Proverbs, Sirach, parts of Ecclesiastes and Tobit), discourses (Job, Ecclesiastes, the Wisdom of Solomon), and stories (e.g., Gen 2-3, Tobit, Jonah, Job 1-2; 42).

PSALMS

The Psalms are classified as part of the wisdom books because they contain wisdom Psalms and fit better there than in the other Old Testament classifications. Because of their importance, accessible nature, and broad relevance, we devoted a whole chapter (twenty-two) to them.

PROVERBS

Though attributed to Solomon, Proverbs is a collection of aphorisms (proverbial sayings) and poetry from several sources. Like Sirach, its optimistic tone contrasts with the stark realism of Job and Ecclesiastes.

Proverbs' Groupings

    I.   Poetic proverbs on various topics (1:1-9:18).

    II.   First Collection of Solomon's proverbs (10:1-22:16).

    III.   Sayings of the wise (22:17-24:22).

    IV.   More Sayings of the wise (24:23-34).

    V.   Second Collection of Solomon's proverbs (25:1-29:27).

    VI.   Words of Agur (30:1-33). (Unknown person)

    VII.   Words of Lemuel (31:1-9). (Unknown person)

    VIII.   Poem in praise of the God-fearing wife (31:10-31).

Highlights of Proverbs

- **3:1-12:** Proper attitudes toward God.
- **3:13-24:** The value of wisdom.
- **3:25-35:** Proper attitudes toward fellow human beings.
- **8:1-21:** Personification and characteristics of wisdom.
- **8:22-31:** Wisdom present at creation. Presents wisdom in the feminine gender as an entity active in creation (cf. Jn 1).
- **8:32-36:** Two beatitudes for those who pursue wisdom.
- **9:1-6:** Wisdom's banquet.
- **30:7-33:** Numerical proverbs.

     As a mnemonic device, the sages would preface and group a collection of related proverbs by their number (cf. Prov 30:7-33). The prophet Amos employs this in Amos 1-2.

- **Prov 31:10-31:** A beautiful poem on the ideal wife that provides a fitting closing to the book.

     This passage is often read at women's funerals. There is a tradition within Judaism of husbands reading this to their wives on the eve of the Sabbath. Why not honor our loved ones while they are still with us?

THE BOOK OF JOB

The book of Job is a literary masterpiece that has been praised by a who's who's list of philosophers, theologians, artisans, and literary critics. Probably written somewhere between 500 and 300 B.C., we know nothing of the author's identity, save his craftsmanship. While referencing Old Testament texts in various parts of the book, it has a universal tone and a Gentile hero, Job. Pope John Paul II offers helpful insights into Job in the first part of one of his finest pastoral letters, *Salvifici Doloris* (On the Christian Meaning of Human Suffering).

Job: The Original Poor Soul

The beginning of the book of Job is familiar and straightforward enough for you to read on your own. Any questions that might arise are usually answered in the biblical footnotes. Our familiarity with its main theme, suffering in light of providence, enables us to identify with Job and his wife, and, to a lesser degree, Job's preachy friends.

Job's Structure

Excluding the prose prologue and epilogue (ch. 1-2 and 42, respectively), Job is a dramatic poem. The book consists of a prologue (ch. 1-2), Job's initial lament (ch. 3), three cycles of speeches featuring Job and his three friends (ch. 4-27), a poem about wisdom (ch. 28), Job's reminiscing and final remarks (ch. 29-31), a rebuttal by Elihu, a young, previously unannounced bystander frustrated with Job and his friends (ch. 32-37) — his speech is probably a later addition to the story — God's response (ch. 38-41), Job's replies (40:1-5; 42:1-6), and the happy ending (42:7-17).

Highlights of Job

- The story of Job (ch. 1-2).
- Job's outburst (ch. 3). Inverts the imagery of Gen 1 and borrows almost verbatim from Jer 20:14-18.
- Eliphaz's first speech (ch. 4-5). Introduces us to the mentality and rhetoric of Job's friends. As they get riled, their speeches recycle arguments and don't add much to

the dialogue. Emotion and insecurity trumps rationality and sensitivity. Their remarks are of interest primarily to biblical scholars and theologians. Sample them, but concentrate on Job's and God's speeches.

- Job's speeches (ch. 6-7, 9-10, 12-14, 16-17, 19, 21, 23-24, 26:1-4, 27:2-6, 27:11-12, 29-31).
- The wisdom poem (ch. 28).
- God's response (ch. 38-41).
- Job's acceptance speeches (40:1-5; 42:1-6).
- The resolution of the story (42:7-17).

The Devil You Say?

In Chapter Twenty-One, I mentioned that the proper name Adam is not present in Gen 2-3. Likewise, the proper name Satan, i.e., the devil, is not found in Job 1-2. Both the Hebrew nouns *adam* and *satan* are proceeded by the definite article *ha* ("the.")

The noun satan means accuser or adversary. It was legal terminology for a prosecuting attorney. The satan in Job acts as a devil's advocate. The term has a similar meaning in Zech 3:1, a prophetic book coming from approximately the same period.

Thus the passage does not portray God bargaining with the devil. The heavenly scene resembles ancient Near Eastern mythological and royalty imagery: the king or God/gods and their court. The satan's function is to disassociate Job's calamities from God's direct will and articulate Israel's growing but still ambiguous awareness of an angelic adversary whose role in human affairs is troublesome.

ECCLESIASTES: PUTTING A WISE GUY IN HIS PLACE

Koheleth is the Hebrew name for the author and the book. It means "preacher," and is derived from the Hebrew word for assembly. Ecclesiastes, the Greek translation, is the more familiar title.

Eccles 12:9 identifies the author as a popular teacher of wisdom. Along with the authors of Job and Jonah, Koheleth displays an intriguing sense of humor, a helpful aid for preaching. The book was attributed to Solomon, but the vocabulary and concepts indicate a much later date of composition. Koheleth was probably written after Job and Song of Songs, approximately three centuries before Christ. Koheleth and Song of Songs were the books that received the most resistance to inclusion in the Hebrew canon of the Bible.

The Style and Message of Koheleth

Koheleth is a potpourri of eclectic philosophizing, succinct proverbs, and sober observations and exhortations. It reads unevenly, but hangs together through its fundamental theme, realistic and pragmatic faith (cf. Eccles 7:15-17). It is a good balance to the Bible's idealism.

- Koheleth is a spiritual pundit. He speaks in short, self-contained bursts that both build upon and seemingly contradict what he said before.
- Koheleth refuses to force life and religion into tidy, comfortable categories. He prefers to take things as they are and make the best of them.

Like most biblical authors and intelligent, mature persons, Koheleth sees various sides of issues. He recognizes life's complexities and ambiguities, and can inspire you to avoid one-sided, hasty evaluations of such mysteries as human motivations and divine providence. When you read Koheleth, keep in mind his philosophy of moderation and discretion, epitomized by Eccles 3:1-11.

Because of his eclectic, non-linear style and weaving together of musings, it is best to digest Koheleth in chunks. Many Bibles provide subheadings to break up the text.

One of the differences between Koheleth and Proverbs is that the latter's proverbs generally can stand alone, whereas Koheleth's musings usually need to be read in context. In one text he advocates enjoyment of life, while in another he portrays life as arbitrary and incomprehensible. His pet expression is "vanity (of vanities)."

PEAK PASSAGES

"Behold, this alone I found, that God made man upright, but they have sought out many devices" (Eccles 7:29). Isn't that the truth!

SONG OF SONGS (CANTICLES)

Song of Songs is a hidden treasure of the Bible. It is known more by reputation than direct encounter. Churchgoers know that it speaks of love and courtship in erotic terms and is read at weddings. Passages such as Songs 2:8-17; 3:1-5; 4:1-15 are wedding standards that capture the moment: "My beloved is mine and I am his" (Songs 2:16).

Literally "the greatest song," Song of Songs has also been called (Canticle of) Canticles (from its Latin Vulgate title) and Song of Solomon (due to its attribution to Solomon). Its vocabulary and style indicates a post-exilic date of composition. I will use the term "Canticles" along with Song of Songs.

Songs' Interpretation Guidelines

Proper interpretation and application of Canticles requires an awareness of the concrete, earthy nature of the Hebrew language (particularly suited to this sensual topic), and ancient courtship and marriage rituals. A commentary and footnotes will help bridge this gap. Make up the rest of the distance by engaging your senses, experience, and imagination.

Canticles does not have a clear-cut, easy-to-follow order. There are three characters, the bride/beloved, the groom/lover, and the daughters of Jerusalem/companions. Without an indication from the translator who is speaking, readers can easily lose their bearings. When Canticles refers to the king, it can mean Solomon, but also, as in Egyptian love poems that may have influenced Canticles, the groom.

Because these speaker designations are not in the Hebrew text, translations vary in their assignment of verses. Some translations do not show these designations, making the text more difficult to follow.

Some of the best commentaries on Canticles have been written by medieval monks and mystics. The most notable are by St. Bernard of Clairvaux and St. John of the Cross.

PEAK PASSAGES

Songs 1:4; 2:8-17; 3:1-5; 4:1-15; 5:9-6:10; 7:1; 7:7; 8:14.

With an inspired source and your own experience and intuitions, the less said here on love and romance the better.

The Greatest Song

Canticles is the greatest of songs not because its poetry is unsurpassed, but because it gives love, courtship, and marriage its proper dignity and context. It promotes sincerity, fidelity, passion, mutuality, romance, playfulness, and persistence. Canticles is a forum for bringing our romantic energies into dialogue with God and (if applicable) our spouse.

In both Jewish and Christian tradition, the mutual affections of the couple have been interpreted as a metaphor for God's love affair with his people. Canticles sets the stage for the letter to the Ephesians' magnificent synthesis of these (cf. Eph 5:21-33).

Almost every aspect of intimate relationships suffering is portrayed in the Bible:

Envy: Sarah, Rachel.

Betrayal: Samson and Delilah.

Adultery: Gomer (Hosea's wife), and David and Bathsheba.

Deception: Rebekah and Jacob.

Rejection: Leah, Jacob's undesired wife.

Loss: the death of Ezekiel's wife and Rachel, Jacob's preferred wife, and of David's and Bathsheba's first child.

Verbal abuse in response to exorbitant stressors and loss: Job and his wife, and Tobit and Anna.

Loneliness: celibate Jeremiah and Jesus.

Infertility: the patriarchs and matriarchs, Hannah and Elkanah, Elizabeth and John.

Incest and Rape: Amnon and Tamar (cf. 2 Sam 13:1-19).

We can identify with them and draw parallels to our experiences, and invite the Holy Spirit to console and guide us.

SIRACH

Originally written in Hebrew around 180 B.C. by the sage Jesus ben Sira, Sirach was translated into Greek (for the Jews in the Diaspora) sometime after 132 B.C. by his grandson, who added a foreword. The foreword noted that ben (i.e., son of) Sira devoted himself "to the reading of the law and the Prophets and the other books of our fathers." Accordingly, the teaching of the book corresponds to the rest of the Old Testament.

It is similar in style, content, and outlook to Proverbs, while being more thematic and easier to follow. Sirach's proverbs come from one source, whereas there are several sources identified in Proverbs. However, Sirach lacks the poetic qualities of some parts of Proverbs.

Tips for Reading Sirach

Many Bibles provide topical headings so that you can break an individual book into manageable and coherent components. Because Sirach is consistent theologically and is organized by theme, these headings are particularly useful. You can read a section and meditate on its overall message or on one or more proverbs that speak to you.

Sirach's organized structure makes it a wonderful self-help resource. Read a selected proverb or grouping slowly, reflect on its relevance to your life (draw personal parallels and make practical applications), pray about it, and try to discern God's message to you, then apply/live it: biblically based personal growth in a nutshell! Apply this approach to Proverbs, the Sermon on the Mount, James, and other wisdom counsel as well.

PEAK PASSAGES

"Never repeat a conversation, and you will lose nothing at all.... Have you heard a word? Let it die with you. Be brave! It will not make you burst" (Sir 19:7, 10)!

"For a wound may be bandaged, and there is reconciliation after abuse, but whoever has betrayed secrets is without hope" (Sir 27:21; cf. 28:13-18).

St. Francis de Sales points out that slander results in three murders: the slandered, the slanderer, and the listener. Some of the advice in the wisdom books is dated, but most is timeless, albeit countercultural.

HIGHLIGHTS OF SIRACH

- Fear of the Lord. This fundamental wisdom movement value is mentioned seventeen times in 1:10-2:17.
- Duties toward parents (3:1-16).
    A classic, must-read passage, appropriately featured in the Feast of the Holy Family liturgy.

THE BIBLE SAYS WHAT?

Sirach has more negative things to say about women than any other book in the Bible (cf. Sir 9:1-9; 25:12-26:18). Its discriminatory values reflect its patriarchal culture.

Sirach also makes negative comments about men and positive comments about women. Its counsel on discipline of children is likewise out of sync with some contemporary standards (cf. Sir 30:1-13; 42:9-14).

When encountering culturally conditioned parts of the Bible, such as in the areas of sex, violence, and rituals, contextualize the primitive elements, recognize the development of revelation principle, and seek the text's essential and timeless aspects. Humanizing the Bible means recognizing the imperfections and limitations that accompany its human dimension without diminishing its enduring values and divine inspiration.

- Duties toward the poor (3:30-4:10).
- Control of the tongue (5:11-6:5; 19:5-16; 20:18-26: 22:27; 23:7-15; 28:12-26; 37:17).
- Relations with friends and associates (6:6-17; 8:1-19; 9:10-16; 11:29-12:18; 13:1-14:2; 22:19-26; 36:18-37:15).
- Moderation (11:7-28; 37:27-31).
- A commentary on the creation stories (16:24-17:15).
- Prudence (18:14-29).
- Self-control (18:30-19:4).
- True wisdom (19:17-26).
- Incest and adultery (23:16-27).
- Numerical proverbs (25:1-11).
    Introduction and grouping of thematically related proverbs by their number for mnemonic purposes.
- Respect for physicians (38:1-15).
- Joys and miseries of life (40:1-27).
- Appropriate and false shame (41:14-42:8).
- The majesty of nature (42:15-43:35).

- Recollection of Hebrew heroes and divine providence (44:1-49:16).
- Patience (51:30).

THE WISDOM OF SOLOMON

An inspired book with the title "The Wisdom of Solomon" gets my attention if I am interested in growth and fulfillment. Who better to consult on how to get along in the world?

Entitled "The book of Wisdom" in the Vulgate and "The Wisdom of Solomon" in the Septuagint, it was composed between the first and second century B.C. in Alexandria, the center of Greek learning and culture in the ancient Near East.

Although attributed to Solomon, the book reveals an author steeped in the Jewish tradition, yet familiar with Greek philosophy and culture. His objective is to remind Diaspora Jews of the morality, wisdom, and glory of the Hebrew tradition. It is also designed to console Jews who are experiencing persecution.

Highlights of the Wisdom of Solomon
- God made the world good (1:13-15).
- Wis 2:10-3:9 is a beautiful hymn describing the persecution of the just and God's ultimate vindication of them. Excerpts from it are often used at Catholic funerals. Wis 2:12-20 helped the early Church understand Jesus' scandalous death (cf. Mt 27:41-44).
- Childlessness (3:13-4:6).
- Early death (4:7-19).

THE BIBLE SAYS WHAT?

Look up biblical cross-references among Proverbs, Koheleth, Wisdom of Solomon, and Song of Songs. Observe the unity and diversity of pseudo-Solomonic wisdom.

- Solomon's desire and search for wisdom in 7:1-8:8 parallels the bride's and groom's search for each other in the Song of Solomon. You can read these passages and pray that you will have a similar passion for wisdom and your loved one(s).
- God's fidelity during the Exodus (11:1-19:22).

THE QUEST FOR IDENTITY CONTINUES

The wisdom books offer practical, often countercultural insights into our identity and development, while helping us avoid angelism (denial of bodily realities) and fundamentalism.

Let us now conclude our exploration of the Old Testament by encountering the prophets, Israel's conscience, whose message remains vibrant and compelling. The prophetic books reveal in even more detail than the other Old Testament sections how human and religious identity and integrity can be lost both individually and collectively.

Chapter Twenty-Five

How to Read and Heed the Prophetic Books

Contents of this Chapter

- Learn the different types of prophets and the vocabulary associated with them.
- Distinguish between Jewish and Christian arrangements of the prophetic books.
- Understand and apply the prophetic books.
- Identify key prophetic themes and passages.
- Develop a reading plan for the prophetic books.

PROPHETIC TERMINOLOGY

To comprehend the prophets, we must first define and distinguish them. We'll begin by reviewing the vocabulary and canonical groupings of the prophetic books. Then we'll explore the nature and purpose of biblical prophecy. Finally, we'll survey the prophetic books with an emphasis on key passages and themes.

It is not necessary to commit the terminology to memory; basic familiarity prepares you for its appearance in biblical footnotes and commentaries. Eventually, it will help you see how the prophetic books fit in with one another and the Bible as a whole.

WHAT IS A PROPHET?

In the Bible, the term "prophet" refers to an elect individual who acts as God's mouthpiece. The "prophetic books" refers to the section of the Old Testament containing the writings of what Jews refer to as the "later prophets" (composed of three major and twelve minor prophets), along with Daniel (grouped with the major prophets by Christians) and Lamentations and Baruch (see diagram below). The latter two follow Jeremiah in the canon because they have traditionally been linked to him.

The later prophets are also referred to as classical or canonical prophets because they wrote or were the source for the books named after them. The major prophets (Isaiah, Jeremiah, and Ezekiel) are identified as such because of the length of the books (sixty-six, fifty-two, and forty-eight chapters respectively).

THE EARLY PROPHETS

Prophets and prophecy exist in the Old Testament outside of the prophetic books. Although primarily known as lawgiver, Moses is referred to as a prophet in Deut 18:15-18; 34:10. Samuel is frequently referred to as a prophet, as is Nathan, David's trusted associate. Two of the most famous prophets are Elijah and Elisha.

Yet all of the above prophets are found in the historical rather than prophetic books of the Old Testament. Excluding Moses, they are found in the section of the Old Testament that Jews refer to as the early or former prophets, the books of Joshua, Judges, Samuel, and Kings.

The early/former prophets are concerned with the conquering and settlement of the promised land, and the establishment and eventual division of the monarchy. Of these, only 2 Kings, which narrates the history of the northern and southern kingdoms, overlaps chronologically with the later prophets.

We can distinguish the early from the later prophets primarily through their function. The early prophets (e.g., Elijah and Elisha) were not necessarily authors. They were initiators, politically powerful catalysts who acted in God's name. The later prophets were primarily observers/reactors and mouthpieces, persons who revealed God's perspective on Israel, the (neighboring) nations, and the future, and whose actions were more exhortatory and symbolic than military or miraculous.

Perhaps the best analogy comes from the world of sports. The early prophets were players, or even player-coaches, while the later prophets were primarily coaches or referees. The early prophets initiated events, while the later prophets monitored the proceedings and enforced the rules by instructing and warning Israel.

THE PROPHETIC BOOKS
Isaiah
Jeremiah
Lamentations
Baruch
Ezekiel
Daniel

The twelve minor prophets:
Hosea, Joel, Amos, Obadiah, Jonah, Micah,
Nahum, Habakkuk, Zephaniah,
Haggai, Zechariah, Malachi

THE MOST EXCITING SECTION OF THE BIBLE
Because of the intense language and unfamiliar contexts, idioms, theological issues, and literary styles, the early prophets and the prophetic books are the most difficult sections of the Bible for modern readers.

As with any challenge, they are also eminently rewarding and exciting: judges, kings, and prophets are where the action is. Sex, intrigue, and conflict abound. They are the Bible's version of a James Bond movie: intense, controversial, occasionally humorous, confusing at times, and filled with sex, violence, victims, and megalomaniacs. Some of the finest stories in literature are contained in these sections of the Old Testament.

SAMPLING THE MAJOR PROPHETS

The prophetic books contain some of the most inspiring and hopeful passages in the Bible. As in previous chapters, our objective is to break the prophetic books into manageable portions and concentrate on the most important prophets and passages. Thus, you can avoid being overwhelmed by the breadth and intensity of the material.

If you wish to sample the material, the following are ten prominent major prophets passages:

Is 7:14; 11:1-9; 50:4-9; 52-53; 55; 58; 61:1-7
Jer 31: 31-34
Ezek 34; 37

WHO WERE THE PROPHETS?

Think of the prophets as God's private council. They are privy to his plans and decisions, in what manner we do not know. With Moses as the finest example (cf. Deut 34:10), they are directly familiar with God. Texts that support this notion are 1 Kings 22:18-23; Amos 3:7; Jer 23:18, 22; Ps 82:1; Job 1:6; 2:1; 15:8. Similar texts that portray God sitting on his throne include Ps 2:4; 11:4; 93:2; 97:1-2; Rev 4.

When the prophets are "called" (cf. Is 6:1-11; Jer 1:4-10; Ezek 2) they are invited into God's council/confidence. Biblical accounts of the prophet's call justify their role and influence. There were false prophets in Israel, and the community had to discern who truly spoke for God and who were impostors. The Church has to do the same in every era.

The prophets conveyed God's message to his people in response to their actions. Sometimes this involved future predictions and visions. The prophets dealt with the fate of both Israel and the surrounding nations.

Excluding Moses, the prophets span six centuries, from Samuel in the early tenth century, to Joel in the early fourth century.

The prophets were the conscience of Israel. Since most of the kings and religious leaders led Israel astray, hence the "woe to the shepherds" passages (cf. Is 56:9-12; Jer 12:10; 23:1-4; 25:34-38; Ezek 34:1-10; Zech 11:4-17), it was up to the prophets to remind the people of what God had done for them and what he required.

The prophets were western civilization's first social and economic-justice advocates. There were other activists in ancient cultures, but few so boldly challenged the reigning powers. The prophets were fearless in their denunciations, and ended up paying for it (cf. Jer 38:1-6; 2 Chron 24:20-22; Lk 13:34).

THE PROPHETS' MESSAGE

The prophets frequently chastise the people for exploiting the needy and for cheating in everyday business practices.

Principles of commercial and social justice, with emphasis on the rights of the vulnerable, had been conveyed in the law (cf. Ex 22:21-27). The prophets refreshed the people's memory.

The prophets condemned idolatrous and hedonistic practices.

The prophets criticized false notions of worship and sacrifice, and the dichotomy between external gestures and rituals and behavior toward God and neighbor, including family members. Mic 6:6-8 is a classic text in this regard.

The prophets criticized the people's complacency and excessive nationalism (cf. Jonah) and their tendency to neglect God's word and turn toward foreign powers and political alliances for help.

The prophets frequently warned the false prophets (who undermined the real prophet's credibility) of their impending punishment.

PROPHET PERSONAS

Isaiah is elusive elegance, Jeremiah is sensitive and visceral, and Ezekiel is enthusiastic and eclectic. Hosea (particularly Hos 1-3) tugs at your heart, while Amos grabs you by the scruff of the neck. Malachi gives it to you straight: e.g., God hates divorce (cf. Mal 2:16).

Don't confuse the prophets with angels. Flesh and blood like you and me, their actions and writings reveal their humanity. You'll be drawn to prophets and passages that resonate with your situation and temperament.

THE PROPHET ISAIAH

The books of Isaiah, Job, and Genesis are considered the finest literature in the Old Testament. Isaiah contains several passages that were pivotal in the early Church's understanding of Jesus. Isaiah is the prophet that Jesus reads in the synagogue (cf. Lk 4:16-30), and the only major or minor prophet he mentions by name (cf. Mt 15:7; Mk 7:6). The book is understood by the majority of scholars to be composed of three distinct works:

First Isaiah (Is 1-39) contains the prophet Isaiah's message to the southern kingdom in Jerusalem in the second half of the eighth century B.C. It reveals a powerful, transcendent God.

Second (Deutero-) Isaiah (Is 40-55), also known as the book of consolations, contains prophetic messages to the post-exilic (late 6th century B.C.) community in Babylon during the time of Persian rule. God is presented as working through people, e.g., the suffering servant in Is 52-53.

Third (Trito-) Isaiah (Is 56-66) was most likely written between 538 and 500 B.C. by a prophet familiar with first and second Isaiah. He adapted much of second Isaiah to the post-exilic community in

Jerusalem. His objective is to remind Israel of their sins, console the poor, and proclaim a future time of salvation and accountability. Both the transcendent and incarnational images of God presented in first and second Isaiah respectively are reflected in third Isaiah.

Highlights of First Isaiah

- **2:1-4:** Isaiah's vision of future peace, instruction, and judgment on God's holy mountain. Do I have a positive vision of the future?
- **5:1-7:** The unfruitful vineyard. In what areas of my life am I sour grapes?
- **6:1-10:** Isaiah's vision and call. When God calls, am I reluctant like Jonah, Jeremiah, and Moses, or eager like Isaiah? Why do I respond as I do? Do I let God cleanse me?
- **7:10-25:** Isaiah 7:14 states a "young maiden" ("virgin" in the Septuagint, thereby interpreted by Christians as a prophesy of the virgin birth) will bear a son, Emmanuel ("God with us"). Do I experience God as "with me"?
- **11:1-9:** Vision of messianic kingdom. The traditional list of gifts of the Holy Spirit are found in 11:2-3. The Septuagint and Vulgate list seven by substituting "piety" for the first of two "fear of the Lord" expressions found in the Hebrew text.
- **Chapter 35 and 54:** Restoration of the downtrodden. I can pray these in hopes of my restoration.

Highlights of Second Isaiah

- **40:1-41:20:** Consoling of Jerusalem. How might God comfort me?
- **Ch. 43:** God's protection. Affirms God's "fear not" message. Am I listening?
- **44:1-8, 21-28:** Consolation of Israel. Beautiful images communicating the splendor of God.
- **45:9-12:** How can the clay criticize the potter (cf. Jer 18:1-11; 19:1)? Submitting to God's will and divine providence is one of our greatest challenges.

- **42:1-4; 49:1-6; 50:4-9; 52:13-53:12:** The four Servant Songs are interpreted by Christians as prophesies fulfilled by Jesus.
- **55:1-13:** Invitation to experience God.

Highlights of Third Isaiah

- **Ch. 58:** A compelling integration of spirituality and social justice (cf. Mt 25:31-46).
- **59:20-21:** God will establish an everlasting covenant (cf. Jer 31:31-34).
- **61:1-7:** The deliverance of the downtrodden. Jesus fulfilled this (cf. Lk 4:16-21).
- **65:17-25:** Vision of a new, harmonious creation.

THE PROPHET JEREMIAH

Jeremiah preached for approximately forty years (626 B.C. – 587 B.C.; cf. Jer 1:1-3) amid one of the most turbulent periods in Near Eastern history. He was caught between the fall of Assyria and the rise of Babylon. He observed Zedekiah, the last in a succession of weak and wicked kings, ignore his warnings and react imprudently to the changing political tides, resulting in the destruction of Jerusalem and the deportation of the survivors.

Jeremiah is the most outspoken prophet, wearing his heart on his sleeve and communicating his trademark message "terror on every side" to the dismay and ridicule of his contemporaries. He gives hope to those of us who would prefer that God pick (on) someone else.

Jeremiah's Highlights

- **1:4-10:** God's call of Jeremiah. Do I believe that God has particular plans for me?
- **3:1-4:4:** Israel's infidelity and God's call to repentance.
- **4:19-31; 8:18-22:** Jeremiah's anguish. He takes his job personally, and almost cares too much. Do I care this passionately?
- **9:1-9:** Sins of the tongue. Do I monitor my words so as to avoid verbal violence?
- **12:1-4:** Lamenting the prosperity of the wicked. A stumbling block made less onerous by the Beatitudes and Jesus' redemptive suffering and death.
- **14:19-22:** The people's beautiful plea for forgiveness. I can make this prayer mine.
- **15:15-21:** A classic lament and God's response.
- **16:1-2:** Unprecedented in the Old Testament, Jeremiah's celibacy is called for by God in response to the people's sins. This passage foreshadows Jesus' comments on celibacy (cf. Mt 19:11-12). Persons in involuntary celibate situations may find both consolation and a divine call in this passage.
- The prophet bears the consequences of his own sins as well as those of the people (cf. Jer 10:19; Jer 31:29-30; Ezek 18:1-32; 33:1-20).
- **16:18-23:** Jeremiah's life is in danger, and he prays for revenge. When I serve God's word, I evoke opposition and resentment, including within myself.
- **29:10-14:** One of the most consoling passages in the Bible.

- **31:31-34:** For Christians, this is the most hopeful and important passage in the Old Testament (cf. Heb 8:8-12). It is preceded by seven "the days are coming" prophecies (cf. Jer 7:32; 9:25; 16:14; 19:6; 23:5; 30:3; 31:27), thereby making this passage a spiritual crescendo.
- **32:6-25:** Though he knows the Babylonians are coming, on God's order Jeremiah buys a field. This symbolic action prophesies Judah's eventual restoration. Jeremiah asked God for an explanation. Sometimes even the prophets went on blind faith.
- **Ch. 36:** Jeremiah dictates a scroll, Baruch reads it publicly, the king burns it, so Jeremiah dictates another one with even more foreboding prophecies.
- **38:1-13:** After prophesying Jerusalem's destruction, Jeremiah is thrown into a muddy cistern to die, only to be saved by an Ethiopian eunuch.
- **39:1-10:** The fall of Jerusalem.
- **43:4-7:** Jeremiah is taken to Egypt, where he continues his prophesying to a resistant remnant. The Bible does not disclose details of Jeremiah's death.

PEAK PASSAGES

"And the LORD said to me, "Faithless Israel has shown herself less guilty than false Judah" (Jer 3:11): an ominous omen of the destruction awaiting the southern kingdom.

THE PROPHET EZEKIEL

Ezekiel began preaching in and around Jerusalem in the early sixth century and continued in Babylon after the deportation. He has been called "the father of Judaism" because he foresaw its survival as dependent upon its adherence to the word of God and the covenant.

The majority of scholars believe that some parts of Ezekiel were not written by the prophet. Despite this and the prophet's eclectic personality, the book is orderly enough for beginners to follow. Contrast this with the writings of a prophet who significantly influenced Ezekiel, Jeremiah, whose oracles are scattered throughout the book in no apparent order.

Because of his bizarre behavior (e.g., mysterious visions, gestures, and prolonged silences), Ezekiel has been psychoanalyzed *ad nauseum*. Suffice to say that anyone commissioned by God is different from the norm and is subject to pressures that can manifest unusual behaviors. Taking our cue from Einstein ("I should like very much to remain in the darkness of not having been analyzed."), we would be best to analyze the prophet and ourselves less while listening more to God's word.

Both ancient and modern commentators agree that the book, like its author's personality, is both paradoxical and mysterious. Many aspects, such as date of composition, chronology, and degree of pseudonymity, remain the subject of debate.

Highlights of Ezekiel

- **2:1-3:11:** Call of Ezekiel, initial vision, and eating of the scroll. This prepares us for Ezekiel's bizarre language and gestures.
- **3:12-15:** Ezekiel is sent to grieve among the exiles, doing so for the customary seven days like the comforters/friends of Job (cf. Job 2:14).

- **3:16-21:** Respective responsibilities of the leader/prophet (i.e., Ezekiel) and followers.
- **Ch. 15-16:** Images of Judah as the useless vine and faithless bride (cf. Is 5; Hos 1-4).
- **16:59-63:** The promise of an everlasting covenant (cf. Is 59:20-21; Jer 31:31-34).
- **18; 33:1-17:** Among the Old Testament's mature passages on individual responsibility.
- **24:15-27:** Moving first-person account of the foretold death of Ezekiel's wife. Like Jeremiah (cf. 16:1-2) and Hosea (cf. Hos 1-3), his personal suffering takes on a symbolic meaning, indicating to the people how they are to respond when they undergo personal and national tragedy.
- **28:1-10:** An application of the Adam and Eve story to the arrogant pagan king of Tyre.
- **Ch. 34:** God will replace Israel's evil shepherds with himself (cf. Is 54:13; Mt 18:6-7; 23; Lk 12:48; Jn 6:45; 10).
- **36:22-38:** Cleansing of Israel and the outpouring of God's spirit.
- **37:1-14:** The famous "dry bones" passage immortalized in song. It symbolizes the new life God will give to his people.
- **39:25-29:** Prophesy of the restoration of Israel. Recalls God's new start with humanity (cf. Gen 8:21; Joel 3:1-5; Acts 2).
- **48:35:** The new name for the rebuilt city of God: "Yahweh–is–there" (cf. Is 7:14).

DANIEL

Daniel is an apocalyptic work composed around 200 B.C. It is the latest book accepted into the Hebrew canon. The first half of the book takes place at the Babylonian and Persian courts, and is told from the third-person perspective. The second half contains apocalyptic prophecies related in the first person.

Roman Catholic and Orthodox Bibles contain additional sections in the book of Daniel: the Prayer of Azariah and the Song of the Three Young Men in Dan 3, and the story of Susanna in Dan 13 and of Bel and the Dragon (Babylonian idols) in Dan 14. These are found in the Septuagint. Daniel is one of the Old Testament books that contains a significant portion written in Aramaic (cf. Dan 2:4b-7:28).

Highlights of Daniel

The first six chapters of Daniel are accessible, and the deuterocanonical story of Susanna in Dan 13 is intriguing, but the apocalyptic writings in chapters 7-12 are heavy going. The stories of Shadrach, Meshach, and Abednego in the fiery furnace and of Daniel in the lions' den are in Dan 3 and 6 respectively.

THE MINOR PROPHETS

The minor prophets are one of the overlooked parts of the Bible. They are cited several times in the New Testament as messianic prophecies (cf. Mic 5:2; Zech 11:12-13), though not as often as the major prophets (particularly Isaiah) or the Psalms.

Parts of the minor prophets are so steeped in their historical context and ancient literary genres as to become almost unintelligible to the Bible beginner. Other parts, such as Jonah and much of Amos, Hosea, Micah, and Malachi, are readily accessible. The following table will help you sample the minor prophets and encounter their most prominent passages and themes.

SACRED HUMOR

 A southerner preaching to the north, and a dresser of sycamore trees — fat chance of Amos being heeded. In our day, that would be like a southern peanut farmer trying to evoke a moral response from the sophisticated industrialists of the north.

MINOR PROPHETS' BACKGROUNDS AND HIGHLIGHTS

Prophet	Century	Audience	Suggested Readings	Commentary
Amos (shepherd, dresser of sycamore trees).	Mid 8th	Israel (N)	1:1-2-3 2:4-16 4:1-3 (cf. Is 3:16-24) 7:10-17 8:4-14 9:11-15	Judgment of the nations. Judgment of Israel and Judah. Warning to "cows of Bashan" (prosperous women of Samaria) not to influence their husbands to despoil others. A fertile area on the east side of the Jordan River, Bashan was known for its beefy cattle. Expulsion attempt. Condemnation of the oppression of the weak. Restoration of Israel.
Amos sees little hope for Israel, whereas Hosea experiences bursts of hope.				
Jonah	Mid 8th	Israel (N)	Entire book	Classic short story. Reveals God's love for and outreach to all peoples. Corrects excessive nationalism. Jewish version of Good Samaritan parable in that the hated are the heroes and the hometown boy is the heel.
Hosea	Mid 8th	Israel (N)	Ch. 1-3 6: 14 9-10 11	Classic marital imagery. Call for repentance. Israel's punishment. God's compassion and disappointment.
Like a rejected lover, God vacillates between spurning and forgiving Israel.				

Micah	Late 8th	Judah (S)	1:5	Indictment of Jerusalem and Samaria (south and north capitals).
			2:1-10	Social evils
			3:1-12	Criticism of leaders.
			5:1-4	Bethlehem prophecy used in New Testament in reference to Jesus.
			6:6-8	Authentic worship and offerings.
Nahum	Mid-late 7th	Judah (S)	1:1-8; 3:18-19	Is 10:12 predicted Assyria's downfall, Nahum rejoices in it.
Zephaniah	Mid-late 7th	Judah (S)	1-2	Immediately precedes Jeremiah, whom he influenced. Worship of nature deities was reappearing. Classic description of Judgment Day. Offers reproach and hope for Jerusalem (Ch. 3).
Habakkuk	Late 7th-early 6th	Judah (S)	1:2-4	Classic lament.
			1:5-11	Prophecy of Babylonian military ambitions. Probable contemporary of Jeremiah.
Lamentations	Late 7th-early 6th	Judah (S)	Ch. 3	A lament reminiscent of Job and the individual lament Psalms.
			Ch. 5	A plea for mercy in the spirit of the communal lament Psalms (cf. Ps 44).

Though Lamentations is not one of the twelve minor prophets, for chronological purposes I have included it within this table as a complement to the discussion below.

Continued on page 338 . . .

... continued from page 337

MINOR PROPHETS' BACKGROUNDS AND HIGHLIGHTS (CONTINUED)

Prophet	Century	Audience	Suggested Readings	Commentary
Obadiah	early 6th	Post-exilic Jews	1:15-16 1:17-21	Judgment of nations. Restoration of Jewish people.
Obadiah's 21 verses make it the Bible's shortest book. Its prophecies are among the Bible's sternest.				
Haggai	late 6th	Post-exilic Jews	1:1-11 2:13-14	Oriented around the rebuilding of the temple under Darius I. Rebuilt temple was not as spectacular as first temple. Built quicker.
Zechariah	late 6th	Post-exilic Jews	1:7-17 3:1-2 6:1-8 11:4-17 14	Four horsemen. Satan accusing Joshua. Four chariots. Punishment of shepherds/rulers. The fight against Jerusalem, and her deliverance.
Malachi	Mid 5th	Post-exilic Jews	2:13-17 3:1-4:6	God hates divorce. Applied by Christians to John the Baptist (cf. Is 40:3; Mk 2; Mt 11:14; 17:12).
Joel	Late 5th, early to mid 4th	Post-exilic Jews	2:1-17 2:28-32	Call to penance and vision of the Day of the Lord. Vision of outpouring of God's spirit applied to Pentecost in the New Testament.

LAMENTATIONS

Lamentations consists of five laments over the destruction of Jerusalem and the temple in 587 B.C. It is also known as The Lamentations of Jeremiah because of the prophet's association with that period and his composition of laments (cf. Jer 7:29; 9:9, 19; 2 Chron 35:25). Lamentations comes between Jeremiah and Ezekiel in the Christian canon because of its association with the prophet.

Because the message of Lamentations differs significantly from the book of Jeremiah, modern scholars do not believe Jeremiah is its author. However, both the Latin (Vulgate) and Greek (Septuagint) translations of the Bible present Lamentations as an appendix to the book of Jeremiah.

Although beautiful and inspiring, Lamentations is too heavy and historically rooted for most readers new to the Bible. It presupposes knowledge of the destruction of Jerusalem and the book of Jeremiah, the latter's content being richer and more relevant and accessible.

BARUCH

Baruch is the only prophetic book among the deuterocanonical writings. Like the other deuterocanonical books, excluding the Hebrew version of Sirach and the Aramaic of Tobit, it comes down to us in Greek.

Bar 1:1-4 credits the book to the prophet Jeremiah's secretary, Baruch. His name sounds like the Hebrew word for bless. Its five sections range from prose to poetry, the latter likely composed originally in Hebrew:

I. Prayer of the exiles (Bar 1:1–3:8).
II. Praise of wisdom in the Torah (Bar 3:9–4:4).
III. Jerusalem laments and comforts the exiles (Bar 4:5–29).
IV. Jerusalem comforted: the oncoming liberation (Bar 4:30–5:9).

V: The letter of Jeremiah (Bar 6:1–7).

Most likely the book was written after the lifetime of Baruch as a reflection upon the exilic experience with an eye to conveying the importance of watchfulness and repentance to the present generation. Baruch was a well-known and credible person to use as an authority.

The closing chapter is a distinct work and is known as the Epistle, or Letter, of Jeremiah. Its warnings against idolatry recall Jer 10 and the letter of Jeremiah in Jer 29.

This sincere and passionate letter is not distinguished by any new teachings or outstanding literary quality, and is not an essential stop for a beginner's reading tour of the Bible.

THE BIBLE SAYS WHAT?

 Dates ascribed to Old Testament books written after the time of the return from Babylon (ca. 538 B.C.) are educated guesses. An individual book's vocabulary, concepts, and relationship to the rest of Scripture enable us to hypothesize within a century or two.

CANONICAL CRITICISM

An evolving area of biblical studies that has emerged in the last thirty years is known as canonical criticism. Unlike the historical critical methods discussed in Chapter Nine, it is more concerned with the present state of the canon, its final form and content, than with its development over time. This is known as synchronic (same time) analysis, whereas the former are known as diachronic (on account of time).

Canonical criticism recognizes that a book's message is not only historically and pastorally conditioned, but that it has a universal application, given its normative status as part of the canon. It also considers the significance of the position of a biblical book within the canon and its relationship to the other books and the Bible as a whole.

One straightforward application of canonical criticism involves the different way Jews and Christians conclude their Hebrew canons.

The Christian Old Testament ends with Malachi, largely because it contains prophecies cited in the New Testament in reference to John the Baptist and Jesus. Its harsh criticism of Jewish males' propensity to divorce their wives resembles Jesus' in Mt 19:3-9. Malachi serves as a relatively smooth transition to the New Testament.

The Jewish Bible ends with 1 and 2 Chronicles, which gives an account of the monarchy from the death of Saul and David's succession to the fall of Jerusalem. The Jews' dynamic faith as they await David's successor (the messiah) is symbolized by Chronicles' backward glance and reshaped perspectives corresponding to Israel's evolving theology and circumstances.

PEAK PASSAGES

"… and they shall beat their swords into plowshares, and their spears into pruning hooks; nation shall not lift up sword against nation, neither shall they learn war any more" (Is 2:4b).

"Beat your plowshares into swords, and your pruning hooks into spears; let the weak say, 'I am a warrior' " (Joel 3:10).

The biblical version of different strokes for different folks in different times. Each situation requires unique responses. See Mt 12:30, Mk 9:40, and Lk 9:50 for New Testament examples of seemingly contradictory messages that in reality reflect subtle differences in wording and circumstance.

POINTERS FOR PRAYING THE PROPHETS

- Abandoned or betrayed spouses may find praying Hos 1-3 therapeutic and cathartic, an opportunity to let God's word put intimate bitterness into perspective and inject hope.
- The book of Nahum, which exults over the destruction of Nineveh (known in the ancient near east as the "bloody city" (cf. Nah 3:1)), is good for praying your anger against oppressors and putting it in God's hands.
- Micah 6:6-8 is a concise reminder of the true nature of spirituality.
- When you are down, read Ezek 37 and imagine your bones coming to life.
- Pray Jer 12:1-4 and Hab 1:2-4 when you are sick of seeing the bad guys win.
- Pray Jon 4:6-11 when you lose something precious.

READING THE PROPHETS

Develop a game plan for reading the prophetic books. Consider beginning with the highlighted passages of Isaiah, Jeremiah, and Ezekiel, and balance them with selections from Daniel, Amos, Hosea, Micah, and Malachi. Read Jonah whole.

If you wish further background, consult Richard T. A. Murphy, O.P.'s *An Introduction to the Prophets of Israel*. It is the finest introduction available.

In the next and final chapter, we will discuss the culmination of the interactive and holistic Catholic approach to the Bible, the application of prophetic sensibilities (intuition, intelligence, and integrity) and passion to contemporary life.

Chapter Twenty-Six

——— How to Bring the Bible to Life: ———
Reading the Signs of the Times

SPIRITUAL DISCERNMENT

In the previous chapter, we encountered the biblical prophets,
who, often through symbols and signs, communicated God's message to the Hebrews. They also looked at what was happening in
Israel and the world around them, and interpreted its meaning
and consequences for the people.

Because few of us encounter God face-to-face like Moses, or
in intimate counsel like the prophets, we have to make judicious
interpretations not only of God's word but of the circumstances of
our lives.

We have to "read" these properly, or in biblical terms, exercise
the spiritual gift of discernment (cf. 1 Kings 3; Ps 119:144, 169;
Prov 16:21; Mt 10:16; 1 Cor 2:6-16, 12:10; Phil 1:9; 1 Jn 4:1,

5:20). The Bible, Tradition, the magisterium and fellow Christians, along with experience, journaling, spiritual direction or pastoral counsel, and judicious use of the human sciences and faculties, help us do so.

THE SIGNS OF THE TIMES

The New Testament term for these human and divine signs in our midst is "the signs of the times," an expression found in Mt 16:3 and prominent in the documents and implementation of Vatican II. Jesus observed that the religious leaders sought spectacular signs from the heavens, but could not discern the signs that God had given them (cf. Mt 12:38-42; Lk 16:19-31).

By exercising the gift of spiritual discernment, we can read "the signs of the times," that is, the meaning and significance of life events from the perspective of God's word. The *lectio divina* and *pardes* models help us holistically interact with these signs as they manifest themselves in the Bible and life. We thereby fulfill our prophetic function as persons entrusted with a vocation and message from God. God communicates himself through each person.

"The signs of the times" have both daily and eternal ramifications and contexts. The Bible and the Greek language refer to the former as *chronos* (chronological time) and to the latter as *kairos* (moment of crisis/decision). We receive both major jolts/signs at crucial junctures in our life and subtle prompts in daily matters that accumulate and become major. Through faith and reason, we try to discern God's will for our overall life direction or a particular situation.

The reflective (faith), interpretive (reason), and communal (church) principles and activities we explored in this book help us in this endeavor. Let us conclude by reviewing these ways of bringing the Bible to life, and sustaining our spiritual reading and living.

CATHOLIC GUIDELINES FOR INTERPRETING THE BIBLE

- Look up the cross-references in your Bible and this book. This enables the Bible to interpret itself. You will get a balanced view of the Bible and a reservoir of inspiration to refresh yourself during difficult times. Resolve to read the Bible more than books about the Bible, including this one.

- Interpreting the Bible contextually includes the post-biblical interpretive context of the community of believers. Consider how a passage has been interpreted historically/traditionally, particularly by authorities such as the magisterium, doctors of the Church, the saints, and esteemed scholars.

  Just as there is a development of revelation within the Bible, so this development continues through the maturing interpretations and applications of believers. The Church articulated its recognition of the evolving way in which truths are understood and expressed in the 1973 document *Mysterium Ecclesiae*, promulgated by the Congregation for the Doctrine of the Faith.

  Analogously, consider how you as an individual gain greater insights into the Bible and your life as you gain experience and maturity. Conversely, pride and complacency are to be avoided. When we think we've arrived, look out: "Therefore let any one who thinks that he stands take heed lest he fall" (1 Cor 10:12).

- Expect wholeness and integrity, not perfection and linear consistency, from the Bible. It is a human as well as divine document, and like everything human, it has its rough edges. Even Jesus lost his composure over human obstinacy, tragedy (Lazarus' death; cf. Jn 11:33-35), and imminent suffering (the agony in the garden). Stories such as Jesus' temptations in the desert and the cursing of the fig tree (cf. Mt 21:18-22), which have a symbolic interpretation, also reveal that Jesus was not exempt from the deprivations and ambiguities that we experience.

Keep in mind the parallel between Jesus' and the Bible's human nature. Both were subject to human limitations and conditions, but that doesn't mean either is flawed or less than divine. Jesus and the Bible don't transcend limitations as much as they transform them (cf. 2 Cor 5:21).

- As affirmed by Vatican II and subsequent magisterial teachings, the human sciences can have a legitimate bearing on the proper interpretation and application of the Bible, providing they do not supersede, demean, or contradict the Bible.

- Particularly when confronted with difficult passages that on the surface seem to contradict biblical and Catholic values, consider the Bible's historical context as well as the author's theological and pastoral objectives.

  For example, when the Bible uses exceedingly harsh expressions, it is usually because the people have gone astray and have tuned out gentler ways of correction. God's passionate attempt to soften stony hearts in the Bible should be distinguished from puritanical fire and brimstone rhetoric that motivate through fearsome images of God.

- Writing in your Bible or journal is a good way to record insights and feelings and to engage all your faculties. It helps you interpret and respond appropriately to significant events and circumstances in the Bible and life. A wide-margin Bible makes this convenient.

  See my book *Journaling with Moses and Job* for guidance on using *lectio divina* and biblically based potential-fulfillment principles in conjunction with journaling.

- Affirm yourself and thank God when you read or apply/live the Bible despite feeling low. Make the necessary adjustments and corrections when you find yourself getting away from the Bible, and don't dwell on your failures and laxity. Ask God for help and forgiveness, and move forward. He forgets our sins infinitely faster than we do (cf. Is 43:25; Ps 103:12; Heb 10:17).

    I have found low points to be the contexts of my greatest insights into the Bible and life. As reflected throughout the Bible, the Lord loves to help us when we are down, and expects us to reciprocate with one another.

- Get involved in some sort of communal Bible reading and sharing. Just two or three makes a community (cf. Mt 18:20). The Bible is a community book.

- Don't let the Bible become a burden. Use your creativity to make it as enjoyable as possible. As with any other significant undertaking, inject levity and variety as appropriate. Make the best of whatever time you have to read the Bible without letting it chronically get squeezed out by incessant activities or lower priorities.

AN INTIMATE ANALOGY

Taking a cue from Scripture, remember that your relationship with God or the Bible is like an intimate human relationship:

- Things go in cycles. Perseverance enables you to endure valleys and navigate peaks, and eventually arrive at level ground.
- You see yourself reflected in your partner.
- It is a vocation and not a picnic.
- Be realistic in your expectations of your partner, yourself, and the experience in general. Keep your ideals high, but do not lose heart over disappointments and mistakes (cf. Prov 3:11-12; 24:16; Heb 12:5-13).

- Both prosper in an atmosphere of truth. However, whereas even intimate relationships require a certain amount of reserve and discretion, God can handle whatever is in your heart and life.

LINKING THE BIBLE WITH LIFE AND LOVE

In order to sustain and optimize your interactions with the Bible, you must continually look for its links with life and love. These connections ward off staleness and boredom. We began and end with this principle, and like the Bible (the last book, Revelation, concludes with references to the beginning of the first book, Genesis), hopefully have come full circle.

The most important activity you can undertake with respect to the Bible is living/applying it: "Love never ends; as for prophecies, they will pass away; as for tongues, they will cease; as for knowledge, it will pass away" (1 Cor 13:8). Ultimately, it is not how much you know the Bible, but how much you love.

As a resource and guide for refining our capacity to love and live life to its fullest (cf. Jn 10:10), the Bible is unsurpassed. With Sarah and Tobias (cf. Tob 8:8), we entrust ourselves to God's wisdom and mercy, Amen, Amen.

Bibliography

Boadt, Lawrence. *Reading the Old Testament: An Introduction.* Mahwah, N.J.: Paulist Press, 1985.

Brook, John. *The School of Prayer: An Introduction to the Divine Office for All Christians.* Collegeville, Minn.: The Liturgical Press, 1992.

Brown, Raymond E. *An Introduction to the New Testament.* New York: Doubleday, 1997. Reference work for intermediate and advanced readers.

Brown, Raymond E. *Recent Discoveries and the Biblical World.* Wilmington, Del.: Michael Glazier, Inc., 1983.

Brown, Raymond E. *Responses to 101 Questions on the Bible.* Mahwah, NJ: Paulist Press, 1990.

Brown, Raymond E., Fitzmyer, Joseph A., and Murphy, Roland E. (editors). *The New Jerome Biblical Commentary.* New York: Prentice Hall, Inc., 1990. The best one-volume Catholic commentary.

Bryan, David Burton. *From Bible to Creed.* Wilmington, Del.: Michael Glazier, Inc., 1988.

Burt, Donald X. *The Pilgrim God: A Preacher Reflects on the Story of Jesus.* Collegeville, Minn: The Liturgical Press, 1995.

Charpentier, Etienne. *How to Read the Bible.* New York: Gramercy Books, 1991.

Dumm, Demetrius. *Flowers in the Desert: A Spirituality of the Bible.* Petersham, Mass.: St. Bede's Publications, 1998.

Guardini, Romano. *The Lord.* Chicago: Regnery Gateway, Inc., 1954.

John Paul II. The *Theology of the Body: Human Love in the Divine Plan.* Boston: Pauline Books & Media, 1997.

Keating, Thomas. *Invitation to Love.* Rockport, Mass.: Element Books, 1992.

Kodell, Jerome. *The Catholic Bible Study Handbook: A Popular Introduction to Studying Scripture.* Ann Arbor, Mich.: Servant Books, 2001.

Lienhard, Joseph T. *The Bible, the Church, and Authority: The Canon of the Christian Bible in History and Theology.* Collegeville, Minn.: The Liturgical Press, 1995.

Martin, George. *Reading Scripture as the Word of God.* Ann Arbor, Mich: Servant Books, 1998.

Marshall Editions Ltd. *Great Events of Biblical Times.* New York: Barnes & Noble Books, 1998.

Metzger, Bruce M. and Coogan, Michael D. *The Oxford Companion to the Bible*. New York: Oxford University Press, 1993.

Miller, Charles E. *Together in Prayer: Learning to Love the Liturgy of the Hours*. Staten Island, N.Y.: Alba House, 1994.

Montague, George, T. *The Holy Spirit: Growth of a Biblical Tradition*. Mahwah, N.J.: Paulist Press, 1976.

Montague, George, T. *Understanding the Bible: A Basic Introduction to Biblical Interpretation*. Mahwah, N.J.: Paulist Press, 1997.

Murphy, Richard, T.A. *Background to the Bible*. Ann Arbor, Mich: Servant Books, 1978.

Murphy, Richard T.A. *An Introduction to the Prophets of Israel*. Boston, Mass.: Pauline Books & Media, 1995.

Muto, Susan Annette. *A Practical Guide to Spiritual Reading*. Petersham, Mass.: St. Bede's Publications, 1994.

Vest, Norvene. *Bible Reading for Spiritual Growth*. New York: HarperCollins Publishers, 1993.

Wijngaards, John. *Handbook to the Gospels*. Ann Arbor, Mich.: Servant Books, 1979.

Other Works by the Author

Schultz, Karl A. *The Art and Vocation of Caring for Persons in Pain*. Mahwah, N.J.: Paulist Press, 1994.

Schultz, Karl A. *Calming the Stormy Seas of Stress*. Winona, Minn.: St. Mary's Press, 1998.

Schultz, Karl A. *Job Therapy*. Pittsburgh, Pa.: Genesis Personal Development Center, 1996.

Schultz, Karl A. *Journaling with Moses and Job*. Boston: Pauline Books & Media, 1996.

Schultz, Karl A. *Nourished by the Word: A Dialogue with Brother Andrew Campbell, O.S.B. on Praying the Scriptures and Holistic Personal Growth*. Notre Dame, Ind: Ave Maria Press, 1994.

Schultz, Karl A. *Personal Energy Management: A Christian Personal and Professional Development Program*. Chicago: Loyola University Press, 1994.

Schultz, Karl A. *Where is God When You Need Him?: Sharing Stories of Suffering With Job and Jesus*. Staten Island, N.Y.: Alba House, 1992.

About the Author

Karl A. Schultz is the director of Genesis Personal Development Center in Pittsburgh, Pennsylvania. He is an author, speaker, and retreat leader on motivational, gender relations, biblical spirituality, time and stress management, wellness, and organizational development topics.

Schultz is known nationally for his innovative books and workshops on *lectio divina*, the ancient Christian model of holistic spiritual reading and living. He has pioneered applications of *lectio divina* to suffering, care-giving, inner healing, time management, stress management, gender dialogue and relations, potential fulfillment, and the book of Job.

He is the author of *Where Is God When You Need Him?: Sharing Stories of Suffering with Job and Jesus* (Alba House), *Calming the Stormy Seas of Stress* (St. Mary's Press), *Journaling with Moses and Job* (Pauline Books & Media), and *Personal Energy Management* (Loyola University Press).

Additional resources on the Bible, including audiotapes and videotapes containing the author's presentations on biblical and personal growth subjects, are listed on the website *karlaschultz.com* and can be ordered from Genesis Personal Development Center, 3431 Gass Avenue, Pittsburgh, PA 15212-2239. The e-mail address is karlaschultz@juno.com.

The How-To Book of the Bible: Reading Guide for Individuals and Groups, by Karl A. Schultz, can be downloaded free-of-charge at www.osv.com/howtobible.

Our Sunday Visitor ...
Your Source for Discovering the Riches of the Catholic Faith

Our Sunday Visitor has an extensive line of materials for young children, teens, and adults. Our books, Bibles, pamphlets, CD-ROMs, audios, and videos are available in bookstores worldwide.

To receive a FREE full-line catalog or for more information, call **Our Sunday Visitor** at **1-800-348-2440, ext. 3**. Or write **Our Sunday Visitor** / 200 Noll Plaza / Huntington, IN 46750.

Please send me ___ A catalog
Please send me materials on:
___ Apologetics and catechetics
___ Prayer books
___ The family
___ Reference works
___ Heritage and the saints
___ The parish

Name _____
Address _____ Apt._____
City _____ State _____ Zip_____
Telephone (   ) _____

A49BBBBP

Please send a friend ___ A catalog
Please send a friend materials on:
___ Apologetics and catechetics
___ Prayer books
___ The family
___ Reference works
___ Heritage and the saints
___ The parish

Name _____
Address _____ Apt._____
City _____ State _____ Zip_____
Telephone (   ) _____

A49BBBBP

OurSundayVisitor

200 Noll Plaza, Huntington, IN 46750
Toll free: **1-800-348-2440**
Website: www.osv.com